The 1994 Bo of Jewish Thought

קובץ עיונים בפרשנות המקרא ובמחשבת ישראל

A Journal of Torah Scholarship

SOUTH HAMPSTEAD
SYNAGOGUE

Orthodox Union

Yeshivat Ohr Yerushalayim

Copyright © 1992, 1993 by Orthodox Union and Yeshivat Ohr Yerushalayim.

All rights reserved. No part of this publication may be reproduced, translated, stored in a retrieval system, or transmitted in any form or by any means, electronic, mechanical, photocopying, recording or otherwise, without permission in writing from the editors, c/o Yeshivat Ohr Yerushalayim, Moshav Beit Meir, D.N. Harei Yehudah 90865, Israel.

ISBN 1-879016-16-8

Phototypeset at Targum Press, Inc.
Produced by Olivestone Print Communications, Inc.

PRINTED IN THE UNITED STATES OF AMERICA

CONTENTS

PART I: *Chaim Sh. Eisen and Moshe Ch. Sosevsky, eds.*

KOHELETH REVISITED: *Moshe M. Eisemann* 7
A Vibrant Affirmation of Life

> Megillath Koheleth frustrates more than it illuminates, seemingly providing a message of unrelieved negativism with no structured system to ease our quest for understanding. Drawing primarily upon the insights of Maharal, the author establishes Koheleth as the *megillah* of *yirath HaShem* (awe of G-d). In doing so, the essay elucidates the deeper implications of some of the key phrases that give Koheleth its body and nuance. Through them, Koheleth conjures up an optimistic vision of a life constructively lived — bidding man to exploit his infinite potential by looking "beyond the sun" in terms of his relationship with G-d.

"COME TO CHESHBON": *Aharon Feldman* 25
An *Aggadah* According to the
Vilna Ga'on

> The Torah records the song of victory of Sichon, king of the Emorim, over the king of Mo'av. Why should such a song be worthy of inclusion in the eternal Torah? The Talmud understands it as the key to a far more important battle: the ongoing struggle between man's physical and spiritual natures. Its analysis of the verses, however, seems strained and elusive. The Vilna Ga'on's commentary on this passage, adapted into English by the author, clarifies its underlying concepts. Drawing upon his vast knowledge of all facets of Torah, the Ga'on infers the meaning of the passage's symbols and motifs, allowing us to sense that we have become privy to the profound lessons conveyed here by Chazal.

"YOU WILL BE LIKE G-D":   *Chaim Eisen*   44
Chazal's Conception of the *Yetzer HaRa* (PART I)

>Various sources in Chazal imply that the *yetzer hara* is the very embodiment of evil and the root of all sin. Yet other Talmudic and Midrashic sources portray the *yetzer hara* as "very good," implicating it in loving and serving G-d and indicating that man's ultimate quest for G-dliness — and the very existence of this world — depends upon it. Through analysis of these diverse sources and later rabbinical commentaries, the author presents a coherent view of Chazal's conception of the *yetzer hara* as a divine power, unique to man, which is inherently neither good nor bad. In this essay, the *yetzer hara* emerges as the mediator of all human creativity, imagination, and enthusiasm in this world and the basis of man's unique autonomy and initiative — delivered into the hands of man for his use or abuse.

"LET EVERY LIVING BREATH PRAISE G-D":   *Shmuel Grunfeld*   117
The Finale of Sefer Tehillim

>In the conclusion to Sefer Tehillim, praising G-d with specific musical instruments is presented as the prelude to letting "every living breath praise G-d." But why these particular instruments and not others? Noting parallels with the last *mishnah* in *Seder Kodashim* and with the Gemara in *massecheth Arachin*, the author deciphers the symbolism of this extraordinary orchestra, providing new insights into Tehillim's closing crescendo of G-d's praises.

HUMAN ACTION IN RAMBAM'S THOUGHT: *Yehudah Gellman*   122
Individual Autonomy and Love of G-d

>Many students of Rambam fail to sense coherence between his Halachic and philosophical teachings. Through analysis of both Rambam's philosophical classic, *Moreh HaNevochim*, and his Halachic masterpiece, *Mishneh Torah*, the author discerns an all-embracing system, in which the world and the Torah are intelligible and, as a result, human reason and action are pre-eminent. Therefore, as both philosophical conclusions and Halachic imperatives, self-reliance and individual autonomy in man's relationship with G-d are maximized. This approach is dramatically expressed in Rambam's controversial attitudes toward medicine and magic. The essay concludes with Rambam's conception of true service of G-d — "out of love" — motivated by a sense of such ultimate human responsibility.

PART II: *Moshe Ch. Sosevsky, ed.*

KOHELETH REVISITED II: *Moshe M. Eisemann*   147
On Mortality, Society, and G-d

> In a previous essay, the author established Koheleth as the paradigmatic *megillah* of *yirath Hashem* (awe of G-d). In this essay, he explores the major concerns of the awe-inspired servant of G-d. Despite Koheleth's preoccupation with death and its seemingly utilitarian view of fellowship, the author demonstrates that the *megillah* rings with a positivism not usually associated with it. And although Koheleth's apparent emphasis on man rather than G-d makes it difficult to acknowledge it as a religious work, the author finds in the *megillah* a uniquely spiritual message.

RABBEINU HAKADOSH   *Moshe Tz. Neriyah*   162
AND CHANUKKAH:
Why Chanukkah Was Excluded from the Mishnah

> According to *Ta'amei HaMinhagim*, Rabbeinu HaKadosh (R. Yehudah HaNasi) omitted Chanukkah from the Mishnah because, as a scion of the house of David, he took offense at the non-Davidic Chashmonai family's seizure of the kingship. After discrediting this explanation both logically and historically, the author provides several more plausible solutions to the mystery of why the laws of Chanukkah do not appear in the Mishnah.

SHA'UL AND AMALEK: *Moshe Ch. Sosevsky*   175
Anatomy of a Sin

> Once the prophet Shemu'el assigns Sha'ul the historic task of destroying the wicked nation of Amalek, the king seems to proceed vigorously, quickly conscripting a huge army and marching toward the enemy. Just as we begin to anticipate a resounding victory, however, Sha'ul's resolve appears to evaporate. Indeed, the description of the ensuing battle appears surrealistic. By meticulously analyzing both textual nuances and the words of Chazal, the author endeavors to penetrate Sha'ul's mind and clarify his rationale. In the process, the reader gains a glimpse of Sha'ul's true stature.

THE LAST KING OF YEHUDAH: *Yitzchak Levi, z.l.*   195
The Tragic Saga of King Tzidkiyyahu

> Tzidkiyyahu ben Yoshiyyahu was the last of the glorious line of Davidic kings prior to the destruction of the Beith HaMikdash and the exile into Babylonia. Were these calamities inevitable, or could Tzidkiyyahu have averted the retribution foreseen by the prophets? By carefully weaving the words of Chazal into Scripture, the author illuminates Tzidkiyyahu's character and his relationship with the prophet Yirmeyahu in the context of the king's generation and upbringing.

A MIZMOR FOR SHABBATH?   *Dan Vogel*   229
A Literary View of Mizmor 92

> Mizmor 92 is the only *mizmor* of Tehillim that is textually assigned to a particular day of the week. Furthermore, it is recited no fewer than three times during Shabbath. R. S.R. Hirsch maintains that the *mizmor* conveys the sanctity of Shabbath. Yet not one word in Mizmor 92 refers to Shabbath, nor are its encomiums to the L-rd unique to this *mizmor* or to the day it purports to honor. By examining the structure and imagery of this Biblical poem, the author reveals its relevance both to Shabbath and to man.

TRANSLITERATIONS:

Phonetic transliteration is used throughout, without recourse to anglicized forms or conventional English spelling. Transliterations are italicized, except proper nouns and books of the Bible. Several specific conventions employed in transliteration are listed below.

1. א and ע are ignored, except where interposing between two vowels, whereupon א is indicated by ' and ע by ` to prevent erroneous pronunciation of the vowels as a diphthong.
2. ב and ו are both transliterated as *v*.
3. ח and כ are both transliterated as *ch*.
4. י is usually transliterated as *y*. However, where it follows *kamatz gadol, patach, tzeirei,* and *segol,* at the end of a syllable, it is transliterated as *i*, and where it follows *chirik* at the end of a syllable, it is ignored.
5. כ and ק are both transliterated as *k*.
6. *Dagesh chazak* (forte) is indicated by doubling the letter, except ש (*sh*) and צ (*tz*) and where the letter is a capital.
7. *Dagesh kal* is indicated in ב (*b* vs. *v*), כ (*k* vs. *ch*), פ (*p* vs. *f*), and ת (*t* vs. *th*).
8. *Tzeirei, segol,* and *sheva na* (the vocalized *sheva*) are all transliterated *e*. *Tzeirei* at the end of a word is transliterated *ei* to prevent confusion. *Sheva nach* (the silent *sheva*) is ignored.

ABBREVIATIONS USED IN REFERENCES:

Ag.	— *Aggadah, Aggadath*	*Peth.*	— *Pethichta*
b.	— bar, ben, ibn	*Pir.DeR.E.*	— *Pirkei DeRabbi Eli'ezer*
BeM.R.	— *BeMidbar Rabbah*	R.	— Rabbeinu, Rabbi, Rav
BeR.R.	— *BeReshith Rabbah*	R.	— Rabba, Rabbah
ca.	— *circa* ("about")	*Ru.R.*	— *Ruth Rabbah*
ch., chs.	— chapter, chapters	*Sh.HaSh.R.*	— *Shir HaShirim Rabbah*
com.	— commentary	*Sh.R.*	— *Shemoth Rabbah*
Dev.R.	— *Devarim Rabbah*	*T.DeV.Eli.R.*	— *Tanna DeVei Eliyahu Rabba*
Eich.R.	— *Eichah Rabbah*		
Est.R.	— *Ester Rabbah*	*T.DeV.Eli.Z.*	— *Tanna DeVei Eliyahu Zota*
Hil.	— *Hilchoth*		
ibid.	— *ibidem* ("in the same place")	*Tan.*	— *Tanchuma*
		Tar.	— *Targum*
Koh.R.	— *Koheleth Rabbah*	*Tos.*	— *Tosefta*
lit.	— literally	trans.	— translated
loc. cit.	— *loco citato* ("in the place [passage] cited")	*VaY.R.*	— *VaYikra Rabbah*
		vol., vols.	— volume, volumes
Mid.	— *Midrash*	*Yal.*	— *Yalkut*
Mish.	— *Mishnah*	*Yal.Sh.*	— *Yalkut Shimoni*
n., nn.	— note, notes	*Yer.*	— *Yerushalmi*
p., pp.	— page, pages	*Z.*	— *Zota*
Pes.	— *Pesikta*		

Part I

KOHELETH REVISITED:
A Vibrant Affirmation of Life

Moshe M. Eisemann

1. INTRODUCTION

Koheleth is hard: hard to translate, hard to understand, hard to dredge for its secrets. It frustrates more than it illuminates; it seems not to deliver what we expect from a *megillah*. We find no sharply focused message to engage our minds, no gripping narrative to move our hearts. There seems to be no tightly structured system to ease our quest for understanding. We detect no logical progression from a clearly articulated question to an answer that leaves us informed and satisfied. We are thrown a patchwork of musings and jottings, cleanly etched pictures and shadowy presences, philosophy and elegy, homily and exhortation — and we are hard-put to make sense of it all.

Above all, Koheleth has an image problem. If all is emptiness, something within us tells us that we would rather not know about it. Why expose oneself to a message of such seemingly unrelieved negativism? Koheleth is hard to love.[1]

In this essay, we propose to offer an analysis of Koheleth's

RABBI EISEMANN is the *mashgiach* of Yeshiva Ner Israel of Baltimore. A prolific writer and a leading Torah scholar, his publications include the translation and commentary of the ArtScroll-Mesorah Tanach Series' *Yechezkel* (New York: Mesorah Publications, 1977) and *Divrei HaYamim I* (New York: Mesorah Publications, 1987).

goal and some careful definitions of the key phrases that give it body and nuance. We will demonstrate that it sings with positivism and pulsates with joyful affirmation of life. We will find cohesion and direction, purpose and structure. We will learn to appreciate the exquisite sensitivity of the rabbis in prescribing that we read specifically this *megillah* on Sukkoth, the season of our greatest joy.[2] We will, if we succeed, see something of the true Koheleth.

2. LOVE AND AWE — SHIR HASHIRIM AND KOHELETH

In the first chapter of *Avoth*, there is a series of *mishnayoth* in which the ethical teachings of the *zugoth* ("pairs") are preserved. These *zugoth* comprise two men from each of several generations — one the *nasi* (head of the Great Sanhedrin) and the other the *av beith din* (chief of the Court) — who bequeathed these immortal sayings to us. In *Derech HaChayyim*, Maharal subjects their homilies to careful analysis and finds that invariably the sayings of any given *zug* deal with the same essential issue. What differences there are between the respective statements of the two members of the *zug* derive from the fact that the *nasi* presents his treatise from the vantage point of *ahavath HaShem* — love of G-d — while the *av beith din*'s teaching is animated by *yirath HaShem* — awe of G-d — which is the purview of divine worship to which his position obligates him:

> The first ... is [the] *nasi* ... and the office of *nasi* is a lofty exaltation. And one upon whom G-d bestowed [such] lofty exaltation and greatness loves G-d [in gratitude] for the exaltation that G-d bestowed upon him. Such a one serves [G-d] specifically through love, for one should bless G-d for the goodness that He did on his behalf. And therefore, his reproof concerned *ahavath HaShem*.
>
> And the reproof of the *av beith din*, who presides over judgment — and is therefore called "*av beith din*" — concerns *yirath [HaShem]*. For inasmuch as his quality is judgment, he has *yirah*. [Similarly, because] Yitzchak's quality was judgment, it is said [by Ya'akov, regarding Yitzchak's perception of G-d], "the *Fear* of Yitzchak was with me" (BeReshith 31:42): for a master of judgment is fearful lest he transgress and violate the *yirah*. Therefore, the reproof of the *av beith din* concerns *yirah*.
>
> (*Derech HaChayyim* on *Avoth* 1:5)

Maharal (ibid.) finds that these two equally valid modes of service flow from the teaching of Antigenos Ish Socho, the mentor of the first of the *zugoth*. His exhortation, *"Do not be as servants who minister to the master in order to receive a reward; be instead as servants who minister to the master in order not to receive a reward ..."* (*Avoth* 1:3), clearly urges us to be motivated by *ahavath HaShem*, insofar as it deplores service based upon ulterior motives; his closing words, *"... and may the awe of heaven be upon you"* (ibid.), add the element of *yirah* to his depiction of the ideal person. Maharal wonders why the division of the two modes of service, each projected by the person most attuned to its nuances — the *nasi* or the *av beith din* — began only after Antigenos taught the need for a synthesis of the two. His explanation is that, at the source, the two modes need to function in counterpoint, each nurturing the other, each drawing upon and being stimulated by the other:

> This statement ... because it includes all [modes of] service of G-d through *ahavah* and *yirah* as appropriate ... is fitting for Antigenos, who is one instead of two [members of a *zug*], because in essence *ahavah* and *yirah* have one root, since a person must love G-d and be in awe of Him — this being what is appropriate for a person — *and it is inappropriate that there be* yirah *without* ahavah *or* ahavah *without* yirah....
>
> To the contrary, since a person should possess *ahavah* and *yirah* together, it is fitting that Antigenos — who comes to reprove man concerning [both] *ahavah* and *yirah* — has no *zug* partner with him. Among the *zugoth* who came afterward, however, one member of the *zug* came to reprove concerning a specific aspect that expresses *ahavah* only, and the other concerning a specific aspect that expresses *yirah* only.
>
> (*Derech HaChayyim* on *Avoth* 1:3)

It is only after *ahavah* and *yirah* have both been established as equally valid, equally necessary components of an ideal relationship with G-d that they can be carried forward as discrete modes, the one preponderating over the other as circumstances may demand or personal predilection may dictate.

With this background, let us consider the following observations of Rambam. In the course of a discussion concerning the unequalled merit of *avodah me'ahavah* (serving G-d out of a sense of love), he notes:

> *Ahavath HaShem* in the hearts of those who love Him should be overwhelming and completely engrossing, as [G-d] commanded us, "[You shall love G-d your L-rd] with all your heart and with all your soul" (Devarim 6:5). To this Shelomoh refers metaphorically: "For I am lovesick" (Shir HaShirim 2:5). *And the whole of Shir HaShirim is a metaphor for this matter.*
>
> (Yad Hil. Teshuvah 10:3)

We may understand this characterization of Shir HaShirim in light of what we learned from Maharal: that, at the source, *ahavah* and *yirah* must be taught by one man and must, through cross-pollination, fructify, stimulate, and foster one another. We therefore propose that King Shelomoh too (as Antigenos Ish Socho was to do centuries later) provided us, in addition to Shir HaShirim, with a *megillah* whose purpose is to instruct us in the need for and appropriate forms of *avodah miyirah* (serving G-d out of a sense of awe). We contend that Koheleth is that *megillah*. It does for *avodah miyirah* what Shir HaShirim does for *avodah me'ahavah*. When it ends with the words, "When all has been said and everything heard, fear G-d and perform His commands because that is all there is to man" (Koheleth 12:13), this is not a fortuitous peculiarity but the calculated and necessary culmination of its central purpose. *Quod erat demonstrandum*, it says to us; we have demonstrated what we had set out to prove. There are problems in life, challenges and predicaments, to which only *avodah miyirah* can provide the correct response.

Given this thesis, we now have a criterion by which to understand the widely disparate issues with which Koheleth grapples. We may be able to discover common ground among them by recognizing them as being clustered around this central theme. Each of them is valid grist for Koheleth's mill. Each poses problems when viewed from the perspective of *avodah miyirah*, and each must find its solution within the compass of *yirah*'s reach. Let us isolate some of the topics that form the substance of the *megillah* and that clearly reflect the *yirah* orientation, which we now anticipate.

3. *YIRAH* AND THIS WORLD

We would do well to begin our analysis with the words of R. E.E. Dessler, who speaks of the two modes of serving G-d represented respectively by the names "Ya'akov" and "Yisra'el":

> There is the mode of "Ya'akov" and the mode of "Yisra'el," and they are two distinct levels in the service of G-d: two different worlds. The mode of "Ya'akov" is in *olam hatachton* [the terrestrial realm], and the mode of "Yisra'el" is in *olam ha'elyon* [the supernal realm]. The level of "Ya'akov" ... is [divine] service in its most perfect form at the level of *olam tachton*. In this mode, the one serving distinguishes [the physicality of] this world as a separate reality, but everything he does in it is really *leshem shamayim* [for the sake of heaven], like a sacrifice offered to the honor of G-d.
>
> (*Michtav MeEliyyahu*, II, 218)

Olam hatachton, the world in which physicality must be faced, is not hospitable to the love relationship with G-d evoked by the name "Yisra'el." In such a love relationship, the intellect may well become an impediment: We delight in our union with the object of our adoration, and that union by its very definition precludes critical analysis, which requires stepping back and viewing from a distance. We may correctly state that we lose ourselves in love.[3] The obligation to become inebriated on Purim to a point at which we can no longer distinguish between good and bad[4] can only be understood in such terms. So, too, the root "שׁגי" (~ engrossed), which occurs within the context of *avodah me'ahavah*,[5] connotes a state of being in which the intellect is, at very best, quiescent. The comparison of this mode with the case in *avodah miyirah* is particularly instructive.

In his analysis of the methods by which a person can come to love and stand in awe of G-d, Rambam teaches us:

> What is the way to the love and fear [of G-d]? When a person contemplates His wondrous and vast deeds and creations and sees therein His infinite wisdom, he immediately loves and glorifies and adores [Him], and has a great desire to know the Great Name.... And when he considers these matters themselves, immediately he recoils in fear and knows that he is a small, lowly, dim creature standing with trivial, minimal knowledge before Him Whose knowledge is perfect.
>
> (*Yad Hil. Yesodei HaTorah* 2:2)

Love, then, is the initial reaction; awe follows only after further consideration.

We associate the modes of love and awe with, respectively, a parent-child and a master-servant relationship. The ecstasy of love, which inheres in the embrace between parent and child, would be violated by the intrusion of inquisitive probing. In contrast, the servant, charged with duties that define his very existence, would do well to examine carefully and understand fully what is expected of him. When we approach G-d as His children in love, we lift ourselves beyond this-worldly considerations. However, when we stand submissively before Him as servants ready to do His bidding, we must open our minds to the countless problems that life — in this endlessly beguiling, endlessly complex, endlessly threatening world in which we find ourselves — serves up to us.[3] Thus, when we offer up a sacrifice to G-d, we affirm that everything this world of ours contains is His. When we seek to serve Him, not in a rapture of *other*-worldliness, but from within the vexing confines of *this* world, we must make sure to use its gifts only *leshem shamayim*: our modest offering upon the altar of His infinite grandeur.

We have, at this point, certainly touched upon one meaning of the *mishnah* in *Avoth*: "If there is no wisdom, there can be no fear [of G-d]; if there is no fear [of G-d], there can be no wisdom" (ibid. 3:17). The two — wisdom and fear — exist symbiotically, each grounded in the other, each both seed and flower, working in endless counterpoint in the quest for perfection.

We now have a key to two of the great themes of Koheleth: His restless experimentation with the correct way of making use of this world's bounties, and his tireless quest for "חכמה" ("wisdom") — a word that does not appear even once in Shir HaShirim. True to his goal of clarifying the contours of *avoda*h miyirah, Koheleth is determined to discover the rights and wrongs of this-worldly life.

We wonder, nevertheless, whether we may be guilty of anachronistic thinking. Are we not attempting to impose a convenient theory upon an intractable reality? Does it make sense to view Koheleth as so vitally interested in a world that he repeatedly describes as "הבל" ("emptiness")?

4. IS OUR THESIS TENABLE?
"Under the Sun" ("תחת השמש")
Versus "Under the Heavens" ("תחת השמים")

The definition of certain constantly recurring motifs in Koheleth is in order. First among these, we will tackle the phrases "תחת השמש" ("under the sun") and "תחת השמים" ("under the heavens"), which seem to be used interchangeably throughout the *megillah*. Our contention is that not only is the use of these phrases not capricious but, on the contrary, they serve as the very beacons by whose light we can navigate the confusing highways and byways of Koheleth's thought. To understand this, we must first determine the connotations of "השמש" ("the sun") and "השמים" ("the heavens").

The sun, source of the energy that sustains all life on earth, is the Torah's pre-eminent metaphor for the this-worldly and temporal. Thus, Maharal writes:

> The sun controls the world of nature, all of which is ordered under its aegis. Thus, in Scripture, when the physical world is described, *"under the sun"* (Koheleth 1:2) is employed.
> (*Tifereth Yisra'el*, ch. 4 [p. 15])

Casting this theme in more explicitly spiritual terms, Maharal also uses it to explain why the gentile world uses a solar calendar while that of the Torah is essentially lunar:

> The power of the "Fourth Beast" [symbolizing Esav and Rome][6] is derived from the power of the sun — "the greater luminary" (BeReshith 1:16) — and he reckons his calendar with respect to the sun. And Ya'akov is called "small" (ibid. 27:15, 42), and he reckons his calendar with respect to the "smaller luminary" [the moon] (ibid. 1:16). Therefore, [Esav] is called "Edom" [lit. "Red"] (ibid. 25:30, 36:1, 8-9, 19, 43) ... because he receives his power from the sun, which is "red" (*Babba Bathra* 84a).
> (*Netzach Yisra'el*, ch. 17 [p. 93])

The sun is appropriate for Esav-Edom because physical size and brute power define the essence of his being. By contrast, Ya'akov has a greater affinity for the smaller, more unobtrusive, and more modest moon. Therefore, it stands to reason that when Koheleth uses the expression "under the *sun*," he is describing the world in its this-worldly, temporal sense: the frame of reference that, as he demonstrates throughout the *megillah*, breeds only futility and stagnation.

However, scattered throughout Koheleth, we occasionally find the expression "תחת השמים" ("under the heavens") replacing "תחת השמש" ("under the sun"). Clearly we ought not to countenance the idea of arbitrariness in the choice of such evocative phrases. Accordingly, let us now attempt a definition of "under the heavens," by clarifying the connotation of "שמים" ("heaven"). In this context, we note Koheleth's warning: "Do not be rash with your mouth, and do not let your heart hasten to utter anything before the L-rd: for the L-rd is *in heaven* (בשמים), and you are on earth; therefore, let your words be few" (Koheleth 5:1). Why should the fact that "the L-rd is in heaven, and you are on earth" elicit such a sense of restraint and caution?

The answer may well lie in Maharal's explanation of an anomalous word usage found in *Avoth*. There, as quoted above, Antigenos teaches, "... and may the *awe of heaven* (מורא שמים) be upon you" (ibid. 1:3). Maharal wonders at the phrase "מורא שמים" ("awe of *heaven*"). Why do we not speak of "awe of G-d"?[7] Conversely, why do we never find the expression "love of *heaven*" used in lieu of "אהבת ה'" ("love of *G-d*")? Maharal's response is that the term "מורא שמים" is particularly apt for expressing awe, which is the essence of *avodah miyirah*:

> [Antigenos in effect] said, even though I reproved you concerning *love*, do not consider G-d like your lover with whom you are familiar. Instead, one should consider that "the L-rd is in heaven, and you are on earth," and thus ... "the awe of heaven [will] be upon you," and the *love* will not negate the *awe*.
>
> Therefore, he said, "And may the awe of *heaven* be upon you," and he did not say, "And may the awe of *the Omnipresent One* be upon you." And everywhere ... "*awe* of heaven" is stated and never "*love* of heaven," because awe mandates that one consider G-d utterly transcendent, while in love one should consider oneself as cleaving to G-d, as it is written, "*to love* G-d your L-rd ... and *to cleave* to Him" (Devarim 30:20).
>
> (*Derech HaChayyim* on *Avoth*, loc. cit.)

Awe derives from an awareness of distance. I stand in awe of that which forever lies beyond my ken, the One Whose otherness is absolute. *"Heaven"* conveys just this sense of distance.⁸ In this sense, *avodah miyirah* and *avodah me'ahavah* are polar opposites. Since love draws its energy from a sense of union, a oneness that knows no barriers,⁹ "love of *heaven*" — the love of a distant, unattainable object — would be a contradiction in terms. Accordingly, we speak only of *ahavath HaShem*. *Yirah* is different. It is a mode of relation to the beyond, a set of attitudes based upon a realization of profound separation and transcendence. Nothing short of "awe of *heaven*" can convey this recognition.

We therefore propose that wherever Koheleth substitutes "תחת השמים" ("under the heavens") for "תחת השמש" ("under the sun"), the passage is to be interpreted in a positive sense, in terms of a person's relationship to G-d within the context of *avodah miyirah*. It signals a discussion of what *avodah miyirah* might demand in a given set of conditions. To illustrate this approach, we consider the initial occurrences of the terms "תחת השמש" and "תחת השמים" in the *megillah*:

"What benefit does man have from all his effort that he exerts under the sun (תחת השמש)*?"* (Koheleth 1:3) — If a person directs his energies to ambitions as they are defined in a this-worldly context, "תחת השמש," he will reap only disappointment and frustration. In contrast:

"And I set my heart to search out and explore through wisdom all that takes place under the heavens (תחת השמים)*"* (ibid. 1:13) — Here Koheleth is seeking to discover meaning that *does* exist in life. He wishes to understand the world into which he has been placed, the society in which he must function — from the point of view of wisdom and its correlate, *avodah miyirah*. In such a context, the appropriate term is "תחת השמים."

"Emptiness" ("הבל")

In this light, we are ready to begin our analysis of the word "הבל" ("emptiness"), which clearly sets the tone for the entire *megillah*. Our examination of "הבל" will take us further afield than one would normally expect, but — considering the inordinate significance that it carries in Koheleth — it is critical that our perceptions of its connotations be very precise.

Aside from "emptiness," "הבל" also literally means "vapor," suggesting the irreducible plasticity of something so insubstantial that it lacks even a shape and form of its own. Furthermore, its obvious relationship to the name "Hevel" implies that it is somehow connected with whatever Adam's second son epitomized. In this context, we note that Hevel appears to be the archetypal follower, possessed of a passive, plastic personality, which permits others to impress their initiatives upon it but is in itself noncreative and nonproductive. Thus, the Torah describes Kayin as initiating the revolutionary mode of divine service expressed in sacrifice; Hevel follows, picks up the idea, and improves upon it.[10] In addition, we note that Kayin grows things from the ground creatively, while Hevel watches the already existing sheep.[11] It appears that "הבל" relates essentially to this passivity embodied by Hevel.

At this point, it is edifying to note a striking parallel between the three sons of Noach and the three sons of Adam. Obviously, accursed Cham parallels murderous Kayin. Shem, projector of the vivifying force of the soul, is the one among Noach's three sons who parallels Adam's son Sheth, progenitor of all men, and ultimately of Yisra'el, the crown of humanity. Among Adam's sons, his birth alone is prefaced with the statement that Adam "begot [a son] in his likeness, with his image" (BeReshith 5:3) — an obvious allusion to the "likeness" and "image" of G-d, with which Adam had been created (ibid. 1:26-27, 5:1, and 9:6).[12] Yefeth (whose name, "יפת," derives from the same root as "יופי" ["beauty"] — a function of the *passive* body) parallels Adam's son, Hevel: exemplar of plastic passivity.

To understand this parallel fully, we must investigate further the respective roles of Noach's blessed sons, Shem and Yefeth. Our quest now takes us back almost to the beginning of history, into Noach's tent as he lies there in the sorry disgrace of his drunkenness. Cham has seen what he has seen — or done what he has done[13] — and has told Shem and Yefeth what happened. These two take a garment and, with exquisite sensitivity, enter backward (so that they not witness their father's shame) and cover his nakedness. There is, however, a significant syntactic anomaly in the Torah's description of their conduct. In lieu of a plural reference to both Shem and Yefeth — "ויקחו" (*"they* took")

— the Torah commences its description with the singular form: "[Shem] took (ויקח)" (BeReshith 9:23). Chazal explain this aberration: The initiative for this act of filial respect and loyalty came solely from Shem.[14] He — *not* he and Yefeth — was moved to act. Yefeth allowed himself to be inveigled into the mission of mercy but had no part in formulating it.[15]

For an understanding of the incident and an examination of its deeper meanings, we turn to Maharal:

> In *BeReshith Rabbah*,[16] [the Midrash] explains that because these two brothers acted honorably in covering their father, they were rewarded with honor: [Yefeth] with burial of the body — that it not be cast in disgrace [i.e., that the hosts of Gog and Magog, descended from Yefeth,[17] will be buried[18] after being slain[19] for waging war against G-d and Yisra'el][20] — and [Shem] with a *tallith* of *tzitzith* [since Avraham is descended from Shem][21] — for a *tallith* dignifies the body....
>
> Obviously, the honor of *tzitzith*, which is a commandment, is greater than that of burial. And because Shem exerted himself in the commandment [of covering his father] more [than Yefeth], he was rewarded with this honor: that his attire — which dignifies a person while his soul is still with him — should be honorable. This is not the case with Yefeth, who was rewarded with honor only for his [soulless] body and did not merit anything [associated with a] commandment.
>
> (*Gur Aryeh* on BeReshith 9:23)

Thus, Maharal differentiates between the reward of Shem, the initiator — from whom the nation of Yisra'el, clothed in the precept of *tzitzith*, is descended — and the reward of Yefeth, the follower — precursor of the Gogian hordes who would one day fall upon the hills of Yisra'el, who would be buried rather than left to lie rotting in the fields. While both rewards were designed to bestow honor upon those who had acted honorably, Shem's reward addressed his soul; for Yefeth, it was sufficient to honor the body and grant it the dignity of burial. The distinction is clear: Active, vital initiation is the province of the soul — the life force, which energizes us — while the passive plasticity of the follower is typified by the body — the eternal servant.

Let us take our analysis further by examining the precept of *tzitzith*, which was granted to the active, initiating Shem but denied to the passive, plastic Yefeth. Concerning *tzitzith*, the

Talmud recounts the following tale:

> A certain man who was careful in [performance of] the commandment of *tzitzith* heard of a prostitute in the coastal towns who would take as her wages four hundred gold coins. He sent her four hundred gold coins and set a time with her. When his time arrived, he came ... to sit beside her, and his four *tzitziyyoth* came and slapped him on his face. He slipped away and sat himself on the ground.... He said to her, "I swear that I have never seen a woman as beautiful as you, but G-d our L-rd commanded us concerning a certain commandment called *tzitzith*, regarding which it is written twice, 'I am G-d your L-rd' (BeMidbar 15:41): I am He Who will exact punishment, and I am He Who will pay reward. Now [my *tzitziyyoth*] have appeared to me like four witnesses [forewarning me not to sin]."
>
> (*Menachoth* 44a)

Specifically the precept of *tzitzith* prevented him, at the very last moment, from hopelessly compromising his standing as a Jew. Maharal explains the pivotal role of *tzitzith* here:

> The principle of this matter is that this commandment brings a person out of mere physical existence to the point where he is worthy of accepting upon himself the commandment of G-d. And they [the *tzitziyyoth*] are on the corner, which is the end and finish of the garment, which is the honor of a person. Therefore, [the Talmud] said here that his four *tzitziyyoth* — which are on the four corners and indicate that man is ready to accept upon himself the commandment of G-d — "came and slapped him on his face."
>
> Thus ... this commandment indicates that man is worthy of reward and of punishment, because he has [the capacity for] departure from mere physicality toward self-actualization. For punishment and reward do not [derive] from the aspect of mere physicality, but man comes out of mere physicality — as indicated by the *tzitzith* that *comes out* of the garment, which is the honor of a person — to the point where he is worthy of reward and of punishment.
>
> Because of this, [the fringes] are called "*tzitzith* (ציצת)," as in the expression "*sprout* (ציץ) of the field" (Yeshayahu 40:6, Tehillim 103:15), namely, "*sprouting* (צמיחה)": because all sprouting is a *coming out* of the ground — which is a merely physical entity — toward self-actualization.
>
> (*Chiddushei Aggadoth*, loc. cit.)

Tzitzith asserts the possibility of growth and expansion beyond that which might otherwise have been expected. While no object seems so absolutely delimited as a rectangular garment, bounded and defined by its four corners, *tzitzith* — threaded into the forbidding corners of the garment — mocks these boundaries. Just as tender shoots push their obstinate way up through the hard, harsh earth clods, announcing to the world the irresistibility of their determined quest for life, *tzitzith* refuses to countenance the proposition that there are limits beyond which a person simply cannot go. The stark boundaries of the garment hold no terrors for it. The *tzitziyyoth* flow on, unhindered and unbounded, into the far reaches of humanity's grasp.

The hero of the story in *Menachoth* had thought that he was no match for his desires. He saw no way to maintain his religious integrity. His *tzitziyyoth* came and slapped him on his face: "There is nothing," they were telling him, "that you cannot do. You are free, free to be yourself, free to say, 'No!' when every feeling inside you screams that you must succumb to the urgings of your baser self."

This was the gift granted to Shem, the man of the soul, and denied to Yefeth, champion of the physical. Yefeth (whose name, "יפת," as we have noted, derives from the same root as "יופי" ["beauty"]) had *beauty*, but it was not the aesthetically delightful harmony of the fully controlled, fully disciplined, fully integrated moral personality. Instead, it was the ephemeral beauty of appearance and form, bewitching to the eye but — in the final analysis — truly emptiness. Like Hevel, it related to the passivity of the body as opposed to the animation of the soul.

We can now return to our analysis of the word "הבל" ("emptiness") as it appears in Koheleth. Our discovery of the Yefeth-Hevel pole introduced above can help us in our quest to obtain a deeper understanding of what "הבל" signifies. In light of Maharal's explanations of Shem and *tzitzith* versus Yefeth and his emptiness, we realize that "הבל" describes a state of moral stagnation, a condition in which we remain what we are, impervious to the invigorating challenge of *tzitzith*, locked forever in a dungeon of turgid lethargy, morally stunted, frustrated and ultimately disillusioned, bitter and full of contempt and loathing for our smallness. It is the quintessential negation of the spiritual vitality embodied by Shem and his descendants, the nation of Yisra'el.

"Man" ("אדם")

Our quest for meaning in Koheleth now leads us to a closer look at the word "אדם" ("man"), one of the ten names by which man is described in Biblical Hebrew. It is clearly an evocative term, since it is variously given pride of place[22] and the lowest, least admirable position among the various possibilities.[23] "אדם" is the word that our *megillah* appears to favor — it occurs approximately thirty times in Koheleth — so it becomes important to plumb the depths of its possible connotations.

Once more we turn to Maharal:

> Man is called "אדם" because he is "dust from the *ground* (אדמה)" (BeReshith 2:7). Now, one ought to question: Are all other existing things not "from the ground" that man should singularly be called by the name "אדם" because of having been created from the ground? [The Torah states explicitly that "G-d the L-rd grew *from the ground* every tree that is pleasant to the sight and good for food" (ibid. 2:9) and that "G-d the L-rd formed *from the ground* every beast of the field and every bird of the heavens" (ibid. 2:19).] However, the matter of man (אדם) relates most to the ground (אדמה). This is because the ground is unique in that it embodies potential, and through it all the things that sprout from it — plants and trees and everything else — emerge toward actualization. [Just as the ground represents] the potential for all this, so the matter of man is that he is potential, and his completeness [must] emerge toward actualization.
>
> (*Tifereth Yisra'el*, ch. 3 [p. 12])

It is not merely because man was created from the ground that he is called "אדם." Rather, it is because he, and only he, shares with the ground one of its salient features. While a clod of earth has very little intrinsic value, it carries within itself the potential for all life. It can be characterized as that which has value only in terms of what it can produce, never in terms of what it is within itself. That is the nature of man in this world: His value lies not in what he is but only in what he can become.

The divine seal of approval, that "the L-rd saw ... that it was good" (BeReshith 1:4, 10, 12, 18, 21, 25), which throughout the Creation narrative testifies to the absolute value of all that He brought into being, is absent after Adam's appearance. G-d's seeing that the given creation "was good" is the expression of

His will that it ought indeed to be as it is.[24] Manifestly, that is not the case with man. As long as there is another second of life within him, he is not yet as he ought to be. There is still work to be done; there are heights to be scaled, worlds to be conquered. Surely it was this idea that Elifaz expressed in teaching that "man (אדם) is born *for exertion*" (Iyyov 5:7). The "exertion" to which he refers is the effort required of us to stimulate the growth that alone can justify our humanity.

"אדם" is thus placed in sharp contrast with "בהמה" ("beast"). "בהמה," teaches Maharal, may be regarded as a combination of two smaller words: "בה מה," meaning *"that which already contains within itself* (בה) *whatever* (מה) *it can ever be"* (Tifereth Yisra'el, loc. cit.). In that context, notes Koheleth:
"The pre-eminence of man (אדם) *over beast* (בהמה) *is naught, for all is emptiness* (הבל)" (ibid. 3:19) — When all is "הבל,"[25] when a person permits himself to stagnate and allows his growth potential to atrophy, then indeed the edge that "אדם" — creature of the unlimited future — has over the circumscribed is nothing. Such a person has relinquished everything that made him human.

5. CONCLUSION

We are ready to return to the question that provoked our quest to define more precisely some of the key words of our *megillah*. We had feared that in reading Koheleth as the *megillah* that attempts to grapple with the physical world as we know it, we had been guilty of anachronistic thinking. We wondered whether King Shelomoh could really wish to know intimately about a world that he so consistently describes as "הבל."

We have now discovered enough about the world view of Koheleth to put paid to this worry. The tone of the *megillah*, the meaning of the dreadful initial assessment that *"all is emptiness* (הבל)" (ibid. 1:2), is set by the opening rhetorical question that follows, which — if our analysis is correct — we are now more fully equipped to understand:
"What (מה) *benefit does man have from all his effort that he exerts under the sun?"* (ibid. 1:3) — Man, the creature of potential, was indeed created to exert himself. But the purpose of the effort that he exerts is to produce a *"benefit"*: an edge over the animal world.

If, instead, he misdirects his energies and defines his accomplishments in terms that are only meaningful in the context of life lived *"under the sun,"* then indeed he is left with *"מה"* ("what"), reminiscent of the stagnant beast — *"בה מה"* — a dreadful void, devastating in its hopeless vapidity.[26]

Thus, not only does Koheleth *not* condemn the world to a depressing *"הבל"* existence, but, on the contrary, it conjures up by implication a radiantly optimistic vision of a life usefully and constructively lived. We are people, creatures of infinite potential; we are capable of vast, constructive efforts. We can make our humanity count and need not submit to an animal-like existence. There is only one condition: Our labors must be informed by the mentality of *avodah miyirah*. We must look beyond the sun if we are to make our lives count.

NOTES

1. On a personal note, my daughter attended one of our major seminaries. I was delighted when she told me that they were studying Koheleth under a great Torah scholar. Some weeks into the semester, she informed me that the course had been dropped. The teacher had found the going too depressing.

2. *Ed. note:* Regarding the custom of reading Koheleth on Sukkoth, which probably dates from the period of the Ge'onim, see *Darchei Mosheh, Tur Orach Chayyim* 490 (citing *Sefer Abbudarham*); *Haghoth Rema, Orach Chayyim* 490:9 and 663:2 (and com., loc. cit.); and *Teshuvoth Rema*, ch. 35.

3. *Ed. note:* For a more detailed treatment of these ideas, see also *Derech HaChayyim* on *Avoth* 1:3.

4. *Ed. note:* Regarding the obligation to become inebriated on Purim, see *Megillah* 7b, *Tur Orach Chayyim* 695, and *Orach Chayyim* 695:2, and see com., loc. cit. Maharal discusses in depth the conceptual implications of such negation of the intellect. See, for example, his introduction to *Or Chadash* (p. 49) and *Or Chadash* on Ester 3:7, ד"ה הפיל פור הוא הגורל (p. 135), and 9:32 (p. 221).

5. See, for example, *Yad Hil. Teshuvah* 10:3, quoted in the text, above.

6. *Ed. note:* The "Four Beasts" allude to the "Four Kingdoms" (Bavel, Madai, Yavan, and Edom — usually rendered as the Babylonian, Median [and Persian], Greek, and Roman empires), which symbolize all worldly greatness. See especially Daniyyel 7-8 and com., loc. cit. (and Ramban on BeMidbar 24:20 [uncensored v.]). The symbolism of the "Four Kingdoms" is invoked by the Midrash in its exegetic analysis of numerous foursomes, conveying

clearly archetypal significance. See, for example, *BeR.R.* 2:4, 16:4, 34:13, 42:2, 4, 44:15, 17, 56:9, 65:13, 70:8, 76:6, 88:6, and 99:2; *Sh.R.* 15:6, 16, 23:11, 26:1, 35:5, and 51:7; *VaY.R.* 13:5, 15:9, and 29:2, 10; *Est.R. Peth.*:2, 4-5; *Sh.HaSh.R.* 3:1 (1), 4 (2); *Eich.R. Peth.*:25 and 1:42; *Koh.R.* 5:15; *Tan. VaYetzei*:2, *VaYechi*:14, *Terumah*:7, *Shemini*:8, and *Tazria*:11; *Mid. Tehillim* 5:6, 22:9, and 78:6; and *Pir.DeR.E.* 28 and 35. See also Rashi on BeReshith 15:10, Rambam (*Yad Hil. Yesodei HaTorah* 7:3), and Ramban on BeReshith 28:12, regarding this symbolism. Maharal discusses the "Four Kingdoms" and what they symbolize at length; the great majority of *Ner Mitzvah* is devoted to this subject. See also *Netzach Yisra'el*, chs. 17-21.

The "Fourth Beast" (i.e., the "Fourth Kingdom") refers to Edom, descended from Esav, traditionally regarded as progenitor of the Roman empire. (See, for example, *Berachoth* 57b, *Rosh HaShanah* 19a, *Gittin* 56b and 57b, *Avodah Zarah* 2b and 11a, *BeR.R.* 63:7 and 83:4, *Est.R.* 3:5, *Mid. Tehillim* 14:3, *Pir.DeR.E.* 38, and the sources cited above regarding the "Four Kingdoms." See also Rashi and Ramban on BeReshith 36:43, and see Ramban on BeReshith 49:31 [citing Josephus, ch. 2], on Shemoth 17:9, and especially on BeMidbar 24:20 [uncensored v.].) Through Rome's ideological role as the foundation of the Holy Roman Empire and Christendom, the ongoing exile of Yisra'el (still predominantly in Christendom) is regarded in classic Jewish thought as an extension of the Roman exile: namely, the exile mediated by the "Fourth Beast," Edom.

7. *Ed. note:* It should be noted that, while in common parlance we always speak of "**יראת שמים**" ("awe of *heaven*"), this usage itself no doubt derives from that of Antigenos in our *mishnah*. By contrast, in the Bible, "יראה" ("awe") in this sense is always associated directly with one of the names of G-d. We are therefore as much in need of Maharal's commentary to explain our expression "יראת **שמים**" as we are to understand Antigenos' expression in the Mishnah.

8. Compare R. S.R. Hirsch's explanation of the word "שמים" ("heaven") as the double plural of "שם" ("there") — emphasizing an absolute and unbridgeable "thereness." See *Yeshurun*, VIII, 274, and com. on BeReshith 1:1, ד״ה את השמים ואת הארץ.

9. *Ed. note:* Compare also R. S.R. Hirsch's analysis of the connotation of "משמשין" ("ministering"), which appears in the first part of Antigenos' statement concerning *avodah me'ahavah*. See com. on *Avoth* 1:3.

10. See BeReshith 4:3-4.

11. See ibid. 4:2.

12. *Ed. note:* See also *Moreh HaNevochim* 1:7.

13. *Ed. note:* Since the Torah tells us that "Noach awoke from his intoxication and knew what his smallest son [Cham] *had done* to him" (BeReshith 9:24), the implication is that some unmentioned act was perpetrated against Noach. See *Sanhedrin* 70a and Rashi on BeReshith 9:22. See also *BeR.R.* 36:7, *Tan.*

Noach:15, *Pir.DeR.E.* 23, and *Yal.Sh.* BeReshith:61. For a more detailed discussion of Cham's crime, see *Gur Aryeh* on Rashi, loc. cit.; *Chiddushei Aggadoth* (Maharal) on *Sanhedrin* 70a, ד״ה חד אמר סרסו וכוי; and *Be'er HaGolah*, *Be'er* 5 (pp. 103-4). See also "Unmasking Avraham's Slave: A Midrashic Analysis of Eli'ezer," *Jewish Thought*, 1, No. 1, 50-51.

14. *Ed. note:* See *BeR.R.* 36:6, *Tan. Noach*:15, *Yal.Sh.* BeReshith:61, and Rashi on BeReshith 9:23.

15. *Ed. note:* Regarding Yefeth's reaction and the values it expressed, see also *Gur Aryeh* on BeReshith 9:23, R. S.R. Hirsch on BeReshith 9:27, *HaTorah VeHaMitzvah* (Malbim) on BeReshith 9:23, and *Ha'amek Davar* on BeReshith 9:23, 26-27. In addition, see "Unmasking Avraham's Slave," p. 76, n. 34.

16. See *BeR.R.* 36:6. See also the sources cited in n. 14, above.

17. See BeReshith 10:2.

18. See Yechezkel 39:11-16.

19. See ibid. 38:18-39:6.

20. See ibid. 38:1-17.

21. See BeReshith 11:10-26.

22. See *Mechilta DeR. Shimon b. Yochai, Tazria*.

23. See *Mid. Tehillim* 9:16, based upon Yirmeyahu 10:14.

24. See Ramban on BeReshith 1:4, ד״ה וירא א-לקים את-האור כי-טוב.

25. *Ed. note:* "For (כי) all is emptiness" is understood here conditionally — "*when* [i.e., *if*] all is emptiness" — in accordance with one of the four standard meanings of "כי." See *Rosh HaShanah* 3a, *Ta'anith* 9a, *Gittin* 90a, and *Shevu'oth* 49b, and see com., loc. cit. See especially Rashi on *Rosh HaShanah*, loc. cit., ד״ה כדריש לקיש, and on *Ta'anith* and on *Gittin*, loc. cit., ד״ה כי משמש ארבע לשונות, and the Tosafoth on *Rosh HaShanah*, loc. cit., ד״ה אי דילמא אלא דהא, where numerous corroborative examples are cited. See also Rashi on BeReshith 18:15 and on Shemoth 34:9. In addition, see Rashi on BeReshith 24:33 and 43:7 and on BeMidbar 20:29.

26. *Ed. note:* Significantly, Chazal expound this verse from Koheleth similarly:

> "What benefit does man have from all his effort that he exerts under the sun?" — Said R. Shemu'el b. Nachmani: ... From *his* effort there is no benefit, but from the effort of *Torah* [study] there is benefit. Said R. Yudan: [From effort that he exerts] *under* the sun he has no [benefit], but [from effort that he exerts] *beyond* the sun he has [benefit].
>
> (*VaY.R.* 28:1, *Koh.R.* 1:3)

Indeed, it is this understanding of Koheleth's message that justifies in part Chazal's assessment that Koheleth's "beginning is words of Torah and its conclusion is words of Torah" (*Shabbath* 30b).

"COME TO CHESHBON":
An *Aggadah* According to the Vilna Ga'on

Aharon Feldman

The essay that follows is based upon the sources provided below:

Therefore the rulers say,
   "Come to Cheshbon;
   be built and established, city of Sichon.
	על־כן יאמרו המשלים,
	באו חשבון;
	תבנה ותכונן, עיר סיחון:

"For a fire has gone forth from Cheshbon,
   a blaze from the fortress of Sichon;
   it has consumed Ar of Mo'av,
   the masters of the high places of Arnon."
	כי־אש יצאה מחשבון,
	להבה מקרית סיחן;
	אכלה ער מואב,
	בעלי במות ארנן:

And Cheshbon lost its power until Divon;
   it was laid waste as far as Nofach,
   which [reaches] until Meideva.
   (BeMidbar 21:27-28, 30)
	ונירם אבד חשבון, עד־דיבן;
	ונשים עד־נפח,
	אשר עד־מידבא:

RABBI FELDMAN, a well-known Torah scholar residing in Yerushalayim, is the author of *The Juggler and the King* (Yerushalayim: Feldheim, 1990), an English adaptation of *Perush al Kammah Aggadoth* (*Commentary on Several* Aggadoth) — which comprises interpretations of some of the most bizarre and cryptic Aggadic passages in the Talmud — by R. Eliyyahu of Vilna (the Vilna Ga'on, 5480-5558 [1720-1797]).
"Come to Cheshbon" is the author's adaptation of one of the most complex of these passages, which was omitted from *The Juggler and the King* for reasons explained in the author's introduction. *Jewish Thought* is privileged to present it to its readership as a sampling of the Ga'on's remarkable insights.

אמר רבי שמואל בר נחמן אמר רבי יוחנן:[1]

R. Shemu'el b. Nachman said in the name of R. Yochanan:[1]

מאי דכתיב, **על־כן יאמרו המשלים**, וגו'?
המשלים — אלו המושלים ביצרם.
באו חשבון — בואו ונחשב חשבונו של עולם: הפסד מצוה כנגד שכרה ושכר עבירה כנגד הפסדה.

What is the meaning of the verses *"Therefore the rulers say,"* etc.?
"The rulers" — These are the rulers over their *yetzer* [(evil) inclination].
"Come to Cheshbon (חשבון)*"* — [They say,] "Come and make the supreme reckoning ['חשבון' also means 'reckoning']: the loss incurred by a *mitzvah* against its profit and the profit gained by a sin against its loss."

תבנה ותכונן — אם אתה עושה כן, **תבנה** בעולם הזה **ותכונן** לעולם הבא.
עיר סיחון — אם משים אדם עצמו כעיר זה שמהלך אחר סיחה נאה, מה כתיב אחריו:

"Be built and established" — If you do this, you will be *"built"* in this world and *"established"* in the world to come.
"City (עיר) *of Sichon* (סיחון)*"* — [You will be established in the world to come by means of] one who conducts himself like a young donkey (עיר)[2] pursuing an attractive female donkey (סיח)....[3]

כי־אש יצאה מחשבון וגו' — תצא אש ממחשבין ותאכל את שאינן מחשבין.
ולהבה מקרית סיחן — מקרית צדיקים שנקראו שיחין.

"For a fire has gone forth from Cheshbon" — A fire will go forth from those who make a reckoning and consume those who do not make a reckoning.
And *"a blaze from the fortress of Sichon* (סיחן)*"* — [This refers to a blaze going forth] from the fortress of the righteous, who are called *"trees* (שיחין)*."*[4]

אכלה ער מואב — זה המהלך אחר יצרו, כעיר זה שמהלך אחר סיחה נאה.
בעלי במות ארנן — אלו גסי הרוח. דאמר מר, כל אדם שיש בו גסות הרוח נופל בגיהנם.

"It has consumed Ar (ער) *of Mo'av"* — [Ar refers to] one who follows his lust for physical gratification like a young donkey (עיר)[5] pursuing an attractive female donkey.
"The masters of the high places of Arnon" — These are the conceited. For the master has taught, "Whoever is conceited falls into Geihinnom."

ונירם — אמר רשע, אין רם.
אבד חשבון — אבד חשבונו של עולם.
עד־דיבן — המתן עד שיבא דין.[8]
אמר הקדוש ברוך הוא,[9] **ונשים עד־נפח** — עד שתבא אש שאינה צריכה ניפוח.
עד־מידבא — עד שתדאיב נשמתן....

"And ... its power (ונירם)*"* — The wicked man says, "There is no [Most] High (אין רם)."[6]
"Cheshbon lost" — "The supreme reckoning is lost.

"Until Divon (דיבן)" — "Wait until suffering comes (יבא דין)[7] [upon you, the righteous]."[8]

The Holy One Blessed be He says [in response to the wicked],[9] " *'It was laid waste as far as Nofach (נפח)'* — [You will be laid waste] to the point of a fire coming that needs no fanning (ניפוח).[10]

"Until Meideva (מידבא)" — "[You will be laid waste] to the point where the souls [of the wicked] will be anguished (תדאיב)."[11] ...

(*Babba Bathra* 78b-79a)

1. INTRODUCTION

Long before the nation of Yisra'el entered Eretz Yisra'el, Sichon, king of the Emorim, waged war against the king of Mo'av, conquering many of his cities up to Wadi Arnon and annexing them to the land of the Emorim. The Torah records the victory song (BeMidbar 21:27-30) celebrating Sichon's conquest. Why should a war between two Gentile kings be included in the eternal Torah? What importance could there be in a song immortalizing that war?

Chazal explain that the song of the Emori conquerors of Mo'av is the key to understanding another, far more important battle: the ongoing struggle between man's physical and spiritual natures. It is in this light that we confront the Talmudic passage quoted above: This is Chazal's explanation of the song's hidden meaning. Expressed, as always, in their cryptic shorthand, it means little until the underlying concepts have been elucidated.

Upon consideration, difficulties abound in this passage. First, there is an obvious inconsistency in expounding "סיחון" ("Sichon") initially as "סיח" ("donkey") — in reference to "one who follows his lust for physical gratification" — and subsequently as "שיחין" ("trees"), in reference to "the righteous, who are called 'trees.' " More generally, the thrust of many of the Midrashic expositions employed here seems strained at best, often in marked defiance of the implication of both the words and the structure of the verses. Furthermore, the internal logic that binds together the various statements of the *derasha* (exposition) is largely elusive. After raising the above difficulties, the Vilna Ga'on — in his commentary, *Perush al Kammah Aggadoth* — clarifies the underlying concepts in this passage. With him as our guide, we proceed to explicate the *derasha* before us.

2. "COME TO CHESHBON" — THE SUPREME RECKONING

The Gemara begins with an invitation: " 'Come to Cheshbon' — *Come and make the supreme reckoning: the loss incurred by a* mitzvah *against its profit and the profit gained by a sin against its loss.*" This invitation, however, is extended by a specific group: "Therefore *the rulers* say, 'Come to Cheshbon.' " The Gemara clarifies the rulers' identity: " 'The rulers' — *These are the rulers over their* yetzer *[(evil) inclination].*"

This *derasha* raises an obvious question: Why do only those who rule over their *yetzer hara* issue this call to reckoning? Should not everyone be party to such a call? Certainly those who do not rule over their *yetzer hara* would benefit more by taking stock of their actions. Why, then, does the verse associate only those who rule over their *yetzer hara* with "the supreme reckoning"?

The key to this puzzle may be derived from an obscure passage in *Zohar*:

> "Tell the imprisoned, 'Go out!' and those in darkness, 'Be revealed [to the light of day]!' " (Yeshayahu 49:9) — These are the straw and the chaff.
> (ibid., III, 247a)

Zohar's comment seems enigmatic. After all, the verse in Yeshayahu speaks of prisoners and people caught in darkness. How are prisons and darkness related to straw and chaff?

Evidently, on *Zohar*'s level of understanding, Yeshayahu's message is addressed not to those subjected to external imprisonment or physical darkness but to those imprisoned in and encompassed by the darkness of their own spiritual impurities. Man's true self is expressed in his innate drive to seek out and to draw near to G-d's presence. But man can "imprison" this true self, and swallow it up in "darkness," by accentuating materialistic values in life. "Straw" and "chaff" describe the "prison" and the "darkness" of man's inner space.

The Torah tells us that *"man is [like] a tree of the field"* (Devarim 20:19). Grain, the "staff of life" — to which Chazal refer as a "tree"[12] — is a metaphor for human life itself. For grain to become edible, the excess growths that surround it must first be removed through threshing and winnowing. Only then can the true essence of grain — the kernel — be utilized by man for his sustenance. There are two such kinds of undesirable growths in grain: one attached to the head of grain (the straw) and another that covers over the grain (the chaff).[13] These correspond to the two main factors that keep man from expressing his true self — his spiritual essence — and thereby realizing his true potential.

The first results when man is aware of his true goals in life but, due to either habit or peer pressure, he is so preoccupied with materialism that he lacks the strength to change his ways. In other words, he is *"imprisoned"* by the drives of his body and unable to appreciate the great spiritual potential within him. The second results when man rationalizes his materialistic way of life. Materialism has so perverted his thought processes that he is convinced that gratification of his impulses is the proper goal of life. In addition to his "imprisonment," he has become enveloped by a *"darkness"* that blocks out the light of truth. Blind to all but his lusts, he is not even interested in truth. His life exemplifies Chazal's observation that "once a person has committed an offense and repeated it ... it becomes as if permitted to him" (*Yoma* 86b and 87a).

It is to these two major obstacles to spiritual growth that the images of "straw" and "chaff" refer: Straw symbolizes the first factor and chaff the second. Even after grain is harvested, straw represents its original attachment to the earth. The "straw" of man's existence is what binds him to his earthly nature: the material outlook to which he is attached and the habits and drives that are part of him. Just as grain is inedible without threshing, human life is useless until it is separated from this earthly pull and raised above it. The second factor that distances man from G-d — the inability to recognize truth — is symbolized by chaff. Just as chaff hides the edible grain from the light of day, man's spiritual "chaff" blinds him to the light of truth.

This, then, is the meaning of *Zohar*'s comment on the prophet's exhortation, *"Tell the imprisoned, 'Go out!' and those in darkness, 'Be revealed [to the light of day]!'"* *Zohar* tells us that the prophet's words are addressed to both classes of transgressors: *"These are the straw and the chaff."* To those "imprisoned" by bodily-oriented habits of materialism, Yeshayahu says, "Go out!": Free yourselves from your imprisonment. To those whose vision is impaired and who willfully exchange eternity for passing fancies, he says, "Be revealed [*to the light of day*]!" Man must shake off both the straw of materialism and the chaff of falsehood; only then will he be free to develop into the true person he was meant to be.

The order of the two clauses of this verse is clearly significant. To break out of slavery, one must first free oneself from his "imprisonment," by changing his habits and society, before he can begin to see the "light of day." Merely convincing himself intellectually — before his body is ready to respond to what his mind tells him is his obligation — will accomplish nothing, for habit rules man far more than knowledge does.

This distinction between "straw" and "chaff" also clarifies the difference between two terms continually used in Scripture: "תוכחה" ("rebuke") and "מוסר" ("chastisement"). "תוכחה," from the root "הכח" (~ prove), means convincing another intellectually of the wrongness of his actions. By contrast, "מוסר," from the root "יסר" (~ restrict), denotes discipline through either verbal chastisement or corporal punishment, both of which are means to train the body's responses. Likewise, "rebuke" is principally directed to an *intellectual* assessment of the past, while "chastisement" is directed to *behavioral* changes in the present and future. Significantly, we encounter in Mishlei 6:23 the compound expression "תוכחות מוסר" ("rebukes of chastisement"). Ultimately, "rebuke" must be built on a foundation of "chastisement." Only after successfully applying "chastisement" on a behavioral level can fruitful "rebuke" be applied to past actions. As long as bad habits persist, intellectual convictions will remain ineffective. Thus, exhorts the prophet, *"Plow yourselves a field instead of sowing into the thorns"* (Yirmeyahu 4:3).

With this insight provided by *Zohar* and its use of the symbols of straw and chaff, we are prepared to answer the question posed above regarding the "supreme reckoning" that the Gemara enjoins us to make. Why are specifically the "rulers," who rule over their *yetzer*, associated with this reckoning of the true worth of their deeds? Should not those who do not rule over their *yetzer* be involved in such reckoning as well? The answer is that anyone in fact can make this reckoning, but only the "rulers" will find it worthwhile. For the reckoning will influence only a person who has already liberated himself from the fetters of his evil tendencies and habits. No matter how convinced a person is — intellectually — that the profits of *mitzvoth* are preferable to the rewards of sin, his body will not permit him to act out his conviction unless he has trained himself to accept the *rule* of his intellect. Only someone who has removed himself from the imprisonment of the "straw" can begin to make the profitable reckoning that will free him of his "chaff."

3. "BE BUILT AND ESTABLISHED" — THE SHARE OF THE RIGHTEOUS

Our *derasha* continues with the ultimate results of this reckoning, emphasizing a concept that affects the reward of the righteous and the punishment of the evildoers in the world to come: " *'Be built and established'* — If you do this, you will be *'built'* in this world and *'established'* in the world to come." By making the reckoning and living the life of a righteous person, one will have *"built"* his reward. Furthermore, he will have *"established"* his share in the world to come. Since an "establishment" is more than a "building," this passage seems to imply that the righteous person receives even more reward than his actions warrant. What is the basis of this, and how is it possible?

The Talmud records the following exposition in the name of R. Akiva:

> *"The one as well as the other the L-rd made"* (Koheleth 7:14) — ... [G-d] created the righteous; He created the wicked. He created Gan Eden; He created Geihinnom. Each and every person has two portions: one in Gan Eden and one in Geihinnom. A righteous person, through his merit, takes his portion and his [wicked] fellow's portion in Gan Eden. A wicked person, through his guilt, takes his portion and his [righteous] fellow's portion in Geihinnom.
>
> Said R. Mesharsheya: What Biblical verse [implies this]? Regarding the righteous, it is written, *"Therefore in their land they will possess a double portion"* (Yeshayahu 61:7). Regarding the wicked, it is written, *"And destroy them with double destruction"* (Yirmeyahu 17:18).
>
> (*Chagigah* 15a)

Chazal emphasize here that G-d created the world in such a manner that a person's ultimate reward is what he chooses for himself. If he chooses a life of the spirit, a share awaits him in Gan Eden; if he follows a life of materialism, he is implicitly choosing a share in Geihinnom. Moreover, by speaking of the *two* portions prepared for every person, the Talmud tells us what becomes of the righteous person's rejected share in Geihinnom and the wicked person's rejected share in Gan Eden: The righteous person is given his wicked neighbor's "vacant" share of reward, and the wicked person inherits — besides his own punishment — the place left vacant by the righteous person's choice in life.

Initially, we may wonder what justice there is in such a "trade." However, we must realize that each person's actions affect the disposition of evil in the world as a whole. The righteous person's choice of spirituality enhanced the sensitivity of all men to spirituality — even that of the evildoer. Bolstered by the good deeds of the righteous, had the wicked person responded to the call of his spirit, it would have been that much easier for him to have ceased his evil behavior. In spite of this, he continued in his bankrupt ways. He therefore deserves a double portion of Geihinnom: both for the evil ways that he chose and for spurning the good that would have been so easy for him to have accepted. On the other hand, the righteous person deserves an extra share of Gan Eden because of the evildoer's deeds. When the wicked person chose evil, he reinforced evil in the world at large. It thus became more difficult for the righteous person to maintain his ways. Since he nevertheless managed to retain his righteousness, he deserves a double share in Gan Eden: both for his initial choice and for rejecting this strengthened evil.

As a result of this "trade," the wicked person's fate is doubly bitter, for, as the Gemara implies, he inherits the evil that others have abandoned. But the righteous "ruler" finds his reckoning doubly rewarding: Not only is he "built" in this world, enjoying the fulfilling life of producing mankind's spiritual fruit, but he is also "established" in the world to come. Just as an "establishment" is more than just a building, so his share in Gan Eden is even more than the share to which his actions entitle him.

Because of his life's choice, he inherits the good abandoned by the wicked.

Thus, the continuation of the Gemara emphasizes the basis of this "establishment" of the righteous. While it would appear that the *derasha* divides a single clause into two unrelated statements — ascribing *"Be built and established"* to the righteous and *"city of Sichon"* to the wicked — these adjacent expositions are actually causatively linked: *"[You will be established in the world to come by means of]* one who conducts himself like a young donkey pursuing an attractive female donkey." It is through the evildoer's decision to be transformed into the *"city of Sichon"* — a city that epitomized the moral bankruptcy which our *derasha* relates to its name — that the righteous person is *"established"* in the world to come. When the wicked person decided to follow donkey-like his physical drives at the expense of his spiritual drives, he necessarily forfeited his share in Gan Eden, and his righteous counterpart assumed it. It is thus the "city of Sichon" that enhances the righteous person's basic share in the world to come, producing not only a "building" but an "establishment" as well.

But what of the wicked? Have they no arguments to offer in their own defense? Our *derasha* now proceeds to consider their fate.

4. "A FIRE HAS GONE FORTH FROM CHESHBON" — THE PUNISHMENT OF THE WICKED

The Gemara relates the second verse of our passage to the first: " *'For a fire has gone forth from Cheshbon'* — A fire will go forth from those who make a reckoning and consume those who do not make a reckoning." The emphasis is not only on the wicked person's punishment in Geihinnom and his inability to excuse himself for the selfish and evil life he led that necessitated such punishment. In addition, the *derasha* teaches us that this punishment will mirror the righteous person's reward. For besides the wicked person's basic punishment in Geihinnom, he will assume the share in Geihinnom that had been "set aside" for the righteous person as well.

Chazal tell us that when evildoers stand in judgment before G-d, they attempt to justify their conduct as the natural consequence of circumstances over which they had no control:

> The Rabbis taught: [When] the poor and the rich and the wicked come [before G-d] in judgment, the poor man is asked, "Why did you not occupy yourself with Torah?" If he answers, "I was poor and busy with the quest for sustenance," they say to him, "Were you poorer than Hillel?" ...
>
> The rich man is asked, "Why did you not occupy yourself with Torah?" If he answers, "I was rich and busy with my business," they say to him, "Were you richer than R. Elazar [b. Charsom]?" ...
>
> The evildoer is asked, "Why did you not occupy yourself with Torah?" If he answers, "I was handsome and busy with my *yetzer*," they say to him, "Were you more handsome than Yosef?" ...
>
> Thus, Hillel indicts the poor, R. Elazar b. Charsom indicts the rich, [and] Yosef indicts the wicked.
>
> (*Yoma* 35b)

It is the living example of the righteous, who prevailed in similar circumstances, that refutes the protestations of the wicked and ultimately indicts them. Thus, "*A fire will go forth from those who make a reckoning and consume those who do not make a reckoning*": The fire of judgment that consumes the wicked goes forth from the righteousness of the righteous, which demonstrates conclusively that the wickedness of the wicked was indeed a conscious choice.

Furthermore, this punishment of the wicked parallels what we have already seen of the reward of the righteous: "And '*a blaze from the fortress of Sichon* (סיחון)'" — [This refers to a blaze going forth] *from the fortress of the righteous, who are called 'trees* (שיחין).'"[4] The apparent inconsistency in this derasha has already been noted: Initially, "סיחון" ("Sichon") was expounded as "סיח" ("donkey"), in reference to "one who follows his lust for physical gratification" — while here we find the same word expounded as "שיחין" ("trees"), in reference to "the righteous, who are called 'trees.'" Now, however, we can understand the derasha's intent in light of the Talmud's conclusion that the evildoer receives not only his own punishment but the righteous person's vacant portion of Geihinnom as well.

In the Bible, the righteous are likened to trees, as in Tehillim 92:13: "The righteous will flourish like the palm tree; like a cedar in the Levanon he will grow tall." Just as the palm tree, which bears delicious fruit, grows from a seed in which its potential had lain dormant, the righteous express the latent spirituality with which every human being is endowed. Like the cedar, which towers over other trees, the righteous elevate themselves above the rest of humanity by realizing the innate nobility of their souls. Such productivity and stature are achieved by the righteous by restraining their potential for wickedness and by cultivating their potential for goodness instead. In other words, the righteous replace the lustful "סיח" ("donkey") — which they might have been — with "שיחין" ("trees"), to which they can now be likened.

The potential wickedness of the "סיח" banished by the righteous is their unused portion of Geihinnom. As explained above, this portion is transferred to the evildoers as an additional measure of punishment for having chosen evil. This extra retribution is the "blaze" that goes forth "from the fortress of the righteous, who are called 'trees (שיחין)' " to consume the evildoers. "סיחון" has indeed maintained its negative connotation throughout the derasha. While earlier it referred to the wicked themselves, here it refers to the potential wickedness of the righteous, which they never actualized. It was this self-restraint that enabled the "tree" of their righteousness to flourish.

A blaze is more than just a fire. Similarly, the way of life of the righteous will bring a greater catastrophe upon the wicked than would be expected as a result of their evil conduct alone. "From the fortress of the righteous" — the fortress of their righteous resolve — comes a rejected place in Geihinnom and double disaster for those who have directed their lives toward moral bankruptcy.

5. "AR OF MO'AV" AND "THE HIGH PLACES OF ARNON" — DUAL ROOTS OF SIN

The conclusion of this verse, as expounded by the Gemara, identifies the wicked, who are consumed by the fire that emanates from Cheshbon: " *'It has consumed Ar of Mo'av'* — [Ar refers to] one who follows his lust for physical gratification like a young donkey pursuing an attractive female donkey. *'The mas-*

ters of the high places of Arnon' — These are the conceited. For the master has taught, 'Whoever is conceited falls into Geihinnom.' "

All human evil has two basic roots: *ta'avah* (the desire for physical gratification) and *ga'avah* (the desire for power and glory). "Ar of Mo'av," whose name suggests "עיר" ("young donkey"), alludes to someone who sins because his *ta'avah* is out of control. Such a person, who has permitted his animal nature to dominate his life, is appropriately compared to a young donkey chasing after a female of the species. Furthermore, the Torah hints at another aspect of this town's name by reminding us that it is "Ar *of Mo'av*": part of a nation conceived through incest[14] and driven by its quest for hedonistic satisfaction. Mo'av was the nation that declared it the civic duty of its daughters to entice Yisra'el to sin with them.[15] The Midrash relates that even drinking the water of this land intensifies lust.[16] In contrast, "the masters of the high places of Arnon" alludes to those who sin out of *ga'avah*. For these "masters," life's goals are self-aggrandizement and arrogance. The consequences of their sin are no less disastrous than those of Ar. Both "Ar of Mo'av" and "the masters of the high places of Arnon" — and what they symbolize — are consumed by the fire of judgment that emanates from the righteous.

Nevertheless, in spite of the apparent equivalence between the lustful "Ar of Mo'av" and the prideful "masters of the high places of Arnon," the Gemara emphasizes a distinction in their fates: *"For the master has taught, 'Whoever is* conceited *falls into Geihinnom.'* " We can better understand this distinction in light of the correlation that must exist between a crime and its punishment.

The punishment meted out for man's sins after his death is not vengeful but rehabilitative; its ultimate purpose is to reform him. Having spent his life doing evil and developing all the anti-spiritual strains of his character, man is left unable to come close to the divine presence. The punishment of the afterlife is designed to remove the evil that clings to him. Not surprisingly, the retribution for the two major categories of sin — lust and pride — corresponds to their respective natures.

Sins of physical gratification — the "fire" of lust — are punished by the *"fire"* of Geihinnom. Geihinnom is, of course, a spiritual punishment; "fire" is merely its nearest analogy in earthly terms. Just as, on earth, fire is used to remove forbidden impurities absorbed in utensils,[17] so the "fire" of Geihinnom purifies sinners from the taint of their illicit physical indulgence. On the other hand, whoever has been conceited *"falls"* into Geihinnom: The prideful impurities of the soul are purged by a spiritual experience whose closest earthly equivalent is a constant sensation of falling. The arrogant man spent his lifetime raising his heart high; this attitude must be rectified by a feeling of constant lowering. Accordingly, we are told, "Whoever is conceited *falls* into Geihinnom."

6. "IT WAS LAID WASTE AS FAR AS NOFACH" — THE FINAL DOOM OF WICKEDNESS

Sometimes G-d gives a wicked person free rein. In fact, Chazal say that one should not even attempt to oppose an evildoer at the height of his success:

> Said R. Yitzchak: If you see a wicked person when times are going well for him, do not provoke him, as it is said, *"His ways are always prosperous"* (Tehillim 10:5). Furthermore, he will win any suit [brought against him], as it is said, "Your judgments are far above, away from him" (ibid.). Furthermore, he will see [the downfall of] his adversaries, as it is said, "He puffs [in contempt] at all his adversaries" (ibid.).
>
> (Berachoth 7b)

Even an ordinary righteous person[18] cannot prevail against such good fortune of the wicked.[19]

The evildoer interprets this flow of beneficence to him as a vindication of his belief that G-d does not direct the world and that everything is mere chance. Our derasha presents the wicked person's credo: "The wicked man says, 'There is no [Most] High....' " Implicit in this rejection of G-d is his own self-importance: If there is no "Most High," then it is he who is high, beyond anything else, including G-d. Furthermore, he continues, "... *The supreme reckoning is lost*...." In other words, divine providence is a chimera. Finally, he boasts to the righteous, "... *Wait until suffering comes"*[7] upon you, while I prosper. Wait and see that my way is right. Suffering will come, he predicts, to the point of anguish for everyone else — but not for himself.[20]

But reckoning is not lost, nor does the power of the successful wicked person last forever. The Gemara continues, "The Holy One Blessed be He says [in response to the wicked], ' "*It was laid waste as far as Nofach*" — [You will be laid waste] to the point of a fire coming that needs no fanning, "*until Meideva*" — to the point where the souls [of the wicked] will be anguished.' " When he moves on to the next world, the evildoer will find out what he has done to himself through his insistence on transient pleasures and self-serving pursuits. Having neglected and starved his own soul, what is left of him other than the flesh that he so loved? And what ultimately is the significance of such "flesh"?

The Talmud provides us with an insightful definition of "flesh":

> Said R. Yochanan: Flesh (בשר) [stands for the initials of] "*shame* (בושה)," "*putrid* (סרוחה),"[21] [and] "*worms* (רימה)."
>
> There are those who say [that flesh (בשר) stands for the initials of "*shame* (בושה),"] "*purgatory* (שאול)" [and "*worms* (רימה)"].
>
> (*Sotah* 5a)

Initially, one wonders why Chazal offered two different acrostics for "בשר" ("flesh"). On further reflection, we recognize that the Talmud is not presenting us with alternatives; each acrostic tells us something different about man's material existence.

The first acrostic refers to the meaning of physical existence in this world and shows us how man should approach his life on earth. The Mishnah teaches elsewhere:

> Akavya b. Mahalalel says: Reflect upon three matters and you will not come into the grip of sin. Know whence you came and where you are going and before Whom you will in the future give account and reckoning: "*whence you came*" — from a putrid drop; "*and where you are going*" — to a place of dust, decay, and worms; "*and before Whom you will in the future give account and reckoning*" — before the Supreme King of kings, the Holy One Blessed be He.
>
> (*Avoth* 3:1)

R. Yochanan summarizes this entire paragraph in one three-word acrostic. He reminds us that, in this world, your past is "*putrid* (סרוחה)" — "a *putrid* drop"; your present is "*worms* (רימה)" — a journey "to a place of dust, decay, and *worms*"; and your future is *"shame (בושה)"* — the *shame* of giving "account and reckoning before the Supreme King of kings, the Holy One Blessed be He." All this is so if you are foolish enough to live for your "flesh (בשר)" alone.

The second acrostic relates directly to our *derasha*'s conclusion — revealing the culmination of a life of the flesh by specifying the three sorts of retribution that await sinners after death. The prophet spoke of their gruesome end:

> It shall be that every new moon and every Shabbath
> all flesh will come to bow before Me, says G-d.
> They will go out and see
> the corpses of the people who sinned rebelliously against Me:
> for their worm will not die and their fire will not be extinguished,
> and they will be an abhorrence for all flesh.
> (Yeshayahu 66:23-24)

The second acrostic tersely explains this prophecy, detailing the three components of punishment enumerated by Yeshayahu and providing a mnemonic abbreviation for them (in inverse order). The supremacy that the wicked imagined for themselves will be replaced by a sensation of *"shame (בושה)"* — the *shame* of being "an abhorrence for all flesh"; the pleasures to which they dedicated their lives will give way to the fire of *"purgatory (שאול)"* — the *purgatory* fire that "will not be extinguished"; and the bodies whose welfare they fostered will be attacked by *"worms (רימה)"* — "for their *worm* will not die."

These three punishments — shame, purgatory, and worms — represent the three sorts of punishments that the wicked must undergo after death. As discussed above, punishment after death is not vengeful but rehabilitative: a means to purge the impurities that cling to the souls of those who spent their lifetimes preoccupied with evil. Each of these three punishments is intended to eliminate one category of the impurities that have attached themselves to the souls of the wicked.

As explained earlier, the attitude of the prideful, who devoted their lives to the evils of conceit and self-aggrandizement, is rectified by constant falling: *"The master has taught, 'Whoever is conceited falls into Geihinnom.'"* The acrostic summarizes this punishment as *"shame."* For the lustful, the spiritual "fire" of Geihinnom purges the soul of the impurities born of illicit physical indulgences. They are "consumed" — summarized by the acrostic as "purgatory." Finally, the body, which had been an instrument of evil, must also undergo rehabilitative suffering. The Talmud tells us that "a grave-worm is as painful to a dead man as a needle in the flesh of a living man" (Berachoth 18b, Shabbath 13b and 152a). This is the pain of chibbut hakkever (threshing of the grave), to which the acrostic refers tersely as "worms."

We recall the evildoer's threefold credo as expressed in our *derasha*. During his life, he arrogantly proclaimed, *"There is no [Most] High"* — therefore, no one is higher than I; *"The supreme reckoning is lost"* — therefore, I am free to choose hedonism; and *"Wait until suffering comes"* upon you — for I above all am safe. Our *derasha* concludes with G-d's threefold response. In light of the foregoing, we can appreciate how fitting a response this is.

"It was laid waste...." In other words, *you* will be laid waste before all mankind. "ונשים" (here trans. "it was laid waste") is derived from the root "שמם" (~ desolate), which can also mean "horrify," as in "they will clothe themselves in trembling, they will sit on the ground; they will tremble every moment, *and be horrified* (ושממו) over you" (Yechezkel 26:16). Although you said that no one is as great as you, in the end — as Yeshayahu prophesied — you *"will be an abhorrence for all flesh."* "Shame (בושה)" will be your lot as all mankind watches in horror while you fall from your selfish pride through endless realms of emptiness — until, finally, humility enters your soul.

"[You will be laid waste] to the point of a fire coming that needs no fanning." You said that there is no reckoning, but the fire of *"purgatory* (שאול)" will be fed by your own misdeeds: No other fanning will be necessary. You thought that pleasure was all; now see how the reward of sin weighs against its final loss, as you and your hedonistic life-style are purged through a fire that *"will not be extinguished."*

"[You will be laid waste] to the point where the souls [of the wicked] will be anguished." Destruction will even strike your most beloved possession of all: your precious body. You said that the righteous, whom you scorned, would suffer — but never you. But now your soul will be anguished by the *"worms* (רימה)" that devour your flesh. You thought that you alone would be safe,

but now it is specifically the grave-worm that *"will not die"* as it consumes your body.

7. CONCLUSION — THE POWER OF TORAH STUDY

The Gemara warns us of the consequences of sin so that we may seek the only ultimate protection from them — the study of Torah. Indeed, at the conclusion of our *derasha*, the Gemara warns that one who leaves the study of Torah will eventually be overcome by both major roots of sin. Concerning the temptation of lust, it states:

> R. Yehudah said in the name of Rav: Whoever abstains from words of Torah *is consumed by fire*, as it is said, "I shall set My countenance against them; they have gone forth from the fire [i.e., from the Torah (Rashi)], and the fire will consume them" (Yechezkel 15:7)....
>
> (*Babba Bathra* 79a)

Likewise, with respect to pride, it continues:

> ... When R. Dimi came, he said in the name of R. Yochanan: Whoever abstains from words of Torah *falls into Geihinnom.*
>
> (ibid.)

By abandoning Torah study, one is exposed to the temptations of lust and pride — and the consequent punishments of being consumed by fire and falling into Geihinnom.

Conversely, whoever is diligent in the study of Torah is spared from these two evils. Therefore, regarding the drive toward lust and physical gratification, the Talmud relates:

> The Holy One Blessed be He said to Yisra'el: My children, I created the *yetzer hara*, and I created Torah as its spice [i.e., antidote].
>
> (*Kiddushin* 30b)

Similarly, regarding man's drive toward pride and glory, we note that — among the elements in the progression of spiritual refinement initiated by Torah — Chazal specify:

> Torah engenders ... *humility....*
>
> (*Avodah Zarah* 20b)

"Therefore the rulers say, 'Come to Cheshbon.'" If a man does not rule over himself, all his victories must some day turn to defeat. The wise man, who has conquered his self-defeating habits, calls

the world to account: "Come and make the supreme reckoning: the loss incurred by a *mitzvah* against its profit and the profit gained by a sin against its loss."

NOTES

1. This version of the text appears in the standard Vilna (Romm) version of the Talmud Bavli and accords with the Vilna Ga'on's reading. According to *Massoreth HaShas* (loc. cit.), however, the text should read, "אמר רבי שמואל בר **נחמני** אמר רבי **יונתן**" ("R. Shemu'el b. *Nachmani* said in the name of R. *Yonathan*").

2. "עיר" is expounded as "עיר" ("young [male] donkey").

3. "סיחון" is expounded as "סיח" ("donkey").

4. "סיחן" is expounded as "שיחין" ("trees"), since "ס" and "ש" are often interchangeable, as in n. 21.

5. "ער" (like "עיר," in n. 2) is also expounded as "עיר" ("young [male] donkey").

6. "ונירם" is expounded phonetically as "אין רם" ("there is no High"), referring to the "Most High," G-d.

7. By transposition of its letters, "דיבן" is expounded as "יבא דין" ("suffering comes"). Note that "דין" (lit. "judgment") is translated contextually here as "suffering," in accordance with the Vilna Ga'on's reading. (Compare the text readings according to the standard Vilna [Romm] version of the Talmud Bavli, and according to *Haghoth HaBach*, cited in n. 8.)

8. This version of the text accords with the Vilna Ga'on's reading. In the standard Vilna (Romm) version of the Talmud Bavli, however, the text reads, "אמר הקדוש ברוך הוא, המתן עד שיבא דין" ("The Holy One Blessed be He says [in response to the wicked], 'Wait until judgment comes [upon you].' "). According to *Haghoth HaBach* (loc. cit.), the text reads, "אמור לו, רשע! המתן עד שיבא דין" ("Say to him, 'Wicked one! Wait until judgment comes [upon you].' ").

9. This version of the text accords with the Vilna Ga'on's reading. In the standard Vilna (Romm) version of the Talmud Bavli, however, the words "אמר הקדוש ברוך הוא" ("The Holy One Blessed be He says [in response to the wicked]"), which already introduced the previous statement (see n. 8), are not repeated here.

10. "נפח" is expounded as "ניפוח" ("fanning").

11. By transposition of its letters, "מידבא" is expounded as "תדאיב" ("will be anguished").

12. See, for example, *Sanhedrin* 70b and Rashi on *Rosh HaShanah* 16a, ד"ה שתי הלחם.

13. The third undesirable part of wheat — the bran — is not germane to the present discussion. See my discussion of bran in *The Juggler and the King* (Yerushalayim: Feldheim, 1990), pp. 158-60.

14. *Ed. note:* Regarding Mo'av's incestuous roots and its legacy of licentiousness and immorality, see BeReshith 19:33-37; *Sifrei* on Devarim 33:2; *BeR.R.* 51:10; *BeM.R.* 20:23; *Ru.R.* 5:14; *Tan. Balak*:17; and *Yal.Sh.* BeReshith:86, BeMidbar:771, Devarim:951, and Yirmeyahu:331.
15. See BeMidbar 25:1-2, 15, and com., loc. cit. See also *Yer. Sanhedrin* 10:2 (37b) and *Tan. Balak*:17-18 and *Pinchas*:2.
16. See BeMidbar 25:1 and *Tan. Balak*:17.
17. The process of *libbun* (heating to a glow) renders utensils fit for use through purification by fire: *burning out* any impurities absorbed within them.
18. This is as opposed to a *tzaddik gamur*, a completely righteous person, who has no sins to his discredit. (See *Berachoth*, loc. cit.)
19. We might well wonder what could justify such overwhelming success for an essentially wicked person. While a more extensive treatment of this subject is beyond the scope of this essay, some understanding of this issue is warranted. An evildoer who has done some acts of good in his life deserves reward for them. G-d is just and will not deny him his due. But he cannot receive his reward in the world to come, which he has implicitly rejected with his choice of life. There is nothing left but to give him his reward in this world. However, the Talmud teaches that "there is no reward for *mitzvoth* in this world" (*Kiddushin* 39b, *Chullin* 142a): The dimensions of this world are insufficient to contain such an enormous reward. Of course, the wicked person's *mitzvoth* are always tainted with self-serving motivations, so their reward is less. Nevertheless, when these *mitzvoth* must be rewarded within the limitations of this world, the evildoer will be so successful that none will be able to stand against him. Even the courts will find any judgment against him in his favor, and his enemies — the righteous — will earn his contempt by appearing to be less fortunate than he.
20. *Ed. note:* It is noteworthy that a correspondence clearly exists between these three statements of the evildoer in our *derasha* and the three components of R. Yitzchak's statement (*Berachoth* 7b), quoted above.
21. The "ש" of "בשר" is expounded as "סרוחה," since "ס" and "ש" are often interchangeable, as in n. 4.

"YOU WILL BE LIKE G-D":
Chazal's Conception of the *Yetzer HaRa*
(PART I)

Chaim Eisen

1. INTRODUCTION

According to Chazal, scarcely hours after man was created,[1] human nature underwent its most dramatic transformation ever: By eating of the forbidden fruit of the "tree of knowing good and evil,"[2] man internalized the *yetzer hara*, the so-called drive toward evil. Rashi comments:

> Even though [man] was given abstract knowledge with which to name [the animals], he was not given the *yetzer hara* until he ate of the tree [of knowing good and evil] and the *yetzer hara* entered him....
> (com. on BeReshith 2:25)[3]

Irrevocably, man was changed: "The eyes of both [Adam and Chavvah] *were opened* (ותפקחנה), and they *knew* that they were naked" (BeReshith 3:7). Explains Rambam:

RABBI EISEN, formerly of the faculty of Yeshivat Hakotel, has lectured extensively in *machsheveth Yisra'el* and *parshanuth HaMikra* at post-secondary institutions in Israel. He teaches at Yeshivat Ohr Yerushalayim and at the OU-NCSY Israel Center, and he is editor of *Jewish Thought*. He wrote this essay in memory of his maternal grandmother — מרת הינדא צביה בת ר' משה דב-בער ע"יה — on the לעלוי נשמת occasion of her tenth *yahrtzeit*.

> [The Torah] does not state, "The eyes of both were opened, and they *saw*," for what they saw initially [is what] they saw ultimately ... but [man] obtained a different character through which he apprehended ... what he had not apprehended ... before. And know that this word — namely "פקח" (~ open) — is never stated except with regard to *conceptual innovation*, not with regard to initiation of the sense of sight.[4]
>
> (Moreh HaNevochim 1:2)[5]

Man had rendered himself incapable of apprehending reality as he had moments earlier and unsuited for the world of perfection in which he had been placed. As the psalmist laments, "Man in glory does not endure" (Tehillim 49:13).[6]

Aside from its immediate consequences (the individual punishments of Adam and Chavvah and their banishment from Gan Eden),[7] this transformation was obviously to man's detriment on multiple levels.[8] Certainly the most glaring, however, is the acquired "evil" of the *yetzer hara*, which has lurked within mankind ever since that fateful moment. We need search no further than *parashath BeReshith* to confront the Torah's assessment that "all the *yetzer* [drive] of the thoughts of [man's] heart is exclusively *for evil*, continuously" (BeReshith 6:5). Indeed, the Torah informs us that G-d Himself concedes, "The *yetzer* of man's heart *is evil* from his youth" (ibid. 8:21), to which the Talmud adds dismally, "[How] hard is the *yetzer hara*, inasmuch as even its Creator called it 'evil'!" (*Kiddushin* 30b).[9] In the same vein, the Midrash comments almost bitterly, "Wretched is the dough whose baker testifies that it is evil — '*for the* yetzer *of man's heart is evil from his youth*' " (*BeR.R.* 34:10).[10] Furthermore, Chazal liken the yetzer hara to "an alien god in your midst" (Shabbath 105b, Yal.Sh. Tehillim:831) and identify it as both "the accusing angel [Satan]" and "the angel of death" (Babba Bathra 16a).[11] Considering that its role is to "entice man in this world and testify against him in the world to come" (Sukkah 52b, *Yal.Sh.* Mishlei:962), we might well surmise that the *yetzer hara*, as the very embodiment of evil,[12] is the ultimate impediment to any positive human development.

It seems astounding, then, that the Mishnah understands the Torah's commandment to "love G-d your L-rd *with all your heart*" (Devarim 6:5) as mandating loving G-d "with both your drives

— with the *yetzer tov* [drive toward perfection] and with the *yetzer ra"* (*Mish. Berachoth* 9:5).[13] Even more emphatically, *Zohar* implicates the *yetzer hara* as the basis of "rejoicing in the discussion of Torah laws" (*Zohar*, "*Mid. HaNe'elam*," I, 138a).[14] Moreover, the Midrash apparently extends such dependence on the *yetzer hara* to essentially every human endeavor. Noting the singular evaluation climaxing the Torah's account of Creation — "behold, it was *very* good" (BeReshith 1:31) — the Midrash comments:

> "And behold, it was ... good" — This [refers to] the *yetzer tov*.
>
> "Very [good]" — This [refers to] the *yetzer hara*.
> Is the *yetzer hara* then "*very* good"? Astonishing! However, this teaches you that were it not for the *yetzer hara*, a person would not build a house and would not marry and would not procreate and would not deal in business.
>
> (*BeR.R.* 9:7, *Koh.R.* 3:11 [3])[15]

Surely we do not regard these activities — much less loving G-d and learning Torah — as inherently evil. How then can they be predicated upon a drive that G-d Himself describes as "evil from [man's] youth"?

This paradox appears to be related to an earlier one, which strikes at the very root of our subject. In its seductive presentation of the fruit of the "tree of knowing good and evil" — which precipitated man's acquisition of the *yetzer hara*[16] — the serpent guaranteed that "on the day you eat from it, your eyes will be opened, and *you will be like G-d*"[17] (BeReshith 3:5). The Midrash adds dramatically, " '*You will be like G-d*' — Just as He does, creating worlds ... so you will be able to create worlds" (*Pir.DeR.E.* 13).[18] Yet, despite the criminality of this almost blasphemous seduction, Chazal inform us that the snake "spoke the truth" (*Pirka DeR. HaKadosh*, cited by Ramban on BeReshith 2:9). (In fact, as noted above, the Torah states explicitly that, after Adam and Chavvah ate, "the eyes of both *were opened*" [BeReshith 3:7], just as the serpent predicted.)[19] Is acquisition of the *yetzer hara* the prerequisite of being "like G-d"? What are we then to conclude about this so-called drive toward evil? Evidently, there is more to the *yetzer hara* than meets the eye.

2. "DELIVERED INTO YOUR HANDS"

We seem to be faced with an intractable dilemma. How can we reconcile a fundamentally optimistic view of the *yetzer hara* as the basis of all constructive — and even G-dly — human action with the bleak conclusion that "even its Creator called it 'evil' — as it is said, *'for the* yetzer *of man's heart is evil from his youth'* " (*Kiddushin* 30b)?[9] While these disparate assessments must ultimately derive from a single underlying principle,[20] what positive features can possibly cohere with such a thoroughly negative perspective?

The Midrash responds with an astounding revelation:

> "G-d the L-rd said, 'Behold, man [has become like one of Us,[21] knowing good and evil]' " (BeReshith 3:22) — This [should be understood in light of] what Scripture said, "Lo, only this I found: that the L-rd made man upright [but they sought many contrivances]" (Koheleth 7:29): The Holy One Blessed be He, Who is called "Righteous and Upright" (Devarim 32:4), did not create man "with His essence"[22] (BeReshith 1:27) except in order [for man] to be righteous and upright like Him.
>
> Perhaps you will say: Why did He create the *yetzer hara*, about which it is written, "for the *yetzer* of man's heart *is evil* from his youth" (BeReshith 8:21)? You say that it is evil; who can make it good?
>
> Said the Holy One Blessed be He: *You* make it evil! Why is it that a child of five or six or seven or eight or nine does not sin, but only from age ten and on — and then he cultivates the *yetzer hara*?
>
> Perhaps you will say: No one can safeguard himself [from being corrupted]!
>
> Said the Holy One Blessed be He: *You made it evil!* Why is it that, when you were a child, you did not sin and, when you grew up, you sinned? And [furthermore] there are so many things in the world that are more refractory than the *yetzer hara* and more bitter than it, and you sweeten them. Nothing is more bitter than the lupine, and you diligently seethe it and sweeten it in water seven times until it becomes palatable — and likewise mustard and capers and many [other] things. And if you sweeten for your use [intrinsically] bitter things that I created, how much more so [could you sweeten] the *yetzer hara, which is delivered into your hands*!
>
> (Tan. BeReshith:7)

The Midrash obliges us to concede that the *yetzer hara* is *not* intrinsically evil. Instead, it is "delivered into your hands";[23] if it is evil, it is only because "you made it evil" yourself. Our "*yetzer*," explains R. Avraham b. Ezra, refers collectively to "our *consequences*" (com. on Tehillim 103:14). Similarly, R. S.R. Hirsch notes linguistically that "*yetzer* (יצר)" should literally be rendered not as "drive" but as "that which is formed" (com. on BeReshith 6:5 and 8:21); the *yetzer hara* is not what *drives us* toward evil but what *we ourselves have driven* toward evil.[24] It is not surprising, then, that the Talmud states, "Avraham made [his] *yetzer ra* good" (*Yer. Berachoth* 9:5 [60a], *Yer. Sotah* 5:5 [25b]), since nothing ever constrained it to be bad.

As the Midrash observes, this conclusion is practically stated explicitly in Koheleth. "... *The L-rd made man upright* ..." (ibid. 7:29): The human condition is essentially untainted and pure. Man enters the world in innocence, unencumbered by any "original sin" or consequent "damnation." If man's initial state is "upright," it is impossible to countenance a conception of the *yetzer hara* — or of any other aspect of human nature — as being inherently bad.[25] Any evil associated with man is necessarily of his own design through exercise of his free will: "... *but they sought many contrivances*" (ibid.).

Moreover, the original verse expounded by the Midrash records G-d's concluding response to man's (sinful) acquisition of the *yetzer hara* itself: "Behold, man has become *like one of Us, knowing good and evil*" (BeReshith 3:22). Clearly, this acquisition is not incidental to the *midrash*'s initial statement that "the Holy One Blessed be He, Who is called 'Righteous and Upright,' did not create man 'with His essence' except in order [for man] to be righteous and upright *like Him*." In particular, while we might have postulated that the Midrash was emphasizing that this affirmation is true *in spite* of the *yetzer hara*, the context of the *midrash* — in the wake of the *yetzer hara*'s very acquisition — belies this assumption: The assertion that man was created with G-d's essence "in order to be righteous and upright *like Him*" is true specifically *because* of the *yetzer hara*. Far from being accessory to the thrust of the *midrash*, the *yetzer hara* is its foundation and pivot. Again, this conclusion is practically explicit in Scripture. It is, after all, G-d Who says that "man has become *like one of Us, knowing good and evil*" — by virtue of having eaten the fruit of the tree of "*knowing good and evil*" and having acquired the *yetzer hara*.[16]

The echo of the serpent's seduction is now terrifyingly resonant. The snake's assurance that "on the day you eat from [the fruit of the tree of knowing good and evil] ... *you will be like G-d*" (ibid. 3:5) has received the ultimate approbation — from G-d Himself: "Man has become *like one of Us*"![26] As Chazal informed us, the snake indeed "spoke the truth" (*Pirka DeR. HaKadosh*, cited by Ramban on BeReshith 2:9). Yet, incredibly, the inner meaning of this likeness to G-d that derives from acquisition of the *yetzer hara* is that "the Holy One Blessed be He, Who is called 'Righteous and Upright,' did not create man 'with His essence' except in order [for man] to be righteous and upright like Him"!

What then is the *yetzer hara*, which enters man at birth[27] as the basis not of wickedness but of G-dliness? The Midrash provides a key in G-d's rhetorical exclamation: "Why is it that a child of five or six or seven or eight or nine does not sin, but only from age ten and on — and then he cultivates the *yetzer hara*?" What is the status of the *yetzer hara* in "a child of five or six or seven or eight or nine," and what critical change takes place "from age ten and on"?

3. "YOU WILL BE ABLE TO CREATE WORLDS"

"A Ten-Year-Old"

We readily appreciate the significance of "age ten" in both biological and cognitive domains. Biologically, it approximates the onset of puberty and of physical maturation in general.[28] Correspondingly, it marks a distinct threshold of cognitive development[29] and maturation.[30] In the latter sense, age ten figures prominently in the Mishnah, initiating a qualitatively discrete stage of life: "A five-year-old [is of age] for [studying] Mikra [Scripture]; *a ten-year-old [is of age] for [studying] Mishnah*" (*Avoth* 5:21, *Tan. Kedoshim*:14). The difference between Mikra and Mishnah lies in the dichotomy between *Torah shebikethav* (the written Torah) — to which Mikra inclusively refers — and *Torah shebe'al-peh* (the oral Torah) — of which the Mishnah is the first written codification. *Torah shebikethav*, as its medium of presentation implies, records the concrete, static, and immutable truths and principles of G-d revealed to the world. *Torah shebe'al-peh* analogously comprises the dynamic process of development predicated upon the truths and principles of Torah applied and reapplied throughout time. Whereas *Torah shebikethav* requires our unmitigated passive receipt, *Torah shebe'al-peh* demands our active involvement and innovative effort as well.[31] Thus, Mikra — from the root "קרא" (~ read) — literally means "that which is read," emphasizing the passive absorption of reading; Mishnah — from the root "שנה" (~ study repeatedly) — may emphasize the creative struggle of the nascent scholar.[32] While the Mishnah considers a five-year-old capable of absorbing Mikra, the cognitive faculties and innovative prowess that are the hallmark of the ten-year-old are deemed indispensable for interacting with Mishnah.

The nature of this cognitive leap is obviously linked to the biological maturation noted above (puberty), which enables one human being to *create* another. Herein also lies the related significance of "age ten and on" in the development of the *yetzer hara*, as is perhaps intimated by *Zohar*'s cryptic comment that "*Torah shebe'al-peh* is from the aspect of the tree of knowing good and evil" (*Zohar*, I, 27a).[33] What mastery of *Torah shebe'al-peh* requires and what a ten-year-old acquires is what the *yetzer hara* represents: *the creative capacity of man.*[34]

Again the serpent's precognition echoes hauntingly, especially through the mouthpiece of Chazal: " '*You will be like G-d*' — Just as He does, *creating* worlds ... so you will be able to *create* worlds" (*Pir.DeR.E.* 13).[18] In this sense, the *yetzer hara* is indeed the basis of G-dliness in man. Through it, man acquires a divine faculty shared with no other being save the Creator: Man — like G-d, so to speak — becomes a *creator* himself. Thus, "*yetzer* (יצר)" derives from the root "יצר" (~ create),[35] clearly emphasizing the creative dimension of man that it embodies.[36] Fundamentally, it is the root of all human creativity in this world.

The "Fire" of Creativity

The context in which the *yetzer hara* originally appears in the Torah suggests creativity on the most elemental biological level, sexuality: the capacity to *create* a human being. Thus, the seduction of the snake is framed by the Torah's conclusion that "man leaves his father and his mother and cleaves to his wife, and they become one flesh" (BeReshith 2:24) — which Rashi understands as an allusion to "the offspring, formed through both [parents], wherein their flesh is made one" (com., loc. cit.).³⁷ And man's consequent eating of the fruit of the "tree of *knowing* good and evil" is framed by the Torah's record that "the man *knew* Chavvah, his wife, and she conceived and bore Kayin" (ibid. 4:1).³⁸

Furthermore, the serpent is introduced on the heels of the Torah's observation that "they were both naked, the man and his wife, and not ashamed" (ibid. 2:25).³⁹ And the most immediate consequence of the resultant internalization of the *yetzer hara* was that "the eyes of both were opened, and they knew that they were naked" (ibid. 3:7). Sexuality per se is not essentially contingent upon acquisition of the *yetzer hara*; animals procreate without possessing such a force.⁴⁰ Human sexuality, however, with its concomitant self-perception of nakedness, modesty, and shame, is uniquely human — and explicitly within the province of the *yetzer hara*. Therefore, "until [man] ate of the tree [of knowing good and evil], and the *yetzer hara* entered him," comments Rashi, "*they did not know the way of modesty* [to refrain from nakedness]" (com. on BeReshith 2:25, quoted above).³

Amplifying this theme, the Talmud speaks explicitly of "the *yetzer* of [sexual] transgression" and describes the consequences of the ill-fated attempt by the men of the Great Assembly to "imprison it" (*Yoma* 69b, *Sanhedrin* 64a):⁴¹ After three days, "they sought a fresh egg in all of Eretz Yisra'el for a sick person and found none" (ibid.). In the absence of the *yetzer hara*, even the most minimal level of biological creativity — at least as it impinged on man — ground to a halt. Understandably, the Talmud relates that the men of the Great Assembly had been forewarned by the prophet Zecharyah: "See that if you kill [the *yetzer* of sexual transgression], the world will be destroyed" (*Yoma*, loc. cit.; *Yal.Sh.* Nechemyah:1071). It was man's acquisition of the *yetzer hara* that precipitated his banishment from Gan Eden and his entry into this world; this world is predicated upon the creative capacity conferred by the *yetzer hara*.⁴² Without that creativity, the world as we know it cannot exist.

In this light, we can readily appreciate an alternate version of the Midrashic exposition quoted earlier concerning G-d's evaluation of all that He had created:

> *"And behold, it was very good"* (BeReshith 1:31) — This [refers to] the *yetzer hara*.
>   Is the *yetzer hara* then called "good"? However, this teaches that, were it not for the *yetzer hara*, a person would not marry and would not beget children, *and the world would not endure*.
>   (*Mid. Tehillim* 9:1, *Yal.Sh.* Tehillim:643)[43]

While G-d could have created a world whose existence would not be contingent upon the sexual creativity of the *yetzer hara*, the world *as we know it* could not endure otherwise.

On a deeper level, we realize that human creativity certainly has far broader implications than sexuality alone. The version of this *midrash* quoted earlier also stated that "were it not for the *yetzer hara*, a person *would not build a house ... and would not deal in business*" (*BeR.R.* 9:7, *Yal.Sh.* BeReshith:16). It should now be clear why these activities as well are portrayed as dependent upon the *yetzer hara*: While neither relates directly to sexuality, both are fundamentally creative acts and therefore mediated by the *yetzer hara*, the root of human creativity.[44]

We can now better understand what the *midrash* quoted earlier regards as the ultimate expression of the *yetzer hara*: " 'G-d the L-rd said, "Behold, man [has become like one of Us, knowing good and evil]" ' — ... The Holy One Blessed be He, Who is called 'Righteous and Upright,' did not create man 'with His essence' except in order [for man] to be righteous and upright like Him" (*Tan. BeReshith*:7). The Creator's righteousness and uprightness are manifest to us continuously through His manifold acts of ongoing Creation: *"In His goodness He renews every day continuously the work of Creation"* (*"Shacharith"* daily service). Likewise, man can only be righteous and upright — "like Him," so to speak — through positive actualization of his creative potential. Thus, the Mishnah concludes that we are required to love G-d "with the *yetzer tov* and with the *yetzer ra*" (*Mish. Berachoth* 9:5);[13] any attempt at such positive expression as loving G-d in this world in the absence of the *yetzer hara* would necessarily be deficient. To be righteous and upright means to live and to create; to live and to create means to activate (*positively*) the *yetzer hara*.

It is not surprising, then, that we find the *yetzer hara* depicted in the Talmud as "fire" (*Kiddushin* 81a). While fire may represent passion in general and sexual passion in particular, the symbolism here suggests additional connotations. Significantly, the Talmud relates that man's mastery of fire took place only after eating the fruit of the "tree of knowing good and evil," whereupon, at nightfall, "the Holy One Blessed be He gave abstract understanding to Adam, a reflection of the heavenly model [G-d's creativity]" (*Pesachim* 54a).[45] Fire is the symbol of human creativity, the paradigm of human initiative, and the hallmark of man's power and his mastery over nature; it becomes his possession only once "man has become *like one of Us, knowing good and evil*" — by virtue of having eaten the fruit of the tree of "*knowing good and evil*" and having acquired the *yetzer hara*.[16] Fire represents not mere passion but the impassioned *creative power* of man — "a reflection of the heavenly model." Above all, *this* is the *yetzer hara*.

The "Lion of Fire"

Fire appears elsewhere in the context of the *yetzer hara* as well. We recognize that creativity has far broader applications than merely exerting mastery over nature through building houses and dealing in business. It is in this sense that the Talmud speaks of the fiery "*yetzer* of idolatry"[46] and its subjugation by the men of the Great Assembly at the beginning of the period of the second Beith HaMikdash (prior to their imprisonment of the "*yetzer* of [sexual] transgression," discussed above):

> They said, "Woe! Woe! It is this [*yetzer* of idolatry] that destroyed the Temple and burnt His Sanctuary and killed all the righteous and exiled Yisra'el from its land, and still it is dancing among us? Did You not give it to us only to receive reward through it? We do not want it, and we do not want its reward!"
>
> A note fell down to them from heaven, upon which "*Truth*" was inscribed. (Said R. Chanina: Infer from this that the seal of the Holy One Blessed be He is "*Truth*.")
>
> They sat in fasting three days and three nights. [The *yetzer* of idolatry] was delivered to them. It came out as a lion of fire from the chamber of the Holy of Holies.
>
> Said the prophet [Zecharyah] to Yisra'el, "It is the *yetzer* of idolatry!" ... As they seized it, a hair was loosed from its mane, and it raised

its voice, and its roar went through four hundred parasangs.

They said, "What shall we do? Perhaps, G-d forbid, heavenly mercy is upon it [protecting it]!"

Said the prophet [Zecharyah] to them, "Cast it into a leaden caldron, and cover its mouth with lead, because lead absorbs sound." ...

(*Yoma* 69b, *Sanhedrin* 64a)[41]

While the divine "cue" to this enterprise (the note "upon which 'Truth' was inscribed") will be discussed, G-d willing, in the sequel to this essay, it is crucial that we consider presently what Chazal are teaching us here about the *"yetzer* of idolatry" and its mitigation.

When the men of the Great Assembly embarked on their campaign against the *yetzer hara*, they were obviously not motivated by any failure to appreciate its vital import. To the contrary, after they realized the devastating destructive potential of the *"yetzer* of idolatry," their appeal began, "Did You not give it to us only to receive *reward* through it?" There is "reward" in the creative power of the *yetzer hara*.[47] How else could the men of the Great Assembly conclude that "perhaps ... heavenly mercy is upon it," protecting it?

Significantly, the *"yetzer* of idolatry" is depicted "as a *lion* of *fire*." The symbolic role of *fire* as the creative power of man has already been discussed; even more so, the *lion*, as "king of the beasts" (*Chagigah* 13b),[48] symbolizes the overwhelming power[49] that the *yetzer hara* embodies. It is this awesome faculty that enables a person to take a *physical* place and *create* a counterfeit sanctuary consecrated to a false *spiritual* force. But considering that the Talmud portrays the *"yetzer* of idolatry" as emerging "from the chamber of the Holy of Holies," we may suspect that this power has other, worthier applications as well.[50]

The boundary between sacred Temple and idolatrous shrine is subtle indeed. Thus, where the Torah reiterates its prohibition of idolatry, "gods of silver and gods of gold you shall not make for yourselves" (Shemoth 20:20), the Midrash comments:

> *"Gods of gold"* — Why is this stated? Since it is stated, "You shall make two *keruvim* of gold" (Shemoth 25:18), [lest one say] "I am making four," the teaching [of the text] implies, *"gods of gold"*: If you have added to two [*keruvim*], they are like [idolatrous] gods of gold.

> "*Gods of silver*" — Why is this stated? Since we have found [regarding] all vessels of the Temple that if one does not have [vessels] of gold, one [is to] make them of silver, I [might] infer that even [regarding the] *keruvim* this is so; the teaching [of the text] implies, "*gods of silver*": If they are not of gold, they are like [idolatrous] gods of silver.
> (*Mechilta* and Rashi on Shemoth, loc. cit.; *Yal.Sh.* Shemoth:303)

Similarly, when the Beith HaMikdash was destroyed, the Midrash relates in even more blatant terms:

> Ammonim and Mo'avim ... entered the chamber of the Holy of Holies and found there two *keruvim*. They took them and put them in a box and were parading them around in the streets of Yerushalayim and saying, "Were you not saying that this nation does not serve idolatry? See what we found of theirs and what they were serving!"
> (*Eich.R. Peth.*:9, *Pes. DeR. Kahana* 19 [138a])[51]

The "*yetzer* of idolatry" also "came out ... from *the chamber of the Holy of Holies*" — which of course implies that, together with the *keruvim*, it had been lurking there (of all places!) all along. What the pagan eyes of Ammon and Mo'av refused to acknowledge was the distinction between unrestrained application of man's capacity for spiritual creativity — by creating idolatrous gods — and quasi-divine application *of the same capacity* — by creating sacred *keruvim* in the Holy of Holies in compliance with G-d's explicit directives.[52] Nevertheless, since it is essentially the same faculty (the so-called "*yetzer* of idolatry") that enables both applications, there is no more appropriate repository for it than the chamber of the Holy of Holies of the Holy Temple:[50] a testimonial to the "*yetzer* of idolatry" as its greatest (*positive*) achievement.

The "*yetzer* of idolatry," then, is a creative force as well, subject to man's use and abuse. Just as the "*yetzer* of [sexual] transgression" is the basis of humanity's *physical* creativity, the "*yetzer* of idolatry" is the basis of humanity's *spiritual* creativity.[53] We readily appreciate the "reward" that ought to have been received through this *yetzer hara* "that destroyed the Temple and burnt His Sanctuary," had it been properly used: Paradoxically, this reward included the Temple and Sanctuary themselves. Yet the men of the Great Assembly were forced to concede that people had shown themselves unreliable in their utilization of this faculty, which was still frivolously "dancing among" them. While the potential reward may have been sacred, the dangers of abuse were too catastrophic.[47]

Having resolved to forgo both the *yetzer hara* and its reward, "they sat in fasting three days and three nights." Of what relevance is such extreme — and nearly suicidal — conduct? The men of the Great Assembly certainly recognized the extent to which the creativity embodied by the *yetzer hara* is inextricably linked to the very essence of life in this world,[42] such that without the *yetzer hara* "the world would not endure" (*Mid. Tehillim* 9:1, *Yal.Sh.* Tehillim:643).[43] As a result, they were constrained to withdraw from life in this world — practically killing themselves by fasting[54] — in order to subdue the *yetzer hara*, whereupon it "was delivered to them ... as a lion of fire [coming out] from the chamber of the Holy of Holies."

What became of this "lion of fire"? Presumably, ever since the confrontation between it and the men of the Great Assembly, it has remained confined in "a leaden caldron ... [with] its mouth [covered] with lead, because lead absorbs sound." What and where is this caldron, and why are the acoustic properties of lead so crucial to its function? Realizing that this cryptic epitaph is intended to provide us with keys to understanding human nature through to our own "leaden" times, we must strive to decipher the cosmic implications of the imprisonment of this *yetzer*.

Muffling the Lion's "Roar"

The imprisonment of the *"yetzer* of idolatry" resulted from an appreciation that it could not be destroyed: "Perhaps, G-d forbid, heavenly mercy is upon it [protecting it]!" Since the *"yetzer* of idolatry" is the root of man's spiritual creativity, for better and for worse, "heavenly mercy" must be protecting it. Inasmuch as "everything that the Holy One Blessed be He created in His world, He created solely for His honor" (*Avoth* 6:11, *Avoth DeR. Nathan* 41:16),[55] a physical universe can never be self-justifying. Since "for His honor" is obviously not expressive of divine egoism (an oxymoron), we recognize that the *baraitha* is referring not to any personal "honor" of G-d but to the honor of spirituality, which G-d (from our perspective) represents. Rephrased, the physical universe was created solely as a mechanism for honoring the spiritual; everything physical is a means to the realization of spiritual ends. In this sense, a world purged of the *"yetzer* of idolatry" — and thus purged of its capacity to attain its spiritual goals — would not endure. "Heavenly mercy" insures the endurance of the *"yetzer* of idolatry," just as heavenly mercy guarantees in general that the objectives of Creation will ultimately prevail. In this world, the *"yetzer* of idolatry" cannot be destroyed.[56] At most, it can be (and was) muffled.[57]

The purpose of the "leaden caldron" is stated explicitly (albeit cryptically) in the Talmud: "lead absorbs sound." It is the lion's "roar" — which "lead absorbs" — that symbolizes the lion's far-reaching impact: "As they seized it, a hair was loosed from its mane, and it raised its voice, and *its roar went through four hundred parasangs*." The implication of the "leaden caldron" is that this "roar" continues unabated; we are, however, less likely to hear it.

The Talmud informs us that the dimensions of Eretz Yisra'el are *"four hundred parasangs by four hundred parasangs"* (*Megillah* 3a).[58] We may conclude, then, that the primary impact of the "roar" of the *"yetzer* of idolatry" corresponds to Eretz Yisra'el. We recall the aforementioned continuation of the Gemara in this light: "[After] they imprisoned [the *yetzer* of sexual transgression] for three days, they sought a fresh egg *in all of Eretz Yisra'el* for a sick person and found none." The motif of Eretz Yisra'el in both cases is self-evident. In this context, we consider the Talmud's conclusion that the *yetzer hara* "leaves alone the nations of the world and *lets itself loose upon ... Yisra'el"* (*Sukkah* 52a, *Yal.Sh.* Yo'el:535 — in com. on Yo'el 2:20). Likewise, the Midrash emphasizes the centrality of the *yetzer hara* particularly in Yisra'el's realization of its mission: "Were it not for the *yetzer hara*, there would be none of that honor [foretold by the prophets] *for Yisra'el"* (*T.DeV.Eli.R.* 16). By extension, the *land* of Yisra'el is the land upon which the *yetzer hara* "lets itself loose." The bases of both physical and spiritual creativity are focused principally here — on the breeding ground for what ought to be the ultimate accomplishments of human creativity. Thus, the lion's "roar went through four hundred parasangs," its impact reverberating throughout Eretz Yisra'el.

It was from this impact that the men of the Great Assembly

deduced that "perhaps ... heavenly mercy is upon [the *yetzer* of idolatry, protecting it]." But it was also this impact, misdirected, "that destroyed the Temple and burnt His Sanctuary and killed all the righteous and *exiled Yisra'el from its land.*" If the creative energy inherent in the Land is misused, the Land itself is forfeit. Therefore, concluded the men of the Great Assembly, although this power cannot be destroyed, it must be blunted. The "*yetzer* of idolatry" had been an overwhelming roar; now it is a faint whisper. We must listen with redoubled sensitivity if we are to hear its sustained creative message.

4. "THIS ONE CORRESPONDING TO THAT ONE THE L-RD HAS MADE"

"Ari'el": The Lion's Legacy

As discussed above, the consequences of the lion and its roar extend far beyond idolatry. To understand the "leaden" world in which we live, we must reckon with the full and far-reaching implications of this "roar," however muffled it is today. In Tehillim, for example, the lion's roar becomes a paradigm for prayer: "The young lions roar for prey, *beseeching the L-rd for their food"* (Tehillim 104:21). By extension, human prayer as well is described as "roaring": "My L-rd! My L-rd! Why have you forsaken me; far from my salvation are *the words of my roaring"* (ibid. 22:2). If the "roar" of the "lion of fire" is a metaphor for spiritual power, then prayer is certainly one of its most dramatic expressions, through which man forges metaphysical bonds between the mundane and the Divine, between himself and the Absolute.[59] In this sense, even G-d is anthropomorphically depicted as "roaring" in prayer: "G-d *roars* from on high, and from His holy Temple He raises His voice; He *roars incessantly* for His dwelling place" (Yirmeyahu 25:30);[60] "G-d *roars* from Tziyyon, and from Yerushalayim He raises His voice" (Yo'el 4:16, Amos 1:2).[61]

Moreover, we observe that G-d's "roar," so to speak, issues from the "lion's den": "G-d roars *from Tziyyon,* and *from Yerushalayim He raises His voice."* Fittingly, Yerushalayim itself is called "Ari'el" (lit. "Lion of G-d"; see Yeshayahu 29:1-2, 7, and com., loc. cit.).[62] The Mishnah understands this as an allusion to the

Sanctuary, which was "narrow in back and wide in front, resembling a lion" (*Middoth* 4:7); the Talmud analogously portrays the fire on the altar of the first Beith HaMikdash as "crouched like a lion" (Yoma 21b).[63] We have already noted that the Talmud describes the *"yetzer* of idolatry" emerging "as a lion of fire from the chamber of the Holy of Holies" of the Sanctuary. We note here that the symbolism of the lion applies to the Sanctuary — and, by extension, to all of Yerushalayim — as a whole: the supreme realization of man's capacity for spiritual creativity, positively applied. Thus, comments Maharal, "The Beith HaMikdash is called 'Ari'el' because of the great power that it embodied" (*Netzach Yisra'el*, ch. 55 [p. 203]).

We readily appreciate the "great power" expressed in erecting a Temple of G-d. As King Shelomoh emphasized at the dedication of the Beith HaMikdash, "For will the L-rd indeed dwell with mankind on earth? Behold, the heavens and heavens' heavens cannot contain You, even more so this house that I have built" (Divrei HaYamim II 6:18, Melachim I 8:27). Yet, in the same context, he summarized the objective of his unprecedented construction effort, "I have surely built a heavenly palace for You, an establishment for Your eternal dwelling" (Melachim I 8:13, Divrei HaYamim II 6:2). Only through the G-d-given gift of (spiritual) creativity can man accomplish this impossibility, namely, to transform "this house that I have built" into "an establishment for Your eternal dwelling" — for You Who transcend all establishments and all dwellings and even "the heavens and heavens' heavens."[64]

And what became of the "lion" Ari'el when the "lion of fire," which spawned it, "came out" of its midst? Compared with the first Beith HaMikdash, the second Beith HaMikdash lacked more than just the "lion of fire," which no longer lurked within its Holy of Holies. The comparison, in fact, was quite devastating to the newly returned exiles, even at the climax of the joyous dedication of the new Temple: "And many of the Kohanim and the Leviyyim and the heads of households — the old men who saw the first House when it was [still] founded — [upon seeing] this House with their own eyes *were crying in a loud voice*" (Ezra 3:12). The deficiencies were clearly on a deeper plane than that of mere physical grandeur. The very focal point of the Beith HaMikdash, the holy ark of the covenant,[65] was missing from the Holy of Holies as well.[66] Chazal note that various aspects of the first Beith HaMikdash were lacking in the second[67] — including the altar fire "crouched like a lion" (*Yoma* 21b);[68] unquestionably most significant was the absence of the Shechinah (G-d's Presence).[69] The greatest objective of man's spiritual creativity is to transform "this house that I have built" into "an establishment for Your eternal dwelling," a Sanctuary for the Shechinah; an incapacitated *"yetzer* of idolatry," with but a muffled roar, is surely insufficient to attain this goal.[70]

"A Lion Has Roared": The Power of Prophecy

Finally, we confront one additional connotation of the lion and its roar in the Bible, which clearly has the most dramatic implications for the *"yetzer* of idolatry" and its ultimate positive and negative consequences as they relate to us. The faculty that enables a person to *create* a counterfeit sanctuary consecrated to a false god is obviously also the basis of man's ability to *create* an image of G-d or gods and convey to his people the resultant "prophetic" message. It is certainly no accident that the demise of the false prophecy that had been so rampant in the period of the first Beith HaMikdash coincided with the imprisonment of the *"yetzer* of idolatry."

Like idolatry, false prophecy significantly affected the course of history, and we dare not underestimate its potency. Furthermore, by no means were the false prophets of whom we read continually in the Bible mere charlatans. As R. Yerucham HaLevi of Mir observed, "Had they been simple impostors, the Torah would not have called them 'prophets' " (quoted in *Michtav MeEliyyahu*, I, 238).[71] Thus, the Talmud faults the false prophet Tzidkiyyah ben Kena'anah[72] not with lying but with failure "to examine carefully" the circumstances of his prophecy, which — he ought to have realized — indicated a spurious source (*Sanhedrin* 89a, *Yal.Sh.* Melachim:221). And even more emphatically, the Talmud states that Chananyah ben Azzur, the infamous false prophet who publicly defied Yirmeyahu,[73] "was a true prophet" who misinterpreted a legitimate prophecy of Yirmeyahu (*Yer. Sanhedrin* 11:5 [41b], *Sanhedrin* 90a).[74] It is not surprising, then, that the "conspiracy of her [false] prophets" (Yechezkel 22:25) represents an awesome power, likened to "a *roaring lion* tearing prey" (ibid.).[75]

In this light, let us consider true prophecy. We recognize that the equation noted above — between the force that spawned the abominable shrines of idolatry and that which enabled establishment of the holy Temple of G-d — also mandates a correspondence between the driving forces of false prophecy and true prophecy as well. The source of one is inextricably linked with the source of the other. *"This one corresponding to that one the L-rd has made"* (Koheleth 7:14) is an inexorable law of this world.[76] Indeed, we cannot fail to hear the "lion's roar" reverberating most loudly in the words of the true prophets of G-d: "Will a *lion roar* in the forest without his having prey? Will a *young lion raise his voice* from his den unless he has seized? ... *A lion has roared; who will not fear? G-d the L-rd has spoken; who will not prophesy?"* (Amos 3:4, 8).

Even more intensely, apropos of the roaring "lion of *fire*" emerging from the chamber of the Holy of Holies, Yirmeyahu speaks of the overwhelming might of his prophecy, which — in spite of the derision he suffers for it — cannot be silenced: "And I said, 'I will not mention Him, and I will no longer speak in His name.' But it was in my heart *like a burning fire* shut up in my bones, and I wearied of containing it, and I could not" (Yirmeyahu 20:9).[77] The spiritual dynamo to which Yirmeyahu refers is reminiscent — so to speak — of the fire of creative inspiration by which every artist is possessed and animated.[78] But the analogy to any creative domain ostensibly falls completely flat: While creativity may play a role in the fantastic fabrications of *false* prophecy, what purpose could it possibly serve in the realm of *true* prophecy, passively conveying to the nation the words of G-d Himself?

"By the Hand of the Prophets I am Imagined"

While creativity, in the sense of any personal input, surely seems antithetical to prophecy, the Talmud presents us with a confounding puzzle whose resolution challenges this assumption:

> Menasheh ... said to [Yeshayahu], "Mosheh, your master, said [in G-d's name], *'For no man can see Me while alive'* (Shemoth 33:20). And you said, *'I saw G-d sitting upon a throne, High and Uplifted'* (Yeshayahu

6:1)!" ... The verses contradict one another.... [The resolution is] as we have learnt: *All the [other] prophets gazed through unclear glass;*[79] *Mosheh Rabbeinu gazed through clear glass.*

(*Yevamoth* 49b)[80]

The implication of the Talmud is astounding: After asking how Yeshayahu could say that he "saw G-d" (inasmuch as we know from the Torah that this is impossible), the reply is that this image was really an artifact of the "unclear glass" through which Yeshayahu gazed — in other words, *it was not really there* on the "other side" of the "glass." Lest we lack the courage or insight to draw this conclusion ourselves, Rashi states it explicitly:

> "*[All the other prophets] gazed through unclear glass*" — They thought to see and did not see, and "*Mosheh ... gazed through clear glass*" and knew that he did not see Him....
>
> (com., loc. cit.)

While Mosheh at his unique level "knew that he did not see Him," Yeshayahu at the level of "all the [other] prophets"[81] could say that he "saw G-d" — meaning that he "*thought to see and did not see*"!

We must be exceedingly cautious with this realization; it obviously does *not* imply that Yeshayahu or "all the prophets" other than Mosheh Rabbeinu were "hallucinating," G-d forbid. Inasmuch as the source of all prophecy is G-d's Will, any image beheld by a true prophet necessarily accords with that Will. This is, indeed, the most definitive distinction between the legitimate images of true prophecy and the spurious fabrications of false prophets like Tzidkiyyah ben Kena'anah and Chananyah ben Azzur. Yet, while in this sense the divinity of the prophets' visions is beyond question, we are forced to conclude that such visions — with the singular exception of Mosheh's — include aspects that derive not from their *objective* divine source but from the "unclear glass" through which *the prophet* experienced them. While the nature of these aspects extends far beyond the scope of this essay,[82] we must concede that their immediate source lies not so much in G-d, Who "cannot be seen" (Shemoth 33:20, 23), as in the prophet, who nevertheless "saw." Thus, Ramchal states that "prophetic imagery ... relates *to the seer* but is not of the essence of the One Seen" (*Kelach Pithchei Chochmah, Pethach* 7).[83]

This *active* role of the prophets demands further clarification in order for us to understand prophecy and also to appreciate the prophet's extraordinary task.

At the outset of this inquiry, we should consider the significance of such a role; it has, in fact, crucial legal ramifications. It is the basis of the irreducible Halachic differences that distinguish the level of prophecy of Mosheh — through which we received the Torah — from that of all other prophets. Thus, the Torah states as an inviolable principle that "no prophet arose again in Yisra'el like Mosheh" (Devarim 34:10), since all post-Torah prophecies include some limiting element of "unclear glass." As a result, the force of all such prophecies can only be that of temporal — not eternal — instruction,[84] and "no prophet is authorized to innovate anything" to supersede the Torah of Mosheh (*Shabbath* 104a).[85] The Talmud posits further that "we do not learn words of Torah from words of [post-Torah] tradition" (*Chagigah* 10b, *Babba Kamma* 2b),[86] meaning that we do not even deduce interpretations of Torah law based upon analogous statements by the prophets in Nevi'im and Kethuvim. Likewise, concerning the Mishnah's conclusion that the prohibition of eating *gid hannasheh* (the sciatic nerve)[87] "was stated at Sinai" and not merely "to the sons of Ya'akov" (*Mish. Chullin* 7:6, *Yal.Sh.* BeReshith:133), Rambam notes that "everything from which we refrain [as prohibited] or that we do [in fulfillment of the commandments] nowadays, we do only *by the command of the Holy One Blessed be He through Mosheh Rabbeinu*, not because the Holy One Blessed be He had said so to prophets who preceded him" (com. on *Mish. Chullin* 7:6).

Belief in the qualitative supremacy of Mosheh's prophecy is thus one of the fundamental principles of Judaism, listed among Rambam's "Thirteen Foundations" of Jewish faith.[88] Ultimately, because of the intrinsic boundedness of all other prophets, "the Nevi'im and the Kethuvim will be nullified in the future, but the five volumes of Torah will not be nullified in the future" (*Yer. Megillah* 1:5 [7a]).[89] Rambam emphasizes, "The obligatory call to the Torah derives solely *from that level of perception* [unique to Mosheh].... Therefore, according to our outlook, there neither was nor will be any *torah* [instruction] other than the one Torah, which is the Torah of Mosheh Rabbeinu" (*Moreh HaNevochim* 2:39).[90]

In addition, the Midrash differentiates between the prophecies of Mosheh (the Torah), which include the singular expression "*this* (זה) is the matter that G-d commanded" (BeMidbar 30:2, etc.), and those of all other prophets, which are replete with the less pointed expression "*thus* (כה) said G-d" (*Sifrei* and Rashi on BeMidbar, loc. cit.; *Yal.Sh.* BeMidbar:784). In light of all the aforementioned distinctions between Mosheh and all other prophets, R. Eliyyahu Mizrachi explains:

> The word "כה" indicates the [general] intent of the matter, and the word "זה" indicates the matter suggested in itself. And because all the prophets prophesied through only "unclear glass," and they lacked the capacity to receive more than the [general] intent of the matter that was appropriate to them, they were constrained to mention in their [prophetic] language, "*Thus* (כה) said G-d" — meaning the intent of the matters, not the matters in themselves....
> (com. on Rashi, loc. cit.)[91]

"כה" suggests "כזה" ("*like* this"),[92] lacking the precision implied by "זה." When one gazes "through unclear glass," the image one sees through the glass is partially obscured. Concerning the nature of this obscurity, R. Tzadok HaKohen adds:

> This [means] that when all the prophets would receive their prophecies, the prophecy would not be specified but instead *would have an appearance appropriate to the character of the receiver*. Therefore, the prophet has the capacity to say the matters *according to his character*, as Chazal say that [King] Yoshiyyahu sent [messengers to inquire] of Chuldah [the prophetess] (Melachim II 22:12-14) [in lieu of inquiring of Yirmeyahu] "because women are compassionate" (*Megillah* 14b, *Yal.Sh.* Melachim:248).
> (*Peri Tzaddik* on *Mattoth*, ch. 2 [p. 204])

Chuldah's womanly disposition toward compassion would clearly have been irrelevant to the content of her prophecy, would prophecy at large not include an inescapable individual dimension prefaced not by a sharply focused "זה" but by a fitting expression of likeness: "כה."

Moreover, the source of Chuldah's compassion, says the Talmud, lay not so much in what she saw *through* the glass as in what she saw *in* the glass: herself. Inevitably, what obscures the image one sees "through unclear glass" is partially one's own reflection: "Regarding the visions of the prophets," Rema states, "[each] saw the glory [of G-d] as *the likeness of the prophet himself*"(Torath HaOlah 1:14).[93] In particular, concludes Malbim, "[Just as] one who sees the image in a mirror sees in it his own face as well — since he is himself standing before the mirror and his likeness is also imprinted on the mirror — ... [so, too, in] the visions and images that visionaries see, they see also their own likeness and the visions of their imagination, which is imprinted on their vision" (HaTorah VeHaMitzvah on BeMidbar 12:6). Such "unclear glass," then, may be likened to "a mirror in which one sees [both] oneself and whomever one faces ... — as opposed to 'clear glass,' through which one sees [purely] what is on the other side" (Peri Tzaddik [R. Tzadok HaKohen], "Kedushath Shabbath," *Ma'amar* 7 [p. 37]). Thus, notes Ramchal, even though G-d "is certainly the One Revealed to [the prophet] through that [prophetic] vision ... that vision is solely what is generated in the sight of the prophet *as a consequence of his own spirit*" (*Da'ath Tevunoth*, ch. 186).

There is, then, an irrevocably *individual* aspect of prophecy, mediated by the *individual* prophet. Thus, the Talmud asserts:

> All that Yechezkel saw Yeshayahu [also] saw. To what can Yechezkel be likened? To a village dweller who saw the king. And to what can Yeshayahu be likened? To a capital city dweller who saw the king.
>
> (*Chagigah* 13b)

The prophetic descriptions provided by Yeshayahu and Yechezkel surely differ markedly, not only in style but in substance as well. The Talmud (ibid.) proceeds to discuss a discrepancy in the number of "wings" that the two prophets ascribed to the angels — clearly, in the supernal realm of prophecy, anything but a trivial, "numerical" detail.[94] Nevertheless, the Talmud affirms that each was recounting his individual perception of G-d as He revealed Himself to the prophet.

In this context, we can understand an extraordinary dialogue presented by the Midrash:

> The prophets said to Yirmeyahu, "What did you apprehend [that prompted you] to say, '[Who does not fear You,] King *of the nations*' (Yirmeyahu 10:7)? All the [other] prophets call Him 'King

of Yisra'el,' and you call Him 'King *of the nations'*?"

He said to them, "I heard from Him, 'A prophet *for the nations* I appointed you' (ibid. 1:5), so I said, 'King *of the nations.'* "

(Sh.R. 29:9)

Amazingly, an alternate version of this *midrash* ascribes its initial question not to "the prophets" but to G-d Himself: "Said *the Holy One Blessed be He* to Yirmeyahu, 'You call Me "King of the nations"; and am I not King of Yisra'el?' ..." (*Mid. Tehillim* 93:1, Yal.Sh. Yirmeyahu:285). Evidently, while the expressions chosen by Yirmeyahu ultimately conform to G-d's Will (of course), the Midrash attributes at least these expressions not to G-d but to the prophet. "It was," as Yirmeyahu expressed it, *"in my heart like a burning fire"* (Yirmeyahu 20:9). Furthermore, these expressions are not arbitrary, but derive from the prophet's own self-perception: "*I* heard from Him, 'A prophet *for the nations* I appointed you,' so *I* said, 'King *of the nations.'* "[95]

More generally, the Talmud emphasizes the broad application of these observations, extending far beyond the identities of certain prophets (like Yeshayahu, Yirmeyahu, and Yechezkel) and constituting one of the most basic principles of prophecy: *"No two prophets prophesy with the same style"* (*Sanhedrin* 89a, Yal.Sh. Melachim:221). R. Ya'akov Kamenetsky explains:

> What our Rabbis z.l. said, that "no two prophets prophesy with the same style," is because the prophet would receive the [general] form of the prophecy, but the words themselves *the prophet would produce from his own heart*. And since "their minds do not resemble one another,"[96] each one would necessarily express his prophecy in different language from his fellow.
>
> (introduction to *Iyyunim BaMikra* [on the Torah])

The unique style of each prophet emanates from the inexhaustible depth and unfathomable profundity of the prophet's own, unique soul.[97]

Considering this individual component, which emerges as one of the hallmarks of prophecy and necessarily leaves its imprint on the prophet's style, we can appreciate Maharal's conclusion regarding prophecy in general:

> There is a distinction between the speech of [G-d in] prophecy and

speech that [relates] to other people: for the speech of [G-d in] prophecy is *undoubtedly not explicit* like speech that [relates] to other people.

(Avraham Kariv, ed., *Kethavei Maharal MiPrag* [1960; rpt. Yerushalayim: Mossad Harav Kook, 1975], II, 355)

Thus, R. Tzadok HaKohen comments, expounding a verse from Tehillim:

> *"G-d gives the statement; its harbingers are a great host"* (Tehillim 68:12) — One utterance of G-d is extended in the mouth of the prophet to a complete chapter.
>
> (*Resisei Lailah*, ch. 46 [p. 91])

It is to the prophet that we must look for the source of that "great host": what he himself made of the utterance he was given by G-d. Such an understanding of prophecy is obviously predicated upon at least some interpretive function entrusted by G-d to the prophet in expounding his own prophecy. Indeed, following Onkelos's lead, Rashi deduces etymologically that the literal meaning of "נביא" ("prophet") is "interpreter" (com. on Shemoth 7:1, ד"ה יהיה נביאך),[98] designating the prophet's primary role.

Actually, the reality of such a role is practically explicit in the Torah. In characterizing the uniqueness of Mosheh's prophecy, G-d specifies that he perceived an explicit image, *"not in riddles"* (BeMidbar 12:8). We may infer conversely that "for other [prophets, prophecy is] 'in riddles' " (*Da'ath Tevunoth*, ch. 180): "Riddles" (i.e., allegories) *are* the normal prophetic mode.[99] Thus, Rambam states:

> Matters that are made known to the prophet in prophetic vision are made known through allegory — and immediately he inscribes in his heart the interpretation of the allegory in the prophetic vision and knows it.
>
> (*Yad Hil. Yesodei HaTorah* 7:3)[100]

> And among prophetic allegories, the intent of many is not explained in the prophetic vision; however, after awakening, the prophet would know what the intent was.
>
> (*Moreh* 2:43)[101]

Rambam clearly differentiates between the allegorical image, which is "made known" to the prophet in his vision, and its interpretation, which the prophet himself "knows" after awakening.[102]

One obvious example of such allegory and its interpretation by the prophet, cited by Rambam (ibid.), is Yirmeyahu's description of his inaugural prophecy. R. Naftali Tz.Y. Berlin explains this dialogue between G-d and Yirmeyahu — and the prophet's discernment of its intent — along similar lines:

> ... G-d [asked] Yirmeyahu the prophet, "What do you see, Yirmeyahu?" (Yirmeyahu 1:11), and he replied, "I see a rod of an almond tree" (ibid.).... And [G-d's] response was, "You have seen well" (ibid. 1:12), the intent of seeing well being that Yirmeyahu undoubtedly saw before him other objects at that juncture but reasoned that the rod of the almond tree ... was G-d's intent. And therefore G-d said to him, "You have seen well": Your mind is good and fine.
>
> (*Ha'amek Davar* on Shemoth 4:2)

The evaluation that "you have seen well" implies that Yirmeyahu could conceivably have seen otherwise. In fact, the Talmud (*Sanhedrin* 89b) concludes that the prophet Yonah initially failed to comprehend the full significance of his prophecy that "Nineveh will be overturned" (Yonah 3:4).[103] The prophet's capacity to "see" G-d's message results not only from the divine gift of prophecy — which is *"undoubtedly not explicit"* — but also from his own efforts,[104] as G-d's chosen "interpreter" in executing His Will. Maharil Diskin observes that (unlike the "clear glass" through which Mosheh received the Torah) "prophecy also [employs] another faculty: *the interpretation of the human mind*" (*Shuth Maharil Diskin*, vol. II [end]). As a general principle, emphasizes R. Eli'ezer Shach, prophecy that is "through 'unclear glass' ... *required the interpretation of the prophet himself*" (Avi Ezri, vol. I, on Yad Hil. Yesodei HaTorah).[105] Since only "prophecy that was necessary for all generations was recorded" (Megillah 14a),[106] only the consequent message itself was normally preserved and not the complex process that produced it.[107] But we may well surmise from this seminal prophecy of Yirmeyahu that the prophet played much more than a passive role in this process.

This active role, notes the Midrash, reflects the great power not only of prophecy but of the prophets themselves:

> Said R. Yudan: Great is the power of the prophets in that they imagine the likeness of Divine Might as the form of man, as it is said, "I heard the voice of *a man* between [the banks of] Ulai" (Daniyyel 8:16).

> And R. Yehudah b. Simon said: [We derive this conclusion more explicitly] from here: "And upon the likeness of the throne was a likeness similar to the appearance of *a man* upon it from above" (Yechezkel 1:26).
> (BeM.R. 19:4)[108]

We might have thought such "imagining" to be unpardonably audacious if not practically blasphemous. Interestingly, the Midrash uses the same language — "they liken the form to its Former" (BeR.R. 24:1)[109] — not only in lauding the "great power" of the prophets[108] but also in indicting the wickedness of those who blithely imagine that their misdeeds can be as concealed from G-d as they can be from people. "Great power," comments Rambam in explaining this *midrash* (*Moreh* 1:46), is indispensable for a singularly difficult achievement. The capacity to *imagine* G-d — in the literal sense of likening Him to an *image* (let alone a mortal image!) — is indeed a stupendous feat that, if abused, can initiate a precipitous slide toward depravity. It is this same stupendous feat, however, that enables the prophet to climb to the breathtaking heights of prophecy — to think "to see" an image where in reality he knows that "he did not see Him" (Rashi on *Yevamoth* 49b, ד"ה נסתכלו באספקלריא שאין מאירה, quoted above): "for all the perception of the prophets is not in terms of [G-d's] essence, since no thought can grasp Him at all, but only ... *in accordance with the perceptions of [His] creations*, this [referring to] man" (*Takkanath HaShavin* [R. Tzadok HaKohen], ch. 12 [p. 113]). While G-d presumably assists the prophets in their ascent, this capacity is evidence of *their* "great power" (in interpreting their encounter with G-d) and not *His*. Just as the wicked bear sole responsibility for their evil imaginings, the source of prophetic ability lies fundamentally within the prophets themselves.

In light of all the foregoing, we apprehend the truly broad implications of the following Midrashic observation:

> "*I spoke to the prophets, and I multiplied visions, and by the hand of the prophets I am imagined.*"[110] (Hoshea 12:11) — Said the Holy One Blessed be He, "Certainly '*I spoke to the prophets,*' but '*I multiplied visions,*' because [for] each, this one's prophecy does not resemble that one's [prophecy]. In what [sense]?
>
> "Amos sees Me standing, as it is said, '*I saw G-d standing upon the altar*' (Amos 9:1).

> "Michah saw Me sitting, as it is said, '*I saw G-d sitting upon His throne*' (Melachim I 22:19, Divrei HaYamim II 18:18).
>
> "Mosheh saw Me as an overpowering hero, as it is said, '*G-d is the Master of war*' (Shemoth 15:3).
>
> "Daniyyel saw Me as an old man, as it is said, '*And the hair of His head was as [white as] pure wool*' (Daniyyel 7:9)."
>
> Therefore, it is said, "*And by the hand of the prophets I am imagined.*"
>
> (*Yal.Sh.* Yeshayahu:385)[111]

This diversity of prophetic imagery is attributed by the Midrash to the prophets' individual perceptions: "Amos sees," "Michah saw," "Mosheh saw," "Daniyyel saw" — *individually* — for "*by the hand of the prophets I am imagined.*" An unseverable bond links each prophet's imagination with his prophecy.[112]

In this context, we note the extent to which the imaginative faculty is essential to prophecy, as Rambam comments:[113]

> The imaginative faculty ... is the cause of correct visions, and it is itself the cause of prophecy — varying in degree but not in kind. You already know the parallel [drawn by Chazal] in saying, "A dream is one-sixtieth of prophecy" (*Berachoth* 57b),[114] and one does not compare two things that differ in kind.... They reiterated this matter in *BeReshith Rabbah*, and said, "The *noveleth* [unripe fruit, prematurely shed] of prophecy is the dream" (*BeR.R.* 17:5).[115] And this is a wonderful parallel, because the *noveleth* (נובלת) is clearly the fruit itself, except that it has withered (נבל) before its completion and before its time came. Likewise, the action of the imaginative faculty during sleep is [the same as] its action during prophecy, except that it is deficient and has not reached its fruition....
>
> (*Moreh* 2:36)[116]

More specifically, R. Nissim[117] explains the ramifications of the imaginative faculty's involvement in prophetic visions:

> It is known that the faculty that always deceives man is the imaginative faculty, which is wont to exchange one matter for another that has no reality at all. And the prophets [other than Mosheh] would prophesy by means of this faculty, and they would see matters that had no [objective] reality at all.... While the matter intimated and intended [by the prophecy] was real, the vision was not real but imagined.
>
> (*Derashoth HaRan*, Derash 8)

While an extended discussion of the precise role of the imaginative faculty in the mechanics of prophecy is beyond the scope of this essay, evidently G-d's words through Hoshea, "And by the hand of the prophets *I am imagined,*" indicate a theme that is fundamental to our understanding of prophecy in general.[118]

On the one hand, this imaginative element is obviously a shortcoming, introducing an individual, interpretive factor into prophecy and precluding an unadulterated vision of objective Truth. While it was through his imaginative faculty that Yeshayahu said, "*I saw G-d*" (Yeshayahu 6:1), he nevertheless declared, "*And as whom will you imagine the L-rd, and what likeness will you compare to Him?*" (ibid. 40:18).[119] In terms of such imagining, the Midrash paraphrases the Talmud's differentiation — quoted earlier — between the limited level of prophecy of all other prophets (like Yeshayahu) and that of Mosheh:

> All the prophets beheld [G-d] through soiled glass.[79] This is what is written, "*And I multiplied visions, and by the hand of the prophets I am imagined*" (Hoshea 12:11)....
>
> (*VaY.R.* 1:14)[120]

Moreover, the Midrash considers this imaginative dimension of prophecy a deficiency with respect to the more explicit revelations of G-d in history as experienced even by common people:

> "*This is my L-rd, and I shall glorify Him*" (Shemoth 15:2) — R. Eli'ezer says: Whence do you say that a maidservant beheld upon the [splitting of the] sea what was not beheld by Yechezkel and all the other prophets? [We conclude this] for it is said regarding [the prophets], "*And by the hand of the prophets I am imagined.*"
>
> (*Mechilta*, loc. cit.)[121]

> "*For, on the third day, G-d will reveal Himself*[122] *in the sight of all the people upon Mount Sinai*" (Shemoth 19:11) — ... This teaches that they beheld at that time [when G-d gave the Torah] what was not beheld by Yechezkel and Yeshayahu, as it is said, "*And by the hand of the prophets I am imagined.*"
>
> (*Mechilta*, loc. cit.)

Such unmitigated perceptions of Truth — which the Torah describes as G-d revealing Himself "*in the sight of all the people*" — which enabled even a maidservant to exclaim, "*This* (זה) *is my*

L-rd" (reminiscent of the unique level of Mosheh, who prophesied with *"this* [זה]*"* [*Sifrei* on BeMidbar 30:2, quoted above]),[123] necessarily transcend any level of prophecy mediated by a prophet's own imagination and interpretation.

On the other hand, such dramatic experiences as the splitting of the sea and the giving of the Torah resulted solely from G-d revealing Himself, without any commensurate human preparation or readiness.[124] Since such revelations were not essentially predicated upon human effort, they were as ephemeral as they were ethereal. R. Menachem Mendel of Kotzk noted on the *midrash* quoted above, " 'A maidservant beheld ... what was not beheld by Yechezkel and all the other prophets' — She beheld, *but she remained a maidservant,"* unaffected in any abiding, fundamental sense by the overwhelming magnitude of the revelation experienced. As expressed by R. Tzadok HaKohen, " 'A maidservant *beheld* ... what was not beheld by Yechezkel,' but it was only at [the level of] mere [superficial] *beholding,* not at [the level of] a permanent acquisition of the heart" (*Peri Tzaddik*, "Kedushath Shabbath," Ma'amar 7 [p. 53]). By contrast, while the imaginative aspect certainly limits prophecy, it is through this restrictive darkness that the prophet scales the torturous slopes of *his own* spiritual ascent. It is the prophet — not the "maidservant" or any of her equally passive associates — who becomes a man of G-d.[124] As the Midrash comments, "Great is the power of the prophets": To "imagine the likeness of Divine Might" altogether in this world of concealment,[125] where G-d does *not* "reveal Himself in the sight of all the people," is an unfathomably great accomplishment. This *imaginative* enterprise is indeed animated by the "great power" that it so vividly suggests.

Restating this dialectic, we observe that Rambam regards the imaginative faculty as the basis of not only true prophecy. In the preface to *Moreh HaNevochim*, he writes disparagingly of the "imaginative ideas" of the ignorant. Furthermore, as we might well expect, false prophecy too (like idolatry itself)[126] derives from "the power of the imaginative faculty" (*Moreh* 2:37) — where it is uncontrolled by a powerful intellect.[127] The principle cited earlier — *"This one corresponding to that one the L-rd has made"* (Koheleth 7:14) — indeed applies to true prophecy versus false prophecy as well.[76]

The basis of this "correspondence" between the sources of true and false prophecy should now be self-evident. After discussing the tendency of the masses to imagine any of several corporeal features in G-d, Rambam states:

> All this follows from the imagination, which is also the yetzer hara in reality, for any logical or ethical shortcoming is [derived from] the action of the imagination or appended to its action.
>
> (Moreh 2:12)

Rambam could hardly have been more explicit. The imaginative faculty, which we have discussed so extensively — which we have come to appreciate as the mediator of prophecy — is simply the *yetzer hara* by a different name. Conversely, the *yetzer hara* is "the imagination, which the serpent introduced into [man], through saying, 'You will be like G-d' " (*Machshevoth Charutz*, ch. 1 [p. 3]). In fact, the serpent may itself symbolize the imagination and its potentially disastrous consequences.[128]

We could readily have anticipated this conclusion; it simply confirms what we have already discovered in the words of Chazal. While the Talmud's equation of the *yetzer hara* with "the accusing angel [Satan]" and "the angel of death" (*Babba Bathra* 16a)[11] still bears clarification (G-d willing, in the sequel to this essay), the *yetzer hara* — like the imaginative faculty — is *within* ourselves,[129] "delivered into *your* hands" (*Tan. BeReshith*:7, quoted earlier).[23] Moreover, as every artist can testify, human imagination is the basis, by definition, of human *creativity*. (Indeed, by enabling man to fabricate — i.e., *create* — his own "reality," imagination is also the vehicle through which man can fling himself in the face of the most obvious logical and ethical mandates.)[130] If the *yetzer hara* represents the creative capacity of man, it and man's imaginative faculty must be synonymous.

Having unmasked this equivalence between the imagination and the *yetzer hara*, let us consider the consequences. As we discussed at length concerning human creativity and the *yetzer hara*, clearly our imaginative faculty is not inherently evil. We have, in addition, glimpsed some of the prodigious achievements that, Chazal tell us, are within our ken solely by dint of the *yetzer hara*. We can now, however, add a crucial insight to compound these observations: Prophecy, too, among the most sublime levels attainable by man,[131] is mediated by the *yetzer hara*.[113] The torturous path upon which our inquiry has guided us allows us no other conclusion. With all its potential dangers, the imaginative faculty — *"which is also the* yetzer hara *in reality"* — is indispensable not only for fabricating *false* prophecy but for properly "imagining" *true* prophecy as well.[132]

This, if we may so call it, is the creative element of prophecy:[133] the prophet's active role in expounding G-d's transcendent message. On the one hand, it is the basis of the irrevocably individual, interpretive dimension of all prophecy other than that of Mosheh, which imposes essential limitations on the scope and even the Halachic force of all post-Torah prophecy. On the other hand, it is the basis of the *"great ... power* of the prophets, in that they *imagine* the likeness of Divine Might as the form of man" (*BeM.R.* 19:4).[108] In either case, it is to the *yetzer hara* — in particular, to the basis of spiritual creativity, the *"yetzer* of idolatry"* — that we are beholden for this unique prophetic capacity. For a true prophet of G-d, then, the *yetzer hara* is apparently *not* "evil." This is the legacy of Avraham, the first prophet of the nation of Yisra'el, who "made [his] *yetzer ra* good" (*Yer. Berachoth* 9:5 [60a], *Yer. Sotah* 5:5 [25b]). Once again, with renewed force, the echo of the serpent's promise boggles the mind: "On the day you eat from [the fruit of the tree of knowing good and evil], your eyes will be opened, and *you will be like G-d*" (BeReshith 3:5).

Hearkening to the Lion's "Echo"

Armed with this sharpened appreciation of the *"yetzer* of idolatry" and its full implications, we return to the Talmud's surrealistic portrayal of the men of the Great Assembly and the "lion of fire." In light of the above discussion of prophecy, it is especially striking that this nameless beast is identified only by *"the prophet* [Zecharyah, who says] to Yisra'el, 'It is the *yetzer* of idolatry!' " Evidently, recognizing this force was no trivial accomplishment, perhaps since it is the *"yetzer"* of so much more than merely idolatry.[134] R. E.E. Dessler observes:

> This *yetzer* concerns only high levels. Similarly, its semblance — to the [men of the Great Assembly] — as "a lion of fire" ... suggests that this

> *yetzer* comes specifically from enthusiasm in the service of G-d.... The *yetzer* of idolatry belongs specifically at the high level of the flow of prophecy.... Therefore, it is the prophet who recognized this *yetzer hara*.
> (*Michtav MeEliyyahu*, IV, 174)

Inasmuch as this "*yetzer* of idolatry" is the driving force behind not only idolatry and false prophecy but the consecration of the Beith HaMikdash and *true prophecy* as well, no one is better suited to identify it than "*the prophet*" — its greatest user.

Furthermore, it is particularly apt that the "lion of fire," which lies at the root of prophecy, lurked within "the chamber of the Holy of Holies," the inner sanctum of the Temple. From its inception in the Sanctuary erected in the Sinai wilderness, the Holy of Holies served as the focal point of prophecy. This role was explicitly stated when G-d transmitted to Mosheh the initial commands concerning the Sanctuary's construction: "*I shall commune with you there*, and I shall speak with you from above the ark cover, from between the two *keruvim*, which are upon the Ark of the Testimony" (Shemoth 25:22). Thus, the Torah reports in fact: "And when Mosheh would come to the Communion Tent to speak with Him, he would hear the Voice speaking with him from above the ark cover, which is upon the Ark of the Testimony, from between the two *keruvim*" (BeMidbar 7:89). Consequently, throughout the Bible, G-d is repeatedly called the One "Who is enthroned [upon] the *keruvim*" (Shemu'el I 4:4, etc.).[135] Conversely, we find the holy ark itself — the focal point of both the Holy of Holies and Mosheh's prophecy — called "G-d" by Mosheh (*HaKozari* 1:97 — in com. on BeMidbar 10:35-36).[136] The goal of its formation — indeed, the goal of the Beith HaMikdash as a whole — was primarily to establish a permanent framework for divine revelation in the midst of Yisra'el: "They shall make Me a sanctuary, and *I shall dwell among them*" (Shemoth 25:8).[137]

Likewise, as we would anticipate, we find a continuous association between prophecy and the Beith HaMikdash as a whole. The Talmud relates, for example, that "Yonah the son of Amittai was [one] of the festival pilgrims, and [when] he entered the *simchath beith hasho'evah* [the joyous celebration surrounding the water libation in the Beith HaMikdash on Sukkoth] the holy spirit rested upon him" (*Yer. Sukkah* 5:1 [20a], *Yal.Sh.* Yonah:550). Moreover, the Talmud emphasizes that whenever a prophet is introduced in the Bible with "his name and not the name of his city, it is certain that he is from Yerushalayim" (*Megillah* 15a, *BeM.R.* 10:5), from which we may infer that proximity to the Beith HaMikdash generated a proliferation of prophecy. Even more dramatically, the Midrash comments that Yerushalayim is called *"the Valley of Vision"* (Yeshayahu 22:1), meaning "the valley about which all visionaries prophesy, the valley from which all visionaries arise" (*Eich.R. Peth.*:24, *Yal.Sh.* Yeshayahu:421).

In this sense, R. Yehudah HaLevi notes that the Sanctuary, with the holy ark as its focal point, endured "in the midst of Yisra'el *all the days of prophecy*" (*HaKozari* 1:87), implying interdependence between it and prophecy. *Otzar Nechmad* explains this linkage: "for all the prophets absorb the flow of divine [prophecy] from the effulgence of the Temple's glory" (com., loc. cit., ד"ה כל ימי הנבואה).[138] R. Yehudah HaLevi himself states explicitly that all the prophets — even the last of them, at the beginning of the period of the second Beith HaMikdash (which was bereft of the "lion of fire") — "merited the illumination of prophecy by force of the Shechinah, which rested in the *first Beith [HaMikdash]*" (ibid. 3:65). Conversely, "all the days that [the Shechinah] rested in that *[first] Beith [HaMikdash]*, everyone who was ready for it in terms of [individual] quality[139] would attain prophecy" (ibid. 2:14).[140]

Similarly, R. Yosef Albo concludes that "prophecy was prevalent in the nation of Yisra'el ... because, as a result of *the ark and the tablets*, the Shechinah would rest upon [the prophet]" (*HaIkkarim* 3:11). Emphasizes R. Me'ir b. Gabbai, "The great cause of prophecy and the reason for ... the holy spirit and the Shechinah resting upon the worthy was the ark and the keruvim when the first Temple was [still] in existence, and from there the light and the [spiritual] abundance would spread forth.... Thus, the Temple was the great cause of the resting of [the spirit of] prophecy" (Avodath HaKodesh, "Sithrei Torah," ch. 24).[141] If the Beith HaMikdash and especially its Holy of Holies were the primary abode of the "yetzer of idolatry," we would indeed expect them to have been the focus of prophecy — its ultimate expression.

Furthermore, with our heightened understanding of the *"yetzer* of idolatry" and prophecy, we can discern one more crucial implication of the "roar" that issued from the "lion of fire" and "went through four hundred parasangs." We have already discussed the significance of "four hundred parasangs," the dimensions of Eretz Yisra'el:[58] The primary impact of the "roar" of the "*yetzer* of idolatry" corresponds to Eretz Yisra'el. We now consider one of the most far-reaching consequences of Eretz Yisra'el's distinct role in this regard, as the land upon which the *yetzer hara* "*lets itself loose*": *Eretz Yisra'el is uniquely "the land of prophecy"* (*HaKozari* 1:95 and 2:14). Thus, the Midrash observes that "once Eretz Yisra'el was chosen [for prophecy], all other lands were excluded.... The Shechinah is not revealed outside the Land" (*Mechilta* on Shemoth 12:1, *Yal.Sh.* Shemoth:187 and Yechezkel:336).[142] R. Yehudah HaLevi comments categorically, "Everyone who prophesied prophesied solely either in this land or on its behalf" (*HaKozari* 2:14).[143] It is no wonder, then, that the "roar" of the "*yetzer* of idolatry" reverberates specifically "through four hundred parasangs" — throughout "the land of prophecy." Only here can the prophet exclaim, *"A lion has roared; who will not fear? G-d the L-rd has spoken; who will not prophesy?"* (Amos 3:8).

With this apprehension of our resplendent past, we must now painfully direct our gaze to our *yetzer hara*'s relatively dim, pallid present. R. Avraham Y. Karelitz (Chazon Ish) observes:

> We have no conception of how a *yetzer* of bowing to an idol is possible. However, this is not an ascent on our part [with respect to our ancestors] but a descent. For surely the culmination of man is the *yetzer*, and one lacking the *yetzer* is lacking the soul.
>
> (*Kovetz Iggeroth Chazon Ish*, I, 109)

This dismal assessment characterizes the human condition — with its stunted *yetzer hara* — today. In light of our enhanced appreciation of this *yetzer*, it should not surprise us to realize that, when man's obsession with idolatry vanished at the beginning of the period of the second Beith HaMikdash, his capacity to prophesy disappeared as well. The Talmud states that "Chaggai, Zecharyah, and Malachi were the last of the prophets" (*Babba Bathra* 14b); traditionally, the three were also members of the Great Assembly.[144] After they died, "the holy spirit was withdrawn from Yisra'el" (*Tos. Sotah* 13:4).[145] Obviously, this is no coincidence; muffling the "lion of fire" inevitably smothered both true and false prophecy as well. As the Vilna Ga'on states, "Once they 'killed'[56] the *yetzer hara* [of idolatry], prophecy ceased" (*Haghoth HaGra* on *Seder Olam R.*, ch. 30).[146] Explains R. Tzadok HaKohen, "Since there is no [longer] compulsion of the *yetzer* here, it is no longer possible to reach the height [of prophecy] through it (*Sichath Malachei HaShareth*, "*Tan. Parashath Mishpatim*" [pp. 76-77]).[147] That guiding principle of the human condition, "*This one corresponding to that one the L-rd has made*" (Koheleth 7:14), mandates such interdependence between true prophecy and false prophecy. Their sources are not only linked but identical: Both necessarily derive from the "*yetzer* of idolatry" — now, "cast ... into a leaden caldron [covered] ... with lead."

Paradoxically, however, from this somber epitaph of the "*yetzer* of idolatry," we can yet draw a glimmer of hope for our *yetzer hara* and ourselves. As we have seen, the "lion of fire" is *not* extinguished; its "roar" endures withal.[56] The leaden caldron and cover were prescribed "because lead absorbs sound" — and one need mute only what has not yet been irrevocably silenced. Moreover, to the extent that every human being is an *olam katan*, a microcosm of the world,[148] that "roar" is sustained (although muffled) inside each one of us. Within every individual "holy of holies" — the heart of hearts of every person — the "*yetzer* of idolatry" endures, covered with "lead" to absorb its unabated "roar."

We can still hear this persistent echo, but only if we listen with redoubled sensitivity. Thus, despite the imprisonment of the drive toward idol worship, idolatry is yet, regrettably, extant (albeit to a greatly attenuated extent). And, correspondingly, while prophecy itself is no longer accessible, the Talmud reports that "after ... the holy spirit was withdrawn from Yisra'el ... [the Sages] *nevertheless would continue to be informed by divine echo* (בת קול)" (*Tos. Sotah* 13:4).[149] Maharal explains that "this divine echo is inaudible" (*Derech HaChayyim* on *Avoth* 6:3); rather, "it is close to the level of man" (*Chiddushei Aggadoth* on *Babba Metzi'a* 59b). R. Tzadok HaKohen comments that "these voices are extant today as well, *for one who wants to hearken* [to them]. And these are *the thoughts that arise in everyone's heart* every time to return to G-d" (*Tzidkath HaTzaddik*, ch. 221).[150] For those who listen attentively enough, the divine echo resonates with the lion's muffled roar, welling up from the "leaden caldron" in the midst of us all.[151] It is the echo of creativity, the echo of G-dliness, reiterating the serpent's promise that — through the *yetzer hara* — "*you will be like G-d*" (BeReshith 3:5).[16]

5. THE DIVINE POWER WITHIN US

We now hold the key to understanding the *yetzer hara*, root of both G-dliness and wickedness. Equated by Rambam with the imagination (*Moreh* 2:12), it is fundamentally the root of the gamut of self-initiated, creative human action — from sexuality through prophecy — undertaken in this world. As we have noted, "*yetzer* (יצר)" derives from the root "יצר" (~ create),[35] plainly emphasizing this creative dimension.[36] Herein lies its awesome potential for unparalleled greatness — and for unprecedented self-destruction.

In light of the *yetzer hara*'s role as the basis of man's creative initiative, it is particularly fitting that Avraham — the initiator par excellence who, as the first of the patriarchs of Yisra'el, "*from his own self* learned the Torah" (*BeR.R.* 95:3, *Tan. VaYiggash*:11)[152] — is the exemplar of positive exploitation of the *yetzer hara*. As the Talmud Yerushalmi relates, "Avraham made [his] *yetzer ra* good" (*Yer. Berachoth* 9:5 [60a], *Yer. Sotah* 5:5 [25b]).[153] Comments the Vilna Ga'on, "All the acts of Creation [including the *yetzer hara*] are good: for the *yetzer hara* also aids the righteous, and *the essence of their service [of G-d] is through it*, as is known" (*Be'urei Aggadoth* on *Berachoth* 61b).[154]

More generally, we are all enjoined to love G-d "with the *yetzer tov* and with the *yetzer ra*" (*Mish. Berachoth* 9:5);[13] in the absence of the *yetzer hara*, it would be impossible truly to express love of G-d within the sphere of willful, human action. Explains R. Menachem b. Shelomoh HaMe'iri, "The intention of *both* [involvement in the *yetzer tov* and involvement in the *yetzer ra*] should be for one object, *which is love of G-d*" (*Chibbur HaTeshuvah* 1:3 [p. 66]).[155] R. Yisra'el Lipschutz specifies that this love includes "using the fire of the *yetzer hara* — such as desire and longing and anger and pride and jealousy — *to inflame oneself to perform the commandments and do good deeds*" (*Tifereth Yisra'el* on

Mish. Berachoth 9:5). This sense of excitement accords with the Midrash's analogous exposition — on King David's declaration, "I shall thank G-d with all my heart; I shall relate all Your wondrous works. I shall rejoice and exult in You ..." (Tehillim 9:2-3) — that "with all my heart" refers to thanking G-d "with the yetzer tov and with the yetzer hara" (Mid. Tehillim 9:5, Yal.Sh. Tehillim:643). Without the *yetzer hara*, such exultation in G-d would be lackluster and lifeless.

Thus, observes *Zohar*, "the *yetzer hara* is as necessary for the world as rain, for were it not for the *yetzer hara*, rejoicing in the discussion of Torah laws would not be" (*Zohar*, "Mid. HaNe'elam," I, 138a).[14] Just as rain initiates the chain of biological dynamism upon which all life depends, so the *yetzer hara* is the basis of creative involvement in Torah study, which precipitates the dynamic excitement of "rejoicing in the discussion of Torah laws." In fact, Chazal state that there can be no authentic Torah study lacking such creative involvement: "It is inconceivable for a house of study to be without scholarly innovation" (*Chagigah* 3a).[156] Even more emphatically, R. Tzadok HaKohen adds:

> "*Yetzer* (יצר)" means "longing," as it is said, "for the *longing* (יצר) of the thoughts of the heart of Your people" (Divrei HaYamim I 29:18): for G-d created man with a *yetzer* in which the aspect of desire is incorporated.... And it is [written] that "were it not for the *yetzer hara*, rejoicing in the discussion of Torah laws would not be" (*Zohar*, loc. cit.), *since this is the object for which the* yetzer *was created: to be a longing and desire for the Torah.* And this is [what is] written in the Gemara, "If this repulsive one [the *yetzer hara*] meets you, drag him to the house of study" (*Sukkah* 52b, *Kiddushin* 30b), meaning: [you are] to drag the desire into being the desire for Torah.
> (*Peri Tzaddik* on *Terumah*, ch. 8 [p. 152])[157]

The object of the *yetzer hara* is not *evil* but *enthusiasm* — ultimately, as applied to Torah study. No wonder R. Yitzchak b. Shemu'el of Akko comments that "one who has not longed for a woman resembles a donkey and less" (quoted in *Reshith Chochmah*, "Sha'ar HaAhavah," ch. 4). Like a donkey ("חמור"), symbol of an utterly materialistic ("חומר") perspective,[158] one who lacks desire necessarily lacks the real object for which desire was created: enthusiasm for *spirituality*.¹⁵⁹ The " 'lion of fire' ... comes specifically from enthusiasm in the service of G-d" (*Michtav MeEliyyahu*, IV, 174);160 therefore, as we have seen, "the culmination of man is the yetzer, and one lacking the yetzer is lacking the soul" (Kovetz Iggeroth Chazon Ish, I, 109). In conclusion, notes the Midrash, "were it not for the yetzer hara, there would be none of that honor [foretold by the prophets] for Yisra'el" (*T.DeV.Eli.R.* 16). R. Tzadok HaKohen observes that "when [the longing that is derived from the *yetzer hara* is applied] in holiness, there is no holiness greater than it, and it is called *'very good'* "¹⁶¹ (*Takkanath HaShavin*, ch. 6 [p. 30]). The greatness of the people of Yisra'el, realized by virtue of the spiritual wellsprings they initiated, is indeed to be credited primarily to the *yetzer hara*.

Given the *yetzer hara*'s mediation of the unique, creative dynamism that characterizes human nature in this world,⁴² we can readily appreciate its uniqueness to the human condition. On the one hand, "the *yetzer hara* does not rule over the angels" (*BeR.R.* 48:11).¹⁶² On the other hand, "there is no *yetzer hara* in a beast" (*Avoth DeR. Nathan* 16:3).¹⁶³ Yet man is so animated by this dynamism that "no one leaves the world with half of what he *desires* in his possession" (*Koh.R.* 1:13, 3:10). As Elifaz HaTeimani summarizes human nature, "man is born *for exertion*" (Iyyov 5:7; *Sanhedrin* 99b, *Yal.Sh.* Yehoshua:6). Thus, man alone is identified collectively as "moving ones," in contradistinction to the angels, who are characterized as "the standing ones" (Zecharyah 3:7). Likewise, Maharal comments that the name of man, "*adam* (אדם)" — related to "אדמה" ("ground") — symbolizes his dynamic nature: "[The ground] embodies potential, and through it all the things that sprout from it ... emerge toward actualization ... [and] so the matter of man is that he is potential, and his completeness [must] emerge toward actualization" (*Tifereth Yisra'el*, ch. 3 [p. 12]). In a similar vein, R. Tzadok HaKohen (*Machshevoth Charutz*, ch. 4 [p. 13]) relates "*adam* (אדם)" to "אדמה לעליון" ("*I will be like* the Most High" [Yeshayahu 14:14]), expressing the imitative drive that — fueled by the *imagination* ("דמיון") — has spurred human initiative and ambition ever since man submitted to the serpent's seduction to "be like G-d" (BeReshith 3:5). By contrast, the beast ("בהמה") embodies static self-containment: "בה מה" ("something within"), "for the fruition of the matter for which it was created is found within it" (*Tifereth Yisra'el*, loc. cit.).

Significantly, Chazal relate this distinction between man and beast to the observation that "an infant lying in a cradle puts his hand upon a snake or upon a scorpion, which stings him ... [and] puts his hand upon burning coals and is burnt ... only [because of] the yetzer hara in his midst," whereas "a kid or a lamb, upon seeing a well, retreats [from the danger], because there is no yetzer hara in a beast" (Avoth DeR. Nathan 16:3). Lest we erroneously deduce from this contrast that the yetzer hara is essentially no more than a "death wish," we should consider the conclusion of Chazal that, "were [the *yetzer hara*] put within [a human fetus while] still inside its mother's innards [instead of at birth], it would cut through her innards and leave" (*BeR.R.* 34:10, *Sanhedrin* 91b).[164] The Midrash's gruesome image sharply conveys the extent to which one possessed of a *yetzer hara* (and the creative initiative it engenders) is guided by a sense of autonomy[165] so overwhelming that it induces rebellion against nature itself. The secure confinement of the womb — let alone the fetus's dependence on its mother — is antithetical to the *yetzer hara*'s message of initiative and independence. As opposed to such human autonomy, " 'there is no *yetzer hara* in a beast' (*Avoth DeR. Nathan*, loc. cit.), meaning: all its actions are to be completely [determined by] *nature*" (*Chibbur HaTeshuvah* [HaMe'iri] 2:9 [p. 411]). Thus, while a beast avoids danger instinctively and, "upon seeing a well, retreats," a person is, in this context, autonomous from birth; even "an infant lying in a cradle" is a creature independent of instinct, subservient to no nature.

Correspondingly, the Midrash notes that, were a beast to have a *yetzer hara*, "upon seeing a knife in the hand of a person [coming] to slaughter it, it would be *terrified* and die" (*BeR.R.* 14:4, *Yal.Sh.* BeReshith:20). Conversely, *Mattenoth Kehunnah* comments, "Because it has no *yetzer hara*, its ways are *wholesome*" (com., loc. cit.). Its conduct, emphasizes *Yefeh To'ar*, necessarily conforms to "the one *natural* way, without deviating from it right or left" (com., loc. cit).

A sense of terror when confronted with one's mortality is the most elementary consequence of self-awareness: a recognition that one lives (and will cease to live) as a distinct, autonomous being. As but a part of the natural world, motivated by instinct alone, a beast is incapable of perceiving any such autonomy. While animals instinctively avoid pain, they inherently lack the capacity to fear death, for death is the cessation of autonomous existence as "self," an awareness they had never possessed from the beginning. For the same reason, a beast lacks any sense of resistance to nature in general. But even "an infant lying in a cradle" is animated by just such a sense of autonomy. People are not creatures of instinct; through their *yetzer hara*, they have the capacity to initiate action without any recourse to nature — for better and for worse. In this light, we can appreciate R. E.E. Dessler's observation that the *yetzer hara* is called an "angel" — "because it transcends all terrestrial [i.e., natural] forces" (*Michtav MeEliyyahu*, I, 237).

6. CONCLUSION: THE AWESOME FRUIT OF "KNOWING GOOD AND EVIL"

While this capacity of even an infant creatively to assert its autonomy (and be stung or burnt) evokes our awe, it surely provokes our fear as well. In fact, from its inception, the *yetzer hara* is associated not only with creativity and G-dliness but with destruction and sin as well. After all, it was in flagrant violation of G-d's explicit command that man ate the fruit of the "tree of knowing good and evil" and internalized the *yetzer hara* altogether[16] — an act that impelled not only banishment from Gan Eden into this world of creativity,[42] but also the accursed consequences of creativity itself. Thus, Chavvah and womankind were punished with the pains of pregnancy, childbearing, and child rearing:[166] The ultimate creativity in this world — creating and raising the next generation — is fraught with anguish and adversity. Similarly, Adam and mankind were punished with an intractable earth that resists all efforts at cultivation, sprouting thorns and thistles but yielding bread only through sweat and sorrow:[167] Any human attempt to assert autonomy and harness nature involves endless struggle, costly victories, and recurrent defeats. Man's creative capacity, as initiated by the *yetzer hara*, is clearly a mixed blessing at best. Understandably, Chazal caution, "[Concerning the] *yetzer* ... *let the left hand push it away and the right hand draw it near*" (*Sotah* 47a, *Sanhedrin* 107b).[168]

In spite of our interim conclusions concerning the awesome power of the *yetzer hara* — and perhaps because of them — we dare not forget that the *yetzer hara* is also the root of all sin. Indeed, on the one hand, the *yetzer hara* is implicated in building houses, raising families, and running businesses. Furthermore, it is indispensable both in loving and serving G-d and in learning and rejoicing in Torah. Prayer, the Beith HaMikdash, and prophecy — hallmarks of man's "great power" — all depend upon it. Ultimately, man's quest for G-dliness — and, in fact, all enthusiasm for spiritual pursuits in general — derives from the *yetzer hara*; as a result, the very endurance of this world is predicated upon its continued existence. On the other hand, the *yetzer hara* spawns destruction and death, mediating sexual transgression, idolatry, false prophecy, and — more generally — *all sin*.

Moreover, we recall the Talmud's dismal assessment, "[How] hard is the *yetzer hara*, inasmuch as even its Creator called it 'evil'!" (*Kiddushin* 30b),[9] concluding, " *'Evil'* refers solely to the *yetzer hara*" (*Chagigah* 16a). How can the very basis of man's capacity for G-dliness be "evil"? Is it this creative power that Chazal brand "an alien god in your midst" (*Shabbath* 105b, *Yal.Sh.* Tehillim:831), identified as both "the accusing angel [Satan]" and "the angel of death" (*Babba Bathra* 16a),[11] whose role is to "entice man in this world and testify against him in the world to come" (*Sukkah* 52b, *Yal.Sh.* Mishlei:962)? While this bitter conclusion seems unacceptable, why does the Midrash comment, regarding the basis of human creativity, "Wretched is the dough whose baker testifies that it is evil!" (*BeR.R.* 34:10)?[10] Still more perplexing, how can the Talmud enumerate the *yetzer hara* as one of four entities that "the Holy One Blessed be He *regrets having created*" (*Sukkah* 52b)?[169]

Obviously, no perspective presented here is incorrect. Each, however, taken singly and superficially, is incomplete. These disparate sources in Chazal clearly do not demonstrate incoherence or inconsistency; rather, they indicate a yet-unfathomed complexity.[20] Why was the *yetzer hara* (i.e., the fruit of the "tree of knowing good and evil") forbidden to Adam and Chavvah, its acquisition resulting solely from their defiance of G-d's will? In what sense altogether is the *yetzer hara* the basis of sin? Does evil lurk in man's capacity to create? In addition, what role is there for the elusive *yetzer tov*, which we have as yet hardly mentioned? Finally, if Torah is supposedly the antidote to the *yetzer hara*, what is to be its impact on this faculty — and on human creativity in general? Toward what conception of G-dliness is the Torah advancing us? Evidently, in the quest to explicate the nature of the *yetzer hara* and human creativity, our work is not yet complete. In fact, it is only beginning.

This essay is the first of a three-part series by the author on Chazal's conception of the yetzer hara.
The next installment will appear, G-d willing, in the upcoming issue of
Jewish Thought: A Journal of Torah Scholarship.

NOTES

1. See *Sanhedrin* 38b; *Avoth DeR. Nathan* 1:8; *BeR.R.* 11:2, 12:6, 18:6, and 21:5; *Sh.R.* 32:1; *VaY.R.* 29:1; *Tan. Shemini*:8; *Pes. Rabbathi* 46 (187b); *Mid. Tehillim* 92:3; *Pir.DeR.E.* 11 and 19; and *Yal.Sh.* BeReshith:15, 25, Shofetim:57, and Tehillim:758.

2. See BeReshith 2:16-17 and 3:1-6. I refer to the forbidden tree as the "tree of knowing good and evil" to emphasize that it was *not* knowledge per se that was forbidden to man, but specifically "knowing good and evil" — a paltry level indeed, notes Rambam (*Moreh HaNevochim* 1:2), involving only relative concepts determined by human consensus — compared with the G-dly knowledge of absolute truth and falsity that man initially had by virtue of having been created with the "essence and likeness" of G-d (BeReshith 1:26-27, 5:1, and 9:6). See also *Mid. Tadshei*, ch. 7 (quoted in *Michtav MeEliyyahu*, I, 127).

The distinction between man's spiritual and intellectual nature prior to eating the forbidden fruit and afterward is discussed in numerous Talmudic, Midrashic, and rabbinical sources. See, for example, *Chagigah* 12a; *Sanhedrin* 38b; *BeR.R.* 8:1, 12:6, 16:1, 19:8-9, 21:1, 3-4, and 24:2; *Sh.R.* 32:1; *VaY.R.* 14:1, 18:2, and 20:2; *BeM.R.* 11:3 and 13:12; *Dev.R.* 11:3; *Sh.HaSh.R.* 3:6 (5); *Koh.R.* 8:1 (2); *Tan. BeReshith*:6, *Tazria*:8, and *Acharei*:2; *Mid. Tehillim* 139:5; *Mid. Shemu'el* 17:4; *Pir.DeR.E.* 11; and *Yal.Sh.* BeReshith:27-28, 951, Tehillim:795, 887, Iyyov:907, Ruth:609, and Koheleth:977. See also *HaKozari* 1:95; *Moreh HaNevochim* 1:1-2; Ramban on BeReshith 2:9 and on Devarim 30:6; R. Bachyai on BeReshith 3:5, 6, 22; R. Eliyyahu Mizrachi on BeReshith 2:25; R. Ovadyah Seforno on BeReshith 2:25 and 3:7; *Derech HaChayyim* (Maharal) on *Avoth* 3:15; *Or HaChayyim* on BeReshith 2:25; *Derech HaShem* 1:3-4 and 2:4; *Da'ath Tevunoth*, chs. 78 and 126; *Nefesh HaChayyim* 1:6, הגה״ה ד״ה והענין כי קודם החטא (and *Ruach*

Chayyim on *Avoth* 3:3); R. S.R. Hirsch on BeReshith 2:17 and 3:7-8; *HaTorah VeHaMitzvah* (Malbim) on BeReshith 2:9, 17, 25, 3:1, 5, 7-11, 19, 22, and 8:21, ד״ה ועץ הדעת טוב ורע, *Ha'amek Davar* on BeReshith 2:9, ד״ה כי יצר לב האדם רע מנעריו; and 3:1, 6-7; R. Tzadok HaKohen (*Tzidkath HaTzaddik*, chs. 218 and 258; *Dover Tzedek*, ch. 4 [pp. 120-25]; *Machshevoth Charutz*, chs. 1, 9, 13, 15, and 18 [pp. 3, 69, 102, 118, 151-53, 156]; *Takkanath HaShavin*, chs. 6 and 15 [pp. 65, 142-43, 165]; *Resisei Lailah*, ch. 35 [p. 57]; *Yisra'el Kedoshim*, ch. 9 [p. 112]; *Likkutei Ma'amarim*, chs. 14 and 16 [pp. 147, 156]; and *Peri Tzaddik*, "Kedushath Shabbath," *Ma'amar* 3 [p. 15], on *BeReshith*, ch. 8 [p. 8], and on *Zachor*, ch. 1 [p. 173]); *Meshech Chochmah* on BeReshith 3:4-5, בא״ד ארבעה מתו בעטיו של נחש; *Sefath Emeth* on *BeReshith* (5644); *Shem MiShemu'el* on *BeReshith* (5671, 5673-74, 5676, 5678); and *Michtav MeEliyyahu*, II, 137-49, and III, 210-11, 228, and 320-22.

In this essay, we focus on one aspect of this transformation — the internalization of the *yetzer hara* — although the broader implications of eating the fruit of the "tree of knowing good and evil" are certainly related to it.

3. See R. Eliyyahu Mizrachi, *Levush HaOrah*, and *Sifthei Chachamim* on Rashi, loc. cit. See also Rashi on Yeshayahu 5:7 and *Zohar*, I, 35-36.

  In later commentaries, this idea is greatly expanded. See, for example, R. Avraham b. Ezra on BeReshith 3:6; Ramban on BeReshith 2:9 and on Devarim 30:6; R. Bachyai on BeReshith 3:6, ד״ה וכי תאוה הוא לעינים; R. Ovadyah Seforno on BeReshith 2:25 and 3:7; *Or HaChayyim* on BeReshith 2:25; *Da'ath Tevunoth*, ch. 126; *Nefesh HaChayyim* 1:6, הגהייה ד״ה והענין כי קודם החטא; *HaTorah VeHaMitzvah* (Malbim) on BeReshith 3:19; R. Tzadok HaKohen (*Tzidkath HaTzaddik*, chs. 218 and 258; *Dover Tzedek*, ch. 4 [pp. 120-25]; *Machshevoth Charutz*, chs. 9 and 18 [pp. 69, 151-53]; *Takkanath HaShavin*, chs. 6 and 15 [pp. 65, 142-43, 165]; *Resisei Lailah*, ch. 35 [p. 57]; *Yisra'el Kedoshim*, ch. 9 [p. 112]; *Likkutei Ma'amarim*, ch. 14 [p. 147]; and *Peri Tzaddik*, "Kedushath Shabbath," *Ma'amar* 3 [p. 15], on *BeReshith*, ch. 8 [p. 8], and on *Zachor*, ch. 1 [p. 173]); *Shem MiShemu'el* on *BeReshith* (5671, 5673-74, 5676, 5678); and *Michtav MeEliyyahu*, II, 137-49, and III, 210 and 320-22.

4. See also BeReshith 21:19, Yeshayahu 35:5 and 42:20, and Yechezkel 12:2, all of which are examples of "פקח" cited by Rambam, loc. cit.

5. See also Ramban, R. Ovadyah Seforno, and *HaTorah VeHaMitzvah* (Malbim) on BeReshith 3:7 and R. Bachyai on BeReshith 3:5, who explain the opening of man's eyes similarly. In addition, see R. S.R. Hirsch, loc. cit., for a comparable interpretation of "פקח."

6. The Midrash exegetically ascribes this verse to Adam's sin and consequent banishment from Gan Eden. See *Sanhedrin* 38b; *Avoth DeR. Nathan* 1:8; *BeR.R.* 11:2 and 12:6; *Dev.R.* 11:3; *Mid. Tehillim* 92:3; *Pir.DeR.E.* 19; and *Yal.Sh.* BeReshith:15, 951, Tehillim:758, and Ruth:609. Rambam and Ramchal also cite this verse in the same context (see *Moreh*, loc. cit., and *Da'ath Tevunoth*, ch. 126).

7. See BeReshith 3:16-19, 23-24, and com., loc. cit.

8. See, for example, the sources cited in n. 2, and see, in addition, *Shabbath* 55b and *Babba Bathra* 17a. Also see, in addition, *Da'ath Tevunoth*, chs. 40, 72, and 158, and *Machshevoth Charutz*, chs. 7, 8, and 19 [pp. 37, 57-58, 160].

9. See also *Sifrei* on Devarim 11:18; *Sukkah* 52a; *Mid. Mishlei* 11:21; and *Yal.Sh.* BeReshith:47, 61, Devarim:870, Yechezkel:375, and Mishlei:947.

10. See also *BeM.R.* 13:4 and *Yal.Sh.* BeReshith:61, Yirmeyahu:290, and Tehillim:859. In addition, see *Sukkah* 52b.

11. See also *Moreh HaNevochim* 3:22. In addition, see *Zohar*, I, 255.

12. Likewise, the Talmud posits, " *'Evil'* refers solely to the *yetzer hara*" (*Chagigah* 16a). See also *Kiddushin* 30b and the sources cited in nn. 9 and 10.

13. See also *Sifrei* on Devarim 6:5 and *Yal.Sh.* Devarim:837. In addition, see *Moreh HaNevochim* 3:22.

    Analogously, the Midrash relates "I shall thank G-d *with all my heart*" (Tehillim 9:2) to thanking G-d "with the *yetzer tov* and with the *yetzer hara*" (*Mid. Tehillim* 9:5, *Yal.Sh.* Tehillim:643 — discussed in the text below).

14. Regarding the implications of this quotation and the *yetzer hara*'s essential role in "rejoicing in the discussion of Torah laws," see the discussion in the text below, and see R. Tzadok HaKohen, in *Tzidkath HaTzaddik*, ch. 229; *Dover Tzedek*, בא״י הי׳ בא״יד והוא עצמו כח היצר (pp. 145-46) and בא״יד וכל הכחות הי׳ בא״י (p.165); *Takkanath HaShavin*, ch. 6 (p. 64); *Resisei Lailah*, chs. 23, 35, and 58 (pp. 29-30, 57, 174); *Yisra'el Kedoshim*, chs. 9 and 10 (pp. 113, 129); *Divrei Soferim*, ch. 38 (p. 45); and *Likkutei Ma'amarim*, ch. 16 (pp. 157, 164, 220); and also in *Peri Tzaddik* on *Terumah*, chs. 2 and 8 (pp. 147, 152); on Pesach, ch. 4 (p. 41); and on Korach, ch. 10 (p. 136).

15. See also *Yal.Sh.* BeReshith:16. While the words "and would not deal in business" do not appear in *Koheleth Rabbah*, compare *BeReshith Rabbah* and *Yalkut Shimoni*, loc. cit. In addition, see *Mid. Tehillim* 9:1 and *Yal.Sh.* Tehillim:643, quoted in the text below. See also *Mid. Tehillim* 37:1.

16. As indicated above, Rashi explicitly links eating the fruit of the "tree of knowing good and evil" with man's acquisition of the *yetzer hara* (com. on BeReshith 2:25 and on Yeshayahu 5:7). See also the sources cited in n. 3.

17. I have translated "והייתם כא-לקים" as "*you will be like G-d*" in conformance with the implication of the Midrash (see the text below and the sources cited in n. 18). See also Rashi, R. Ovadyah Seforno, and R. S.R. Hirsch, loc. cit., and see most translations of the Torah. However, compare *Tar. Yonathan* and *Tar. Onkelos*, loc. cit., and see R. Avraham b. Ezra and R. Bachyai, loc. cit., and *Moreh HaNevochim* 1:2. See also *Ha'amek Davar* on BeReshith, loc. cit.

18. See also *BeR.R.* 19:4; *Dev.R.* 5:10; *Tan. BeReshith*:8, *Tazria*:9, and *Metzora*:2; *Mid. Tehillim* 1:9; *Yal.Sh.* BeReshith:27 and Tehillim:613; and Rashi on BeReshith, loc. cit.

19. Regarding the "opening" of the eyes of Adam and Chavvah and its implications, see *Moreh HaNevochim* 1:2, and see the sources cited in n. 5.

20. Implied here is the principle that "these and those are the words of the Living G-d" (*Gittin* 6b, *Eruvin* 13b). See also *Michtav MeEliyyahu*, III, 353-54 (and II, 68), for a more detailed discussion of this concept.

21. I have translated "ויאמר ה' א-לקים, הן האדם היה כאחד ממנו, לדעת טוב ורע" as "*G-d the L-rd said, 'Behold, man has become like one of Us, knowing good and evil'* " in conformance with the implication of the Midrash (see the text below, and see *BeR.R.* 21:5, *Sh.HaSh.R.* 1:9 [2], and *Yal.Sh.* BeReshith:34) and the punctuation indicated by the *te'amim* (cantillation points). See also R. Avraham b. Ezra, loc. cit., who confirms this interpretation grammatically, and see most translations of the Torah. In addition, see R. Bachyai and R. Ovadyah Seforno, loc. cit. Compare *Tar. Yonathan, Tar. Yerushalmi*, and *Tar. Onkelos*, loc. cit, and see also Rashi, loc. cit., and Rambam (*Yad Hil. Teshuvah* 5:1 and *Moreh* 1:2). In addition, see *Derech HaChayyim* (Maharal) on *Avoth* 3:15 and R. S.R. Hirsch and *Ha'amek Davar* on BeReshith, loc. cit.

22. I have translated "בצלמו" as "*with His essence*" in light of Rambam's demonstration that "צלם" — as opposed to "תאר" and "תבנית" — is employed in the Bible in reference to the essential form and not to a physical image (see *Yad Hil. Yesodei HaTorah* 4:8 and *Moreh* 1:1). See also *Tosefoth Yom Tov* on *Avoth* 3:14 and R. Ovadyah Seforno and *Meshech Chochmah* on BeReshith 1:26. In addition, see Ramban and *HaTorah VeHaMitzvah* (Malbim) on BeReshith 1:26, *Or HaChayyim* on BeReshith 1:27, and *Nefesh HaChayyim* 1:1-3. Compare *Babba Bathra* 58a, *Avoth DeR. Nathan* 2:5, and com., loc. cit.; Rashi on BeReshith 1:27; R. Avraham b. Ezra, *Keli Yakar*, and R. S.R. Hirsch on BeReshith 1:26; *Derech HaChayyim* (Maharal) on *Avoth* 3:14 (pp. 142-43); and *Yeshurun* (R. S.R. Hirsch), VIII, 526.

23. See also BeReshith 4:7 and com., loc. cit. (especially *Tar. Yonathan* and *Tar. Yerushalmi*).

24. Compare the meaning of "yetzer (יצר)" in Yeshayahu 29:16. Thus, "the yetzer of the thoughts of man's heart" means "that which is formed by the thoughts of man's heart." See R. S.R. Hirsch on BeReshith 6:5 (and 8:21).

25. In addition to the various sources in Chazal cited in the text, many rabbinical sources corroborate our contention that the *yetzer hara* is not inherently bad. See, for example, Ma'amar al Odoth Derashoth Chazal (R. Avraham b. Rambam), באי"ד החלק השלישי דרשות; Chibbur HaTeshuvah (R. Menachem b. Shelomoh HaMe'iri) 1:3, 12 (pp. 66, 233), and 2:9 (p. 411); *Ta'alumoth Chochmah* on Koheleth 4:13; Ein Ya'akov (*HaKothev*) on *Berachoth* 64a, באי"ד עוד ראיתי לכתוב; *Be'urei Aggadoth* (Gra) on *Berachoth* 61b; *Torath HaMaggid* (R. Dov Ber of Mezherich), II, on *Kiddushin* 30a (p. 139); *Tifereth Yisra'el* on *Mish. Berachoth* 9:5; R. S.R. Hirsch on BeReshith 2:7, 6:5, and 8:21; R. Tzadok HaKohen (*Tzidkath HaTzaddik*, chs. 218, 229, and 248-49; *Dover Tzedek* on *Berachoth* 3b [p. 24], באי"י באי"ד וכל הכחות הי' [pp. 145-46], and באי"ד והוא עצמו כח היצר [pp. 164-65]; *Machshevoth Charutz*, chs. 4 and 19 [pp. 13, 158]; *Takkanath HaShavin*, chs. 5 and 6 [pp. 17-18, 30, 64]; *Resisei Lailah*, chs. 23, 35, and 58 [pp. 29-30, 57, 174]; *Yisra'el Kedoshim*, chs. 9 and 10 [pp. 112-13, 129]; *Divrei Soferim*, ch. 38 [p. 45]; *Likkutei Ma'amarim*, ch.

16 [pp. 156-57, 164, 220-21]; and *Peri Tzaddik* on *Terumah*, chs. 2 and 8 [pp. 147, 152], on *Zachor*, ch. 1 [p. 173], on Pesach, ch. 4 [p. 41], and on *Korach*, ch. 10 [p. 136]); *Beith Aharon* (R. Aharon Walden) on Tehillim 103, n. 35 (and its analysis of the many sources cited, loc. cit.); *Kovetz Iggeroth Chazon Ish*, I, 109; and *Michtav MeEliyyahu*, II, 211-12, III, 56, and IV, 174 and 289. See also *Moreh HaNevochim* 3:22 and com., loc. cit. In addition, see Prof. Yehudah Levi, "Yetzer Tov VeYetzer HaRa," *HaMa'ayan*, 25, No. 4 (5745), 49-54. See also nn. 28 and 129.

26. See also R. Avraham b. Ezra on BeReshith 3:22.
27. See *Sanhedrin* 91b; *Yer. Berachoth* 3:5 (24b); *Avoth DeR. Nathan* 16:2-3; *BeR.R.* 34:10 and 54:1; *Koh.R.* 4:13 and 9:15 (8); *Mid. Tehillim* 9:5 and 34:2; and *Yal.Sh.* BeReshith:61, Tehillim:723, Iyyov:914, and Koheleth:971. See also *Zohar*, I, 165b; Rashi on BeReshith 8:21 (and *Gur Aryeh*, loc. cit.) and on Koheleth 4:13, ד"ה ממלך זקן וכסיל; *Moreh HaNevochim* 3:22; Ramban on BeReshith 8:21, ד"ה כי יצר לב האדם רע מנעריו; and *Ta'alumoth Chochmah* on Koheleth 4:13.
28. The linkage between the *yetzer hara* and sexuality is indicated and implied throughout Chazal and later rabbinical literature. Indeed, as noted in the text below, the context in which the *yetzer hara* originally appears in the Torah is sexual (see n. 16, and see BeReshith 2:24-25, 3:7, and 4:1). It appears similarly in, for example, *Berachoth* 20a, *Sukkah* 52b, *Sotah* 8a, *Kiddushin* 81, *Sanhedrin* 45a and 107a, *Avodah Zarah* 17b, *VaY.R.* 23:11, *Sh.HaSh.R.* 7:8, and *Pir.DeR.E.* 22. Thus, Chazal speak of the "*yetzer* of [sexual] transgression" (*Yoma* 69b, *Sanhedrin* 64a, *Yal.Sh.* Nechemyah:1071 — discussed in the text below) and implicate the *yetzer hara* in marriage and procreation (see *BeR.R.* 9:7, *Koh.R.* 3:11 [3], *Mid. Tehillim* 9:1 and 37:1, and *Yal.Sh.* BeReshith:16 and Tehillim:643).

Many classic commentators likewise relate the *yetzer hara* to the realm of sexuality. See, for example, R. Avraham b. Ezra on BeReshith 3:6; Radak on Tehillim 103:14; *Ma'amar al Odoth Derashoth Chazal* (R. Avraham b. Rambam), באי"ד החלק השלישי דרשות; Ramban on BeReshith 2:9; *Chibbur HaTeshuvah* (R. Menachem b. Shelomoh HaMe'iri) 1:12 (p. 233); R. Bachyai on BeReshith 3:6, ד"ה וכי תאוה הוא לעינים; *Magen Avoth* (Rashbatz) and *Nachalath Avoth* (R. Yitzchak Abberavanel) on *Avoth* 2:11; *Ta'alumoth Chochmah* on Koheleth 4:13; *Ein Ya'akov* (*HaKothev*) on *Berachoth* 64a, באי"ד עוד ראיתי לכתוב; R. Ovadyah Seforno on BeReshith 2:25 and 3:7; *Or HaChayyim* on BeReshith 2:25; *Keli Yakar* and *Ha'amek Davar* on BeReshith 6:5; R. Tzadok HaKohen (*Tzidkath HaTzaddik*, chs. 218, 229, and 257-58; *Dover Tzedek*, באי"י 'הי הכחות וכל ובאי"ד [*pp. 145-46*] *and* היצר כח עצמו והוא באי"ד [p. 165]; *Machshevoth Charutz*, chs. 9 and 19 [pp. 69, 158]; *Takkanath HaShavin*, chs. 6, 10, and 15 [pp. 28-30, 64-65, 90-92, 142-43]; *Resisei Lailah*, chs. 10, 23, and 35 [pp. 9, 29-30, 57]; *Yisra'el Kedoshim*, chs. 9 and 10 [pp. 114, 129]; *Sichath Malachei HaShareth*, "Tan. Parashath Mishpatim" [p. 76-77]; *Likkutei Ma'amarim*, chs. 14 and 16 [pp. 147, 156-57, 163-64] and "LeSiyyum HaShas" [p. 239]; and *Peri Tzaddik* on *Terumah*, chs. 2 and 8 [pp.

147, 152], on *Zachor*, ch. 1 [p. 173], on Pesach, ch. 4 [p. 41], and on *Korach*, ch. 10 [p. 136]); and *Beith Aharon* (R. Aharon Walden) on Tehillim 103, n. 35 (and its analysis of the many sources cited, loc. cit.). See also "*Yetzer Tov VeYetzer HaRa*," pp. 49-54. In addition, see nn. 3, 25, and 129.

29. As students of psychology will note, the significance of age ten as approximating a threshold in cognitive development was dramatically corroborated in the last generation by the renowned Swiss psychologist Dr. Jean Piaget. In Piaget's model of cognitive development (advanced in many of his more than fifty books and monographs), "age eleven" marks graduation from the "concrete operations" stage, in which a child acquires the capacity to analyze real, concrete events, to the "formal operations" stage, in which this capacity is extended to hypothetical, abstract situations as well. It is, of course, no surprise that modern scientific research can confirm the insights of Chazal (see the text below), recorded almost two millennia ago. (See also nn. 34 and 44.)

Given the biological significance of this stage of human development, one senses a correlation between the onset of puberty and the transition — marked by the initiation of abstract thought — from concrete to formal operations. See also n. 30.

30. According to the Halachah, the age of majority (i.e., one's status as a *gadol* or *gedolah*) normally is explicitly dependent upon puberty. See, for example, *Mish. Sanhedrin* 8:1, *Mish. Niddah* 5:7-8 and 6:1, 11, *Tos. Niddah* 6:2-4, *Yevamoth* 80b, *Yer. Yevamoth* 1:2 (4b) and 13:2 (63b), *Kiddushin* 16b, *Yer. Kiddushin* 1:2 (7b), *Sanhedrin* 68b-69a, and *Niddah* 45b-48b and 52a. See also *Yad Hil. Shevithath Asor* 2:11, *Hil. Ishuth* 2, *Hil. Geirushin* 11:4-6, *Hil. Yibbum VeChalitzah* 1:16-17, *Hil. Nedarim* 11:4, and *Hil. Mamrim* 7:5. In addition, see *Orach Chayyim* 616:2; *Even HaEzer* 155:12-21, 167:3-4, and 169:10-11; and *Choshen Mishpat* 35:1.

31. For a far more detailed treatment of the respective roles of *Torah shebikethav* and *Torah shebe'al-peh*, see my essay "Mosheh Rabbeinu and Rabbi Akiva: Two Dimensions of Torah," *Jewish Thought*, 1, No. 2 (5751), 85-108.

32. Similarly, on the Gemara's exposition, " 'Torah' (Shemoth 24:12) — This refers to Mikra. '*And the* mitzvah' (ibid.) — This refers to Mishnah" (*Berachoth* 5a), Rashi explains:

> "*This refers to Mikra*" — [This means] Chumash, since it is commanded to *read* the Torah.
> "*This refers to Mishnah*" — [This means] that they should *occupy themselves* with the Mishnah.
>
> (com., loc. cit.)

Clearly, Rashi's word choice, associating *reading* with Mikra and *occupying oneself* with Mishnah, is not accidental.

In greater detail, R. Joseph B. Soloveitchik likewise distinguishes between studying *Torah shebikethav* and studying *Torah shebe'al-peh*: While one partially fulfills the commandment of Torah study by simply reading *Torah shebikethav* without comprehension, studying *Torah shebe'al-peh* is of no value unless one understands the subject matter. See R. Yosef Dov HaLevi [Soloveitchik], *Shi'urim LeZecher Abba Mari z.l.*, I (Yerushalayim: Akiva Yosef, 1983), 159-69 and 177, especially:

> Reading *Torah shebikethav* constitutes [fulfillment of] a commandment in itself. There is a special fulfillment of this [commandment of] *reading* even though it comprises no learning because the reader does not understand the content.... However, clearly — and this matter is self-evident — in relation to *Torah shebe'al-peh*, there is no fulfillment [of the commandment of Torah study] at all through reading [alone]. The commandment of *study* is stated regarding *Torah shebe'al-peh*, and its fulfillment is solely through understanding the matters [under study]....
> The first mode of fulfillment — reading without understanding — belongs solely to the realm of *Torah shebikethav*. This mode of fulfillment is not actualized regarding *Torah shebe'al-peh* at all.... By mouthing matters of *Torah shebe'al-peh* without understanding, I have no fulfillment of [the commandment of] study of *Torah shebe'al-peh*.
> (ibid., 159-60)

See also *Shi'urim LeZecher Abba Mari z.l.*, II (Yerushalayim: Akiva Yosef, 1985), 209-13. R. Soloveitchik also discussed this dichotomy in the public *yahrtzeit* lectures in memory of his father, R. Moshe Soloveitchik, that he delivered in 5732 and 5737. (For these last sources, I am indebted to my father-in-law, R. Aaron Rakeffet-Rothkoff.) In addition, see *Shulchan Aruch HaRav*, "Hil. Talmud Torah," ch. 34.

33. R. Tzadok HaKohen discusses this quotation at length. In particular, see *Resisei Lailah*, ch. 46 (p. 93). Elsewhere, he states even more emphatically:

> Had the First Man not sinned, everything would have been "in writing from the hand of G-d Who instructed" (Divrei HaYamim I 28:19) him, and [there would have been] no need for *Torah shebe'al-peh*.
> (*Machshevoth Charutz*, ch. 15 [p. 118])

> *Torah shebe'al-peh* is delivered to [the people of Yisra'el] to the extent that they clarify the matter through their casuistry and scholarship. And this matter came and was innovated specifically through the *yetzer hara*.... Therefore it has no relevance to angels, who have no *yetzer hara*.
> (*Peri Tzaddik*, "Kedushath Shabbath," *Ma'amar* 3 [p. 15])

The deeper implications of this subject extend far beyond the scope of our discussion. See also *Dover Tzedek*, ch. 4 (p. 124), and *Divrei Soferim*, ch. 38 (p. 45).

In addition, R. Tzadok HaKohen discusses how the acquisition of Torah — and wisdom in general — depends upon possession of the *yetzer hara*. See *Takkanath HaShavin*, ch. 2 (pp. 6-7); *Likkutei Ma'amarim*, ch. 16 (p. 204); and especially the sources cited in nn. 14 and 157.

34. Students of psychology will note that this characterization of the *yetzer hara* in terms of man's creative capacity — its full actualization corresponding to that of biological creativity (sexual maturity) — is strikingly analogous to Sigmund Freud's concept of *libido*, the psychic and emotional energy associated with sexuality. Regarding Chazal's concept of libido (and the importance of constructively controlling it), see *Sukkah* 52b, *Kiddushin* 81, and *Sanhedrin* 107a, and see *Yad Hil. De'oth* 4:19. See also n. 28.

    Of particular relevance to our discussion is Freud's description, in *An Outline of Psychoanalysis* (trans. and ed. J. Strachey [New York: Norton, 1969], p. 74), of the *id* — the reservoir of all this psychic energy — striving for its satisfaction and fulfillment: "The id, of course, knows no judgments of value: no good and evil, no morality." While such an amoral assessment has been wantonly extended by the unscrupulous (including Freud himself) to condone immoral behavior, this conception of the id is certainly compatible with the Midrash's evaluation of the *yetzer hara*. As we have seen, initially the *yetzer hara* is indeed amoral: "Delivered into your hands," if it is evil, it is only because "you made it evil" yourself. (See *Tan. BeReshith*:7, discussed above, and see also the sources cited in nn. 23-25.) As noted in n. 29, it hardly surprises a student of Chazal when modern research confirms the Midrash's profound insights. It might be of interest to explore the possibility that Freud, despite his general ignorance of Judaism, might have somehow been influenced by the perspective of the Midrash in developing his psychodynamic theory, but this is not our purpose. See also n. 44.

35. *Metzudath Tziyyon* explains "*yetzer* (יצר)" as "from the language of 'formation (יצירה)' and 'creation (בריאה)' " (com. on Tehillim 103:14; see also *Metzudath David*, loc. cit.).

    In rigorous usage, only "ברא" ("create") denotes divine creation *ex nihilo*. (See Ramban on BeReshith 1:1, ד״ה בראשית, and see R. Ovadyah Seforno and R. S.R. Hirsch, loc. cit., ד״ה ברא. Compare R. Avraham b. Ezra, loc. cit.) Following this initial act of "בריאה" ("Creation"), the creation of form in everything is expressed by "יצר," rendered (in the text) as "create" as well. Understandably, the root denoting the basis of *human* creativity is specifically "יצר," which relates to a this-worldly level and is predicated on the pre-existence of created substance — rather than "ברא," which refers to a level of creation that is within the province of G-d alone.

36. See also R. S.R. Hirsch's analysis of the signification and significance of "יצר" in his commentary on BeReshith 6:5 (and 8:21 and 2:7).

37. See also *Sanhedrin* 58a and Rashi, loc. cit., ד״ה מי שנעשה לבשר אחד, and *Yer. Kiddushin* 1:1 (2a) and *Korban HaEdah*, loc. cit., ד״ה ממקום ששניהם עושים בשר אחד.

38. The association between this verse ("the man *knew* Chavvah, his wife") and man eating the fruit of the "tree of *knowing* good and evil" is even more dramatic — and instructive — in light of Chazal's conclusion that these verses are *not* recorded chronologically. (See *Sanhedrin* 38b, *Avoth DeR*.

Nathan 1:8, *Pir.DeR.E.* 11, *Yal.Sh.* BeReshith:15, and Rashi and com., loc. cit.) In many similar contexts, Chazal invoke the familiar principle that "there is no 'earlier' or 'later' in the Torah" (*Mechilta* on Shemoth 15:9, *Sifrei* on BeMidbar 9:1, *Pesachim* 6b, *Yer. Shekalim* 6:1 [23a], *Yer. Rosh HaShanah* 1:1 [1b], *Yer. Megillah* 1:5 [7a], *Yer. Sotah* 8:3 [35a], *Sh.HaSh.R.* 1:2a [2], *Koh.R.* 1:12, *Tan. Terumah*:8, *Yal.Sh.* BeMidbar:719 [on BeMidbar 9] and Yirmeyahu:264; see also Rashi on BeReshith 6:3, 18:3, and 35:29, on Shemoth 4:20, 18:13, and 24:1, and on BeMidbar 9:1). Obviously, this principle does not imply arbitrariness; rather, the substantive lessons the Torah conveys by juxtaposition of verses take precedence over considerations of chronology.

39. Significantly, the Midrash discerns a causative link between the unabashed nakedness of Adam and Chavvah and the snake's seduction: "Because it saw them occupied in the way of the world [coitus], it desired [Chavvah]" (*BeR.R.* 18:6 and 85:2 and *Yal.Sh.* BeReshith:25; see also Rashi on BeReshith 3:1, ד"ה והנחש היה ערום, and com., loc. cit.).

40. See *Berachoth* 61a, *Avoth DeR. Nathan* 16:3, *BeR.R.* 14:4, and *Yal.Sh.* BeReshith:20.

    It should be noted that, in his essay "*Yetzer Tov VeYetzer HaRa*" (*HaMa'ayan*, 25, No. 4 [5745], 53), Prof. Yehudah Levi argues, based upon the Gemara (*Berachoth* 61a), that a beast does have a *yetzer hara*. However, while the Gemara (loc. cit.) records an objection by R. Nachman b. Yitzchak that presumes the presence of a "*yetzer*" in beasts, the Gemara's reply does not indicate that it subscribes to this presumption, nor does R. Nachman b. Yitzchak specify that the "*yetzer*" to which he refers is the *yetzer hara*. (See, however, *Chiddushei Aggadoth* [Maharsha], loc. cit.) Even if this "*yetzer*" is the *yetzer hara*, R. Nachman b. Yitzchak's position clearly remains a minority view, not only in the Talmud but also with respect to all the other sources cited above, which clearly negate the existence of a *yetzer hara* in beasts. Prof. Levi's inference (ibid.) of the Midrash's position (*BeR.R.* 14:4) does not accord tenably with the context and thrust of the *midrash* (discussed later in this essay) and is at odds with the understanding advanced by all classic commentaries on the *midrash* (especially *Mattenoth Kehunnah, Yefeh To'ar*, and Maharzu, loc. cit.). Furthermore, Prof. Levi bases his analysis of the *yetzer hara* largely on R. Menachem b. Shelomoh HaMe'iri's *Chibbur HaTeshuvah*, which states explicitly that "there is no *yetzer hara* in a beast" (ibid. 2:9 [p. 411], based on *Avoth DeR. Nathan*, loc. cit.).

41. See also *Yal.Sh.* Nechemyah:1071.

42. This world's distinction as the domain of creativity and the *yetzer hara* is accentuated by contrast with man's condition in Gan Eden (prior to eating the forbidden fruit). Adam's principal achievement, as recorded in the Torah and vastly amplified in the Midrash, lay in naming all cattle, birds, and beasts (see BeReshith 2:19-20). Naming all creatures involved comprehending the nature of Creation — a *perceptive*, not *creative*, act (see com., loc. cit.). Chazal continually describe Adam in Gan Eden in this vein; his mission in life was one of attentive perception: "[G-d] said to him, '*See* how becoming

and praiseworthy My creations are! ... *Pay attention* that you not become corrupt'" (*Koh.R.* 7:13). Even his spiritual role in Creation was passive: "Adam was created *as an implement* of the Holy One Blessed be He" (*VaY.R.* 20:2, *Koh.R.* 8:1 (2), *Tan. Acharei*:2); "Adam would *recline* in Gan Eden, and ministering angels would roast meat and filter wine for him" (*Sanhedrin* 59b, *Avoth DeR. Nathan* 1:8). Significantly, the Talmud places Adam's mastery of fire — paradigm of human creativity — specifically after his sin (see *Pesachim* 54a, *Yer. Berachoth* 8:5 [54a], *BeR.R.* 11:2, and see the text below).

Thus, R. Yehudah HaLevi describes Adam in Gan Eden as receiving from G-d "the intellect at the highest level possible for man — given his human condition — and also the divine force that transcends the intellect, namely: the level that, once attained, enables man to cleave to G-d and spiritual concepts and *apprehend truths upon initial thought*, without deliberation and study" (*HaKozari* 1:95). As noted in n. 2, Rambam (*Moreh* 1:1-2) characterizes Adam's level before his sin similarly: Man, created with the essence and likeness of G-d, bore the mark of his Creator particularly through his capacity for *intellectual apprehension*. This capacity enabled Adam to apprehend reality as such, in terms of absolute truth and falsity. Eating the fruit of the "tree of knowing good and evil" resulted in the degeneration of this G-dly intellect into a knowledge of *only* good and evil, relative concepts determined by human consensus. Rephrased, man's interaction with reality was initially one of quasi-divine *perception*: awareness of absolutes. After Adam's sin, his interaction with reality became one of human *creation*; relative concepts of good and evil are essentially fabricated by man, hence Rambam's description of them as determined by consensus. (See also Ramban on BeReshith 2:9 and *Nefesh HaChayyim* 1:6, הגה״ה ד״ה והענין כי קודם החטא [and *Ruach Chayyim* on *Avoth* 3:3], and see *Michtav MeEliyahu*, II, 137-49.) Such creativity is clearly incompatible with the nature of Gan Eden; following this transformation, Adam and Chavvah were banished to this world.

By contrast, this world is pre-eminently a dynamic world of becoming, not a static world of being. "In this world, one who is small can become great, and one who is great can become small" (*Ru.R.* 3:1, 2, *Yal.Sh.* Yechezkel:362 and Koheleth:979 [on Koheleth 9]; see also *Shabbath* 151b, *Sh.R.* 31:14, *VaY.R.* 34:3, *Tan. Mattoth*:6, and *Yal.Sh.* Devarim:898). Chazal characterize this world, as opposed to the next, as "resembling a corridor" (*Avoth* 4:16, *Mid. Mishlei* 6:6) — by definition, a scene of continuous motion. Human nature is so animated by this dynamism that "no one leaves the world with half of what he desires in his possession" (*Koh.R.* 1:13, 3:10). Man in this world is identified as "moving ones," in contrast to the angels, who are characterized as "the standing ones" (Zecharyah 3:7). Chazal repeatedly emphasize that this world alone is the realm of self-initiated spiritual growth: "A person should always occupy himself in Torah and *mitzvoth* before he dies, for once he dies he is suspended from the Torah and the *mitzvoth*" (*Shabbath* 30a and 151b, *Niddah* 61b; see also *Shabbath* 153a; *Eruvin* 22a and 65a; *Pesachim* 50a; *Yoma* 39a; *Mo'ed Katan* 28a; *Kethubboth* 77b; *Babba Bathra* 10b; *Avodah Zarah*

3a and 4b; *Avoth* 4:16; *Ru.R.* 3:3; *Koh.R.* 1:15 [1] and 9:10 [1]; *Pir.DeR.E.* 43; *Mid. Mishlei* 6:6; and *Yal.Sh.* Yeshayahu:454, Yirmeyahu:297, and Koheleth:967). Indeed, in terms of the greatness of such creative growth, Chazal assert that nothing beyond this world can compare to it: "An hour of repentance and good deeds in this world is better than all existence in the world to come" (*Avoth* 4:17, *VaY.R.* 3:1, *Koh.R.* 4:6). While the grandeur of the world to come lies in the attainment of perfection, the hallmark of this world is human creativity: the assertion of autonomy upon which, for better or for worse, life on the level of this world is predicated.

43. Compare also *Mid. Tehillim* 37:1.

44. Apropos of our discussion in n. 34, students of psychology will note obvious parallels between this Midrashic observation — that the *yetzer hara*, as the root of human creativity in general, mediates not only sexuality but also such creative activities as building houses and dealing in business — and Freud's concept of libidinal sublimation. As noted in nn. 29 and 34, such correspondence between contemporary research and Chazal's timeless insights is to be expected.

45. See also *Yer. Berachoth* 8:5 (54a) and *BeR.R.* 11:2.

46. Although, as the Talmud indicates (see the text below, and see *Avodah Zarah* 17a, *Sh.HaSh.R.* 7:8, and n. 56), the *"yetzer* of idolatry" no longer functions as a decisive factor in human action, many sources in Chazal imply that, until this critical juncture during the time of the Great Assembly, the *"yetzer* of idolatry" was at least as powerful as the *"yetzer* of [sexual] transgression."

Perhaps most dramatically, the Talmud relates that, after R. Ashi disparagingly referred to Menasheh — probably the most idolatrous monarch in the history of the kingdom of Yehudah (see Melachim II 21:2-9, 16-17, and Divrei HaYamim II 33:2-9) — as "our peer" (*Sanhedrin* 102b, *Yal.Sh.* Melachim:246), Menasheh appeared to him in a dream and unequivocally established the superiority of his own Torah knowledge to that of R. Ashi. In response to R. Ashi's consequent query, "Since you were so wise, for what reason did you serve idols?" Menasheh told him, "Had you been there [at that time], you would have seized the bottom of your cloak and run after me." Explains Rashi, "You would have raised the hem of your frock from between your legs in order to be more fleet-footed, and you would have run there [after me, to the idolatrous shrine], *because of the* yetzer *of idolatry, which was in control*" (com. on *Sanhedrin* 102b, ד"ה הוית נקוט שיפולי גלימך).

More generally, the Talmud describes the obsessive lust for idolatry that so animated idolaters — prompting them continually to "hug ... and kiss" their idols (*Shabbath* 83b, *Sanhedrin* 63b and 64a, *Yal.Sh.* Shofetim:64 and Hoshea:529) and long for them "like a man who longs for his son" (*Sanhedrin* 63b, *Yal.Sh.* Yirmeyahu:296). Elsewhere, Chazal draw additional parallels between the *yetzer hara* and idolatry. (See, for example, *Shabbath* 105b, *Niddah* 13b, *Yer. Nedarim* 9:1 [25a], and *Yal.Sh.* BeReshith:60 and Tehillim:831.) The subject of the *"yetzer* of idolatry" is also treated by R. Yehudah HaLevi

(*HaKozari* 4:23); Maharal (*Nethivoth Olam*, "*Nethiv HaLashon*," ch. 6; *Netzach Yisra'el*, ch. 3; and *Chiddushei Aggadoth* on *Kiddushin* 30b, 'ד"ה אם אבן הוא נמוח וכו, and on *Sanhedrin* 64a, 'ד"ה הנצמדים לבעל פעור וכו, and 102b, 'ד"ה אוקי אג' מלכים); Maharsha (*Chiddushei Aggadoth* on *Sanhedrin* 102b, 'בא"ד הות נקיט בשיפולי כו); the Vilna Ga'on (Haghoth HaGra on Seder Olam R., ch. 30); R. Tzadok HaKohen (Dover Tzedek, בא"ד וכל הכחות הי' בא"י [pp. 145-46]; *Machshevoth Charutz*, ch. 9 [p. 69]; *Takkanath HaShavin*, chs. 6, 10, and 12 [pp. 28, 90-91, 114]; *Resisei Lailah*, chs. 13, 23, and 35 [pp. 14, 29-30, 57]; *Sichath Malachei HaShareth*, "*Yer. Rosh HaShanah 1*" [p. 72] and "*Tan. Parashath Mishpatim*" [pp. 76-77]; *Divrei Soferim*, ch. 38 [p. 41]; and *Likkutei Ma'amarim*, "*LeSiyyum HaShas*" [p. 239]); R. Me'ir Simchah HaKohen of Dvinsk (*Meshech Chochmah* on BeMidbar 11:17); R. Avraham Y. Karelitz (*Kovetz Iggeroth Chazon Ish*, I, 109); and R. E.E. Dessler (*Michtav MeEliyyahu*, III, 277-78, and IV, 105, 134-35, 174, and 224-25).

This understanding of the "*yetzer* of idolatry" and its "imprisonment" certainly helps explain why idolatrous perversions were so rampant throughout the period of the first Beith HaMikdash yet practically vanished at the outset of the period of the second Beith HaMikdash. Indeed, a significant attenuation took place concurrently in the pagan obsession with idolatry throughout the known world. According to the Talmud (see the text), these global changes resulted from a revolutionary transformation in human nature, effected, at the "heart" of the world, by the men of the Great Assembly.

47. See also *Michtav MeEliyyahu*, III, 277-78, and IV, 105 and 174.
48. See also *Sh.R.* 23:13, *Sh.HaSh.R.* 3:8 (4), and *Yal.Sh.* Shemoth:243. In addition, see *Tan. VaYiggash*:3; *Mid. Tehillim* 22:28; and *Yal.Sh.* Shemoth:182, BeMidbar:769, Yechezkel:337, and Tehillim:688.
49. Throughout Biblical and Talmudic literature, the lion symbolizes power. See, for example, BeReshith 49:9; BeMidbar 23:24 and 24:9; Devarim 33:22; Shofetim 14:18; Shemu'el II 1:23 and 17:10; Yeshayahu 31:4 and 35:9; Yirmeyahu 2:30, 4:7, 49:19, and 50:17, 44; Yechezkel 19:2-7; Yo'el 1:6; Amos 3:12; Michah 5:7; Mishlei 30:30; and Divrei HaYamim I 12:9. See also *Avoth* 5:20, *Tos. Kiddushin* 5:12, *Yer. Shevi'ith* 9:4 (28b), *Shabbath* 111b, *Pesachim* 112a, *Yevamoth* 122b, *Kiddushin* 48b and 82b, *Babba Kamma* 117a, *Babba Metzi'a* 84b, *Babba Bathra* 88a, and *Sanhedrin* 8b, and see com., loc. cit. In addition, see *Zohar*, I, 60a, and the sources cited in n. 48. See also Maharal's discussions of the symbol of the lion: for example, *Tifereth Yisra'el*, ch. 1 (p. 8); *Netzach Yisra'el*, ch. 55 (pp. 202-3); and his introduction to *Or Chadash* (p. 55).
50. See also *Michtav MeEliyyahu*, IV, 174.
51. See also *Yal.Sh.* Yeshayahu:474 and Tzefanyah:567.
52. Likewise, according to R. Yehudah HaLevi, what was essentially sinful in Yisra'el forging a golden calf (Shemoth 32) was *not* worship of "other gods" — since "[no one] denied the divinity of Him Who had brought [Yisra'el]

forth from Mitzrayim" (*HaKozari* 1:97; see Shemoth 32:4) — but only "[the use of] an image, which was forbidden to them" *in the service of G-d* and "[the ascription of] divine force to what they had made with their hands and their will, *without the commandment of G-d*" (*HaKozari*, loc. cit.). Inasmuch as the people of Yisra'el had been promised a tangible symbol *to be designated by G-d* with which to orient themselves toward Him (the Sanctuary, with the two tablets in the ark covered by the *keruvim* at its focal point — see Shemoth 25 and on, and see n. 65), some felt that, bereft of Mosheh (see Shemoth 32:1), they needed to fabricate such a symbol *on their own initiative*. Since, in their frenzy, they regarded such conduct as the epitome of *religious* behavior and *devotion* to G-d, they naturally turned to their (acting) religious leader for direction; why else would they have approached Aharon (ibid. 32:1-5) for guidance in forging an image? Their fatal error lay in thinking that such a symbol could be fabricated *on their own initiative*. In fact, the critical distinction between the golden calf and the golden *keruvim* is precisely that: the one derived from man's unrestrained application of his capacity for spiritual creativity, and the other derived from quasi-divine application (see *Berachoth* 55a) *of the same capacity*, under divine aegis and in compliance with G-d's explicit directives. Indeed, this distinction reflects one of the most central themes of *Sefer HaKozari* (see especially 1:98-99): "Your *intentions* are desirable, but your *actions* are not" (preface to *HaKozari* and throughout the book).

See also R. Avraham b. Ezra on Shemoth 32:1 and Ramban on Shemoth 32:1-5, who advance basically similar explanations of the golden calf. This idea is greatly expanded in later commentaries.

53. In this light, we can appreciate the continual associations that we find between sexual immorality and idolatry. Thus, bemoans Hoshea, regarding both:

> My people inquire of a piece of wood,
> and their staff relates to them,
> for the spirit of licentiousness caused them to err,
> and they strayed licentiously from under their G-d.
> On the mountain tops they sacrifice,
> and upon the hills they burn incense ...
> therefore your daughters stray licentiously,
> and your daughters-in-law commit adultery.
> (Hoshea 4:12-13)

Even more blatantly, the Talmud states: "Yisra'el ... served idols only to legitimate for themselves sexual immorality in public" (*Sanhedrin* 63b).

Regarding the parallel respective roles of the *"yetzer* of [sexual] transgression" on a physical plane and the *"yetzer* of idolatry" on a spiritual plane, see Maharal, in *Nethivoth Olam*, *"Nethiv HaLashon,"* ch. 6; *Netzach Yisra'el*, ch. 3; and *Chiddushei Aggadoth* on *Kiddushin* 30b, 'וכו נמוח הוא אבן אם ד"ה; and see *Michtav MeEliyyahu*, IV, 133-35. See also *Sichath Malachei HaShareth*, "Tan.

Parashath Mishpatim" (pp. 76-77).

54. Common sense would seem to dictate that "fasting three days and three nights" is life-threatening conduct. However, Rambam rules that an oath that one "will not eat anything for *seven* days consecutively" is punishable as an oath taken in vain *(Yad Hil. Shevu'oth* 1:7 and 5:20; see also *Yoreh De'ah* 236:4). Yet his source for the seven-day limit is elusive. *Bayith Chadash* concludes discussion of Rambam's ruling by stating, "The limit of seven days requires [further] consideration as to its source" (com. on *Tur Yoreh De'ah* 236). Moreover, *Kesef Mishneh* quotes the Talmud Yerushalmi as stating that if one takes "an oath that [he] will not eat for *three* days, we wait for him until he eats [to stave off otherwise inevitable starvation] and [then] flog him [for violating his oath]" (com. on *Yad Hil. Shevu'oth* 5:20). Obviously, this Talmudic reference to a three-day limit as manifestly life-threatening highlights the extraordinary behavior of the men of the Great Assembly.

    The Talmud Bavli, however, concludes from Ester's directive to "gather all the Yehudim who are present in Shushan and fast for me, and *do not eat and do not drink for three days, night and day"* (Ester 4:16) that there is nothing miraculous in surviving three days without eating or drinking *(Yevamoth* 121b) — a conclusion clearly incompatible with the statement quoted by *Kesef Mishneh.* Furthermore, I have thus far been unable to locate *Kesef Mishneh*'s source in the Talmud Yerushalmi.

55. See also *Yoma* 38a, *Sh.R.* 17:1, and *Yal.Sh.* Mishlei:953.

56. Our contention that the *"yetzer* of idolatry" has not been destroyed (and indeed cannot be destroyed in this world) is seemingly contradicted by various statements made by Chazal and their commentators. See, for example, *Avodah Zarah* 17a and *Sh.HaSh.R.* 7:8, and see com., loc. cit. See also *Chiddushei Aggadoth* (Maharsha) on *Sanhedrin* 102b, 'באי"ד הות נקיט בשיפולי כו, and *Haghoth HaGra* on *Seder Olam R.,* ch. 30.

    It is instructive in this regard to consider Rambam's discussion (in his introduction to *Moreh HaNevochim*) of the seven possible causes of apparent contradictions in scholarly works. The fifth is that the author, while mentioning a difficult concept in passing, may oversimplify it, pending a more detailed discussion elsewhere. Rambam notes that apparent "inconsistencies in true works of philosophy" derive from this fifth cause.

    Clearly, Chazal's most detailed discussion of the imprisonment of the *"yetzer* of idolatry" and the pursuant transformation of human nature is in the *aggadah* that we are presently analyzing *(Yoma* 69b, *Sanhedrin* 64a, *Yal.Sh.* Nechemyah:1071). Inasmuch as the Talmud explicitly records Zecharyah's advice to "cast it into a leaden caldron, and cover its mouth with lead" as a response to the concern of the men of the Great Assembly that "heavenly mercy is upon it," protecting it, the message is clearly conveyed that this "imprisonment" was intended to circumvent actually causing permanent damage to the "lion of fire," which "heavenly mercy" might forbid. Moreover, Zecharyah's solution — the leaden caldron and cover — is explicitly provided to prevent the lion's *enduring* roar from being heard: "lead absorbs sound." As noted in the text below, one need mute only what has not yet been irrevocably silenced. Indeed, idolatry is still far from extinct today, despite the imprisonment of the *"yetzer* of idolatry"; evidently, this drive continues to affect human nature and action.

We must therefore understand references to the nullification of the *"yetzer* of idolatry" in relative terms — for, while it has been muffled and imprisoned, it has not been (and cannot be) either silenced or destroyed. Significantly, the Midrash depicts G-d "searching" through Yerushalayim in the future world *"to purge it of idolatry and uproot the* yetzer hara" (*Pes. Rabbathi* 8 [29a], *Yal.Sh.* Tzefanyah:567), which suggests that the complete eradication of idolatry — together with the *yetzer* that spawns it — awaits the perfected realm of the future. Furthermore, Maharal, in *Nethivoth Olam*, "*Nethiv HaLashon*," ch. 6, implies that the *"yetzer* of idolatry" is no longer the *primary* root of sin — but that it continues to function as a root of sin nonetheless. (See also his *Chiddushei Aggadoth* on *Kiddushin* 30b, 'ד"ה אם אבן הוא נמוח וכו, where the *"yetzer* of idolatry" is clearly presented as a still-relevant force.) Similarly, R. E.E. Dessler speaks, perhaps guardedly, of the campaign by the men of the Great Assembly "to *reduce* the instigation of the *yetzer* for idolatry" (*Michtav MeEliyyahu*, IV, 105), possibly to imply that the *"yetzer* of idolatry" was not entirely eliminated. (See also ibid., p. 225, where the *"yetzer* of idolatry" appears as a force that is still active.) In addition, see R. Tzadok HaKohen, in *Takkanath HaShavin*, chs. 6 and 10 (pp. 28, 90), and *Resisei Lailah*, ch. 23 (p. 29).

57. Note that, while neither the *"yetzer* of [sexual] transgression" nor the *"yetzer* of idolatry" could be destroyed, only the *"yetzer* of idolatry" could even be muffled. Regarding the *"yetzer* of [sexual] transgression," after "they imprisoned it for three days, they sought a fresh egg in all of Eretz Yisra'el for a sick person and found none" (*Yoma* 69b, *Sanhedrin* 64a): Not even restraint was feasible. Likewise, only with respect to this latter *yetzer hara* did the prophet Zecharyah forewarn the men of the Great Assembly, "See that if you kill it, the world will be destroyed" (*Yoma*, loc. cit.).

While the world's endurance is predicated upon both the *"yetzer* of [sexual] transgression" and the *"yetzer* of idolatry," its dependence on each is distinct. By analogy, while the survival of a human being depends on the fulfillment of many vital needs, deprivation of oxygen is far more immediately deadly than deprivation of food. Similarly, while the *"yetzer* of idolatry" and man's resultant *spiritual* creativity are necessary for the world to reach its ultimate goals of spiritual realization, the *"yetzer* of [sexual] transgression" and consequent *physical* creativity are critical to maintain the minimal level of biological creativity upon which hinges man's immediate existence in this world. Therefore, the world may tolerate the muffling of the *"yetzer* of idolatry" (although certainly not its complete extinguishment), whereas even restraint of the *"yetzer* of [sexual] transgression" is impossible. (The solution of the men of the Great Assembly in dealing with this latter limitation will be discussed, G-d willing, in the sequel to this essay.)

58. According to the Talmud, when Yonathan ben Uzi'el completed his *targum* of Nevi'im, "Eretz Yisra'el quaked *four hundred parasangs by four hundred parasangs*" (*Megillah* 3a; see also *Sotah* 49b, *Babba Kamma* 82b, and *Menachoth* 64b). Rashi assumes these to be the dimensions of Eretz Yisra'el (see com. on BeMidbar 13:25), a conclusion at least implied by the Midrash (see *BeM.R.* 16:15 and *Mattenoth Kehunnah* and Maharzu, loc. cit.; *Tan. Shelach*:8; and *Yal.Sh.* BeMidbar:743). Maharal understands this Talmudic statement similarly, and he discusses in this context the symbolic significance of the number "four hundred" (see especially *Netzach Yisra'el*, ch. 7 [p. 45]; *Chiddushei Aggadoth* on *Gittin* 57b, ד"ה שהרג בכרך ביתר וכו', and on *Babba Metzi'a* 59b, 'ד"ה חרוב זה יוכיח כו; and *Gur Aryeh* on Devarim 1:24, 'ד"ה ארבע אומנין וכו). In commenting on our *aggadah* (*Yoma* 69b), *Chiddushei Aggadoth* (Maharsha) and *Anaf Yosef* (loc. cit.) also relate "four hundred parasangs" to the dimensions of Eretz Yisra'el.

In contemporary units, four hundred parasangs correspond to approximately 1700 kilometers (1500-1900 km.) or 1050 miles (900-1200 mi.), roughly the distance from the mouth of the Nile to the mouth of the Euphrates.

59. Regarding the role of the *yetzer hara* in prayer, R. Dov Ber (the Maggid) of Mezherich homiletically expounds the Talmudic statement quoted above that, when the *"yetzer* of [sexual] transgression" was imprisoned, "they sought a fresh *egg* (ביעתא) ... and found none" (*Yoma* 69b, *Sanhedrin* 64a): Since "ביעתא" ("egg") is related phonetically to "בעותא" ("prayer"), this statement may be interpreted to allude allegorically to the loss of all enthusiasm in prayer. Such enthusiasm is mediated by the *yetzer hara* and is impossible in its absence. (See *Torath HaMaggid*, II, on *Kiddushin* 30a [p. 139]. For this source, I am indebted to my friend and former student Abba Cohen.)

In a comparable vein, R. E.E. Dessler cites the homiletical observation that the letters of "רע" ("evil"), inverted, spell "ער" ("alert," "enthused") — implying that our life's mission is to "invert" (i.e., transform) the "evil" of the *yetzer hara* into "enthusiasm" (*Michtav MeEliyyahu*, IV, 289). Even more explicitly, he explains the symbolism of "a lion of fire" as suggesting "that this *yetzer* comes specifically from *enthusiasm in the service of G-d*" (ibid., IV, 174).

60. See also *Berachoth* 3a; *Yer. Berachoth* 9:2 (57a); *Sh.R.* 29:9; *Mid. Tehillim* 18:12 and 104:25; and *Yal.Sh.* Devarim:836, Shemu'el:158, and Yirmeyahu:307.

61. Regarding G-d "roaring," see also Hoshea 11:10 and Iyyov 37:4.

62. See also *Eich.R. Peth.*:26 and *Yal.Sh.* Yeshayahu:435.

63. Indeed, we also find the altar hearth itself called "Ari'el" (lit. "*Lion* of G-d"; see Yechezkel 43:15-16 and com., loc. cit.). See also *Michtav MeEliyyahu*, IV, 174.

64. Perhaps it is to this inextricable linkage between creativity and the Beith HaMikdash that the Midrash alludes: "Just as the bed is solely for procreation, so everything that was in the Beith HaMikdash *would procreate*.... The Beith HaMikdash was called 'the forest of the Levanon' (Melachim I 7:2) to tell you [that] just as a forest bears fruit, so too the Beith HaMikdash: The

golden forms that were on its walls — for all sorts of trees were designed there — *would bear fruit*" (*BeM.R.* 11:3, *Tan. Naso*:9). Significantly, the Midrash tells us that this bountiful creativity withered when the Shechinah forsook the Beith HaMikdash (see *Tan. Terumah*:11). See also *Yoma* 21b and 39b, *BeM.R.* 12:4, *Sh.HaSh.R.* 1:16 (3) and 3:8 (3), and *Yal.Sh.* Nachum:560 and Shir HaShirim:986.

65. Regarding the centrality of the Holy of Holies in general, see, for example, *Kelim* 1:6-9, *Berachoth* 30a, and *BeM.R.* 7:8. See also *Yad Hil. Tefillah* 5:3 and *Orach Chayyim* 94:1. Regarding the centrality of the ark in particular, see especially *Tan. Kedoshim*:10. See also *HaKozari* 2:26-28 and Ramban on Shemoth 25:1, 10, 21. In addition, see the discussion (in the text below) of the significance of the ark cover and its *keruvim* as the focal point of Mosheh's prophecy in particular (see Shemoth 25:22 and BeMidbar 7:89) and G-d's presence in Yisra'el in general (see Shemu'el I 4:4 and the verses cited in n. 135).

66. See Divrei HaYamim II 35:3 and com., loc. cit. See also *Mish. Shekalim* 6:1; *Mish. Yoma* 5:2; *Tos. Yoma* 2:12-13; *Tos. Sotah* 13:2; *Yer. Shekalim* 6:1 (22a); *Yoma* 21b, 52b, 53b, and 54a; *Yer. Ta'anith* 2:1 (8a); *Yer. Sotah* 8:3 (34a); *Yer. Makkoth* 2:6 (5a); *Horayoth* 12a; *Yer. Horayoth* 3:2 (12b); *Kerithoth* 5b; *Avoth DeR. Nathan* 41:12; *BeM.R.* 15:10; *Sh.HaSh.R.* 3:8 (4) and 8:9 (3); *Tan. BeHa'alothecha*:6; and *Yal.Sh.* Shemoth:367, 388, Devarim:939, Chaggai:567, and Divrei HaYamim:1085. In addition, see *HaKozari* 1:87 and *Yad Hil. Beith HaBechirah* 4:1 and *Hil. Avodath Yom HaKippurim* 4:1.

67. See *Mish. Sotah* 9:12; *Tos. Yoma* 2:13; *Tos. Sotah* 13:2-3; *Yer. Shekalim* 6:1 (22a); *Yoma* 9a, 9b, 21b, and 52b; *Yer. Ta'anith* 2:1 (8a); *Sotah* 48b; *Yer. Sotah* 8:3 (34a); *Yer. Makkoth* 2:6 (5a); *Horayoth* 12a; *Yer. Horayoth* 3:2 (12b); *Arachin* 10b; *Kerithoth* 5b; *Avoth DeR. Nathan* 41:12; *BeR.R.* 36:8; *VaY.R.* 21:9; *BeM.R.* 12:4 and 15:10; *Sh.HaSh.R.* 3:8 (3) and 8:9 (3); *Tan. BeHa'alothecha*:6; *Yal.Sh.* BeReshith:61, Shemoth:388, Chaggai:567, and Divrei HaYamim:1085; and *Pirkei Heichaloth* 27. See also *Yad Hil. Beith HaBechirah* 4:1 (and com., loc. cit.) and *Hil. Kelei HaMikdash* 10:10, and see Radak on Divrei HaYamim II 35:3.

68. See also *Iyyun Ya'akov* (on *Yoma*, loc. cit.), which relates the loss of the altar fire "crouched like a lion" to the absence of the Shechinah (G-d's Presence) in the second Beith HaMikdash (see the text below).

69. See *Yoma* 9b and 21b, *BeR.R.* 36:8, *Yal.Sh.* BeReshith:61 and Chaggai:567, and *Pirkei Heichaloth* 27. See also *Yer. Ta'anith* 2:1 (8a); *Yer. Makkoth* 2:6 (5a); *Yer. Horayoth* 3:2 (12b) and *Penei Mosheh*, loc. cit., ד"ה שמן המשחה ורוח הקדש; *BeM.R.* 15:10; *Sh.HaSh.R.* 8:9 (3); and *Tan. BeHa'alothecha*:6. In addition, see *HaKozari* 2:24, 3:65, and 4:3; *Yad Hil. Beith HaBechirah* 4:1 (and *Hassagath HaRa'avad* and especially *Kesef Mishneh*, loc. cit.) and *Hil. Kelei HaMikdash* 10:10; and R. Tzadok HaKohen (*Tzidkath HaTzaddik*, chs. 93 and 256; *Machshevoth Charutz*, ch. 17 [p. 142]; *Resisei Lailah*, ch. 56 [pp. 158, 160-61]; and *Sichath Malachei HaShareth*, "*Yer. Rosh HaShanah* 1" [pp. 71-72] and "*Tan. Parashath Mishpatim*" [p. 76]).

70. Interestingly, the Midrash describes the restoration of the Beith HaMikdash specifically in terms of the "lion" motif: "A Lion [G-d] will come under the constellation Lion [Leo, the zodiacal sign of the month of Av] and build 'Ari'el' ['Lion of G-d,' the Temple]" (*Pes. DeR. Kahana* 13 [116a], *Yal.Sh.* Yirmeyahu:259). See also *Netzach Yisra'el* (Maharal), ch. 55 (pp. 202-3).
71. See also *Poked Akkarim* (R. Tzadok HaKohen), ch. 2 (p. 9).
72. See Melachim I 22:11-12, 24, and Divrei HaYamim II 18:10-11, 23.
73. See Yirmeyahu 28:1-17.
74. See also *Sifrei* on Devarim 13:3 and 18:19-20 and *Yal.Sh.* Devarim:885, 919.

    Significantly, Yirmeyahu refers six times to "Chananyah *the prophet*" during his conflict with him (see Yirmeyahu 28:1-17), without in any way qualifying this designation or indicating that it was undeserved. In addition, compare the Talmud Yerushalmi's explanation of Chananyah's error (loc. cit.) with that of the Talmud Bavli (*Sanhedrin* 89a, *Yal.Sh.* Melachim:221).

    See also Rashi on Yirmeyahu 23:36, *Moreh HaNevochim* 2:40, *Derech HaShem* 3:4, R. S.R. Hirsch on Devarim 13:2, and *Meshech Chochmah* on Devarim 13:6.
75. Regarding the symbolism of the lion as it relates to false prophecy, compare *Netzach Yisra'el* (Maharal), ch. 55 (p. 203).
76. See also *Divrei Soferim*, ch. 38 (p. 41), and *Michtav MeEliyyahu*, III, 277, which quote this verse in the same context.
77. The motif of fire recurs continually in the context of prophecy. See, for example, BeReshith 15:17; Shemoth 3:2, 19:18, and 24:17; Devarim 4:11-12, 15, 33, 36, 5:4-5, 19, 20-23, 9:10, 15, 10:4, 18:16, and 33:2; Yeshayahu 30:27 and 66:15-16; Yirmeyahu 5:14 and 23:29; and Yechezkel 1:4, 13, and 10:6-7.
78. See also *Moreh HaNevochim* 2:37.
79. I have translated as "glass" the original "אספקלריא," which is derived — according to *HaAruch* — "from the Latin word for clear crystal ... formerly used in place of glass for windows." *Tifereth Yisra'el* likewise specifies the word's origin in "the Greek [i.e., Latin] *specularia*, meaning 'glass' or 'mirror'" (com. on *Kelim* 30:2). The exact connotation of the word as employed by Chazal is, however, subject to broad disagreement.

    Rach (cited by Ramban on *Yevamoth*, loc. cit.) describes the vision of the other prophets as distorted, "like a person whose vision is weak and perceives the short as high and the one as two." Rashi (loc. cit.) explains seeing through "אספקלריא שאינה מאירה" (here trans. "unclear glass") as "they thought to see and did not see" (see the text below). Neither Rach nor Rashi, however, provides an explicit definition of "אספקלריא." Perhaps the earliest (albeit inconclusive) definition can be derived from the Targum on Iyyov, which renders "זכוכית" ("glass") as "אספקלרא" (ibid. 28:17).

    Rambam (com. on *Kelim*, loc. cit.; *Shemonah Perakim*, ch. 7) appears to describe "אספקלריא" either as a lens or as a curved mirror, made of glass or clear crystal, while R. Ovadyah Bartinora (com. on *Kelim*, loc. cit.) defines "אספקלריא" as a glass mirror. *Tosefoth Yom Tov* (loc. cit.) cites both interpretations, concluding that Rambam would render "אספקלריא" as spectacles. *Tifereth Yisra'el* (loc. cit.) challenges *Tosefoth Yom Tov*'s explanation of Rambam on several counts, concluding that Rambam also defines "אספקלריא" as a glass mirror. *Tifereth Yisra'el* accepts this definition, as does HaMethurgeman (in *Ein Ya'akov* on *Yevamoth*, loc. cit.). This view is also supported by R. Bachyai (on BeMidbar 12:6, ד"ה במראה אליו אתודע), by Rema (*Torath HaOlah* 1:14), by Malbim (*HaTorah VeHaMitzvah* on BeMidbar 12:6), and by R. Tzadok HaKohen (*Dover Tzedek*, באייד ולכייא בבראייר [p. 191], and *Peri Tzaddik*, "*Kedushath Shabbath*," *Ma'amar* 7 [p. 37]), who differentiate between "אספקלריא המאירה" ("clear glass") and "אספקלריא שאינה מאירה" (here trans. "unclear glass"), where it is the opaque backing of "*unclear* glass" that makes it function as a glass *mirror*.

See also *Michtav MeEliyyahu*, IV, 53, and see Mordechai Dov Rabbinovitz, ed., *Hakdamoth LeFerush HaMishnah*, by Rambam (1961; rpt. Yerushalayim: Mossad Harav Kook, 1977), p. 196, n. 2. In addition, see nn. 82 and 93.

80. See also *Tan. Tzav*:13 and *Yal.Sh.* Shemoth:360 and Melachim:247. In addition, see *VaY.R.* 1:14; *Yal.Sh.* VaYikra:432 and Hoshea:528 (and Yeshayahu:407); and *Zohar*, II, 23. See also Ramban (com. on BeReshith 18:1; on Shemoth 6:2; and on *Yevamoth* 49b, 'ד"ה כל הנביאים נסתכלו וכו), Maharal (*Derech HaChayyim* on *Avoth* 3:14 [pp. 142-43] and *Chiddushei Aggadoth* on *Yevamoth* 49b, ד"ה משה רבנו נסתכל באספקלריא המאירה), Ramchal (*Derech HaShem* 3:5 [4-5] and *Da'ath Tevunoth*, ch. 188), and Malbim (HaTorah VeHaMitzvah on Shemoth 3:2, 6:2, and 33:11-12, and on BeMidbar 12:6), and see the sources cited in n. 79.

81. Note that Chazal are definitely not implying that the level of prophecy of Yeshayahu, in particular, was limited. To the contrary, the Midrash states, "No prophet [was] greater than Mosheh and Yeshayahu" (Dev.R. 2:4, Ag. BeReshith 14). Thus, no one was better suited to highlight Mosheh's unique level of prophecy than the greatest of all *other* prophets, Yeshayahu.

82. The metaphor of "*unclear* glass" suggests that the opacity of this world — and of the prophet's life within it — precludes true comprehension of G-d; by its very nature, this world is a realm of concealment (see n. 125). Therefore, "no man can see Me *while alive* [i.e., while in this world]" (Shemoth 33:20; see also ibid. 33:23, and see *Sifrei* on Devarim 34:10 and *Zohar*, I, 218). In addition, see *HaKozari* 4:3; *Shemonah Perakim*, ch. 7 (see below), *Yad Hil. Yesodei HaTorah* 1:9-10 and 2:8 and *Hil. Teshuvah* 5:5, and *Moreh HaNevochim* 1:21, 37, 54, 64; *Reshith Chochmah*, "*Sha'ar HaYirah*," ch. 12; *Derech HaShem* 1:1 (2, 5) and *Da'ath Tevunoth*, chs. 46, 184, and 194; and *Michtav MeEliyyahu*, I, 243, II, 67, and III, 28-29 and 281-83. The incomprehensibility of G-d and the inscrutability of His thought are discussed in greater detail in my essay "Mosheh Rabbeinu and Rabbi Akiva: Two Dimensions of Torah," *Jewish Thought*, 1, No. 2 (5751), 70, 72-73, and 97 — especially p. 109, nn. 9 and 11; p. 112, n. 25; and p. 122, n. 109.

As for the actual cause of this *"unclear* glass," evidently, despite their relative spiritual transcendence, the prophets remained encumbered to some degree by an irreducible earthiness, which obscured their view of G-d. In *Shemonah Perakim*, Rambam identifies the root of this boundedness in extremely subtle flaws of moral character — "and all such deficiencies are the partitions that separate man from G-d" (ibid., ch. 7 — in com. on Yeshayahu 59:2) — introducing an inescapably subjective element and precluding a truly objective apprehension of truth. Likewise, Rema explains that "each [prophet] would see in [the 'unclear glass'] as one sees in a mirror, *for the dense physicality of man would stand before the prophet* ... rendering [the 'glass'] a reflective mirror.... And therefore the prophets imagined the glory [of G-d] as the likeness of man, because they saw their own image" (*Torath HaOlah* 1:14). The nature of this subjective element is intimated in the text below (see especially nn. 93, 95, and 104-5). By contrast, Mosheh alone, who was "exceedingly humble [i.e., objective], more so than anyone on the face of the earth" (BeMidbar 12:3) — and free of any such deficiencies — "gazed through clear glass," free of all but the minimal obscurity imposed by his very corporeity: There was nothing within him to mitigate the transparency of the "glass" or introduce subjective "reflections" (see *Shemonah Perakim* and *Torath HaOlah*, loc. cit.; see also *Derech HaChayyim* [Maharal] on *Avoth* 3:14 [pp. 142-43]; *Adir BaMarom* [Ramchal], p. 77b; *HaTorah VeHaMitzvah* [Malbim] on Shemoth 3:2 and on BeMidbar 12:6; *Tzidkath HaTzaddik*, chs. 204-6; and *Michtav MeEliyyahu*, IV, 53).

It should be stressed that this subjectivity, which inheres in all prophecy other than that of Mosheh, does not imply that Yeshayahu, for example, was deceived or deceitful (G-d forbid!) in saying, *"I saw G-d."* True prophets obviously recognized their limitations and had the wisdom and insight to interpret their visions correctly. See *HaIkkarim* 3:9; *Da'ath Tevunoth*, chs. 184-86; *Kelach Pithchei Chochmah, Pethach* 7; and *Michtav MeEliyyahu*, I, 310-12. Regarding the interpretive role of the prophet in his prophecy, see *Yad Hil. Yesodei HaTorah* 7:3 and *Moreh HaNevochim* 2:43; see *Shuth Maharil Diskin*, vol. II (end), and *Avi Ezri* (R. Eli'ezer Shach), vol. I, on *Yad Hil. Yesodei HaTorah*; and see the text below and especially nn. 100-5. Furthermore, just as Mosheh calls the holy ark — the focal point of his prophecy — "G-d" (see *HaKozari* 1:97 — in com. on BeMidbar 10:35-36 [see the text below]), so all the prophets identify the pinnacle of G-d's revelation to them *at their level of prophecy* as "G-d," even though G-d in reality "cannot be seen" (Shemoth 33:20, 23) and ultimately the prophets only "thought to see and did not see" (Rashi, quoted above).

83. See *Michtav MeEliyyahu*, I, 310-12, which quotes and explains this excerpt from *Kelach Pithchei Chochmah*.

84. Thus, while a validated prophet is empowered to abrogate Torah law *temporarily* by dint of divine command received in prophecy (see Devarim 18:15 and *Sifrei* and com. on Devarim, loc. cit.; *Yevamoth* 90b; and *Sanhedrin*

89b), a prophet who attempts to negate any aspect of Torah law *permanently* is demonstrably a false prophet, liable for execution (see Devarim 18:19-20 and *Sifrei* and com., loc. cit., and *Sanhedrin* 89b). One of the most dramatic examples of such temporary abrogation of Torah law, ordained by a prophet (see *Sifrei* on Devarim 12:13, *Yer. Ta'anith* 2:8 [10b], *Yer. Megillah* 1:11 [16a], *Sanhedrin* 89b, *VaY.R.* 22:9, and *Yal.Sh.* Melachim:214), is the sacrifice offered by the prophet Eliyyahu on Mount Karmel (Melachim I 18:20-39), while the Temple was standing in Yerushalayim and such "external sacrifices" were forbidden by Torah law (Devarim 12:5-18; see also *Sifrei* on Devarim 12:8, *Mish. Megillah* 1:11, *Megillah* 10a, *Zevachim* 112b, and *Yal.Sh.* Devarim:881). Regarding the general status of prophetic commands as *temporal* instruction, see Rambam's *Introduction to the Mishnah*, ch. 2, and *Yad Hil. Yesodei HaTorah* 9:1-4.

85. See also *Sifra* on VaYikra 27:34, *Megillah* 2b, *Yoma* 80a, *Temurah* 16a, and *Yer. Megillah* 1:5 (7a). In addition, see Rambam, loc. cit.

86. See also *Niddah* 23a, *Yer. Challah* 1:1 (1b), *Yer. Yevamoth* 2:6 (10a), *Yer. Kiddushin* 3:12 (35a), *BeR.R.* 7:2, *BeM.R.* 19:3, *Koh.R.* 7:23 (4), *Tan. Chukkath*:6, and *Yal.Sh.* Ezra:1069, and see com., loc. cit. In addition, see Rashbam on *Babba Bathra* 123a, ד"ה ת"ש ובני ראובן בכור ישראל.

87. See BeReshith 32:26-33 and com., loc. cit. While the Torah contextually relates the prohibition of eating *gid hannasheh* to an event in Ya'akov's life, the Mishnah stresses that the prohibition itself originates — like the rest of the Torah — in Mosheh's receipt of the Torah from G-d at Sinai and not in Ya'akov or his immediate descendants.

88. See Rambam's *Introduction to Perek Chelek, Yesod* 7.

89. See also *Yad Hil. Megillah* 2:18.
    Concerning the uniqueness of Mosheh's level of prophecy, see also R. Isaac Sender, *Sefer Machazeh Elyon* (New York: n.p., 1987), pp. 72-105. In addition, see "Mosheh Rabbeinu and Rabbi Akiva," pp. 70-71, and pp. 110-11, nn. 15-16, and the sources cited, loc. cit.

90. See also Rambam's *Introduction to the Mishnah*, ch. 2; *Introduction to Perek Chelek, Yesodoth* 8-9; and *Yad Hil. Yesodei HaTorah* 8:3 and 9:1-2; and see Ramban on BeReshith 1:1, (ב') א-לקים ברא בראשית ד"ה; R. Ovadyah Seforno and R. S.R. Hirsch on Devarim 34:10; and *Tifereth Yisra'el* (Maharal), chs. 21-23.
    Indeed, the culmination of the words of the prophets lies in their reinforcement of observance of the Torah: *"Remember the Torah of Mosheh My servant"* (Malachi 3:24, at the conclusion of Nevi'im). Furthermore, Malachi — the last of the prophets — refers to the Torah as that of *"Mosheh My servant,"* emphasizing the unseverable bond between the Torah and the unique prophetic level of Mosheh. (See also *HaKozari* 4:11. In addition, see *Shabbath* 89a and numerous Midrashic references.)

91. See also *Sifthei Chachamim*, loc. cit. In addition, see *Gur Aryeh*, loc. cit., where

Maharal explains the distinction between "זה" and "כה" in the context of Mosheh's unique role in conveying the eternal Torah of G-d at the level of "clear glass." See also *HaTorah VeHaMitzvah* (Malbim) on Shemoth 3:2 and 33:12 and on BeMidbar 12:6, and see *Tzidkath HaTzaddik*, ch. 204.

92. See also Dr. Solomon Mandelkern, *Veteris Testamenti Concordantiae* (1896; rpt. Yerushalayim: Schocken, 1978), p. 532, s.v. "כה."

93. In the same vein, over two hundred years before Rema, *Ra'aya Meheimna* (on Bo) states, "When [G-d] descends [in prophecy] ... He appears *to each [prophet] according to his own sight and vision and likeness*" (quoted in *Torath HaOlah*, loc. cit.). R. Bachyai also notes the symbolism of the mirror in prophecy, albeit more generally: "[Concerning] a glass mirror ... one who gazes into it *sees the likeness of his own form from within it* ... but [in reality] there is nothing within it. Likewise, [in] the prophecy of the other prophets ... imagined [forms] are beheld, and the [prophets] *see their form as the form of man*" (com. on BeMidbar 12:6, ד"ה במראה אליו אתודע). (See also R. Bachyai on Shemoth 34:23.) In addition, see R. Yosef Albo's explanation of the analogy of the mirror in prophecy (*HaIkkarim* 3:9), an analogy initially suggested by the Midrash (*BeR.R.* 4:4), and see his and Rema's explanations of this *midrash* in *HaIkkarim* and in *Torath HaOlah*, loc. cit.

See also *Dover Tzedek*, באי"ד ולכיא בבראיר (p. 191), where R. Tzadok HaKohen quotes and expands upon Rema's statement, and see *Peri Tzaddik*, "Kedushath Shabbath," *Ma'amar* 7 (p. 37). See also *Sh.R.* 29:9 (and *Mid. Tehillim* 93:1 and *Yal.Sh.* Yirmeyahu:285), discussed in the text below, and see n. 95.

94. Regarding the symbolic meaning of the angels' wings, see *Chagigah* 13b and com., loc. cit., and numerous Midrashic references. Compare *Yal.Sh.* Yechezkel:337, where this discrepancy in the number of "wings" ascribed to the angels is also noted, and an alternate explanation is presented. See also *Moreh HaNevochim* 1:43, 49, and *Netzach Yisra'el* (Maharal), ch. 22 (p. 111).

95. In the same sense, on Yechezkel's prophecy — "And upon the likeness of the throne was a likeness similar to the appearance of *a man* upon it from above" (Yechezkel 1:26) — R. Tzadok HaKohen comments: "Understand the secret of the likeness of 'a man' upon the throne [beheld] by Yechezkel — *that this ['man'] is Yechezkel himself*" (Dover Tzedek, באי"ד ולכיא בבראיר [p. 191]). Elsewhere, he notes cryptically that "the likeness of 'a man' that is upon the throne is *the perception of the soul by the soul*" (*Peri Tzaddik*, "Kedushath Shabbath," *Ma'amar* 7 [p. 37]). (See also *Torath HaOlah* 1:14 and the sources cited in n. 93.) Thus, Yechezkel's perception of his prophecy — like Yirmeyahu's — derives directly from his own self-perception. In light of this conclusion, we should consider also the unique title by which Yechezkel is repeatedly addressed by G-d in his prophecies: "Son of *man*!" If, in his greatest vision of G-d, the prophet perceived Him as "a likeness similar to the appearance of *a man* upon it from above," it is particularly fitting that G-d's revelation to him is directed to the "son of *man*." (For this idea and for

the aforementioned sources in R. Bachyai and *Peri Tzaddik*, I am indebted to my esteemed teacher, R. Ch.Y. Hadari of Yeshivat Hakotel.)

96. See *Tos. Berachoth* 6:5, *Berachoth* 58a, *Yer. Berachoth* 9:1 (57a), *BeM.R.* 21:2, and *Tan. Pinchas*:10.

97. Regarding the principle that "no two prophets prophesy with the same style," see also *Halkkarim* 3:9 and *Chiddushei Aggadoth* (Maharal) on *Sanhedrin* 89a, and see *Ha'amek Davar* on BeMidbar 11:25.

98. In support of this conclusion, Rashi (ibid.) cites the root "נוב" (~ express), as in Shemu'el I 10:13, Yeshayahu 57:19, and Mishlei 10:31. See also Rashbam, R. Bachyai, R. Eliyyahu Mizrachi, and *Gur Aryeh* (and compare R. Avraham b. Ezra) on Shemoth, loc. cit., and see Rashi and *Metzudoth* on Nechemyah 6:7.

99. See also Yechezkel 17:2, 21:5, and 24:3. In addition, see Tehillim 49:5 and 78:2, Mishlei 1:6, and Koheleth 12:9, and see *Sifrei* on BeMidbar 12:8. See also the preface to *Moreh HaNevochim*, and see R. S.R. Hirsch on BeMidbar 12:8 and *Peri Tzaddik*, "Kedushath Shabbath," *Ma'amar* 7 (p. 37).

100. See also *Yad Hil. Yesodei HaTorah* 7:6. In addition, see *Da'ath Tevunoth*, ch. 180, which quotes and explains *Yad Hil. Yesodei HaTorah* 7:3.

101. Regarding the role of "allegory and riddle" in prophecy, see also the preface to *Moreh HaNevochim* and ibid. 2:45, 47. In addition, see *Derech HaShem* 3:5 (4) and *Da'ath Tevunoth*, chs. 180, 184, and 190 (and especially ch. 188), and see R. S.R. Hirsch on BeMidbar 12:6, 8; *HaTorah VeHaMitzvah* (Malbim) on Shemoth 3:2 and on BeMidbar 12:6-8; and *Peri Tzaddik*, "Kedushath Shabbath," *Ma'amar* 7 (p. 37).

102. Regarding this dichotomy, see also *Da'ath Tevunoth*, chs. 180 and 188.

103. See also *Derech HaShem* 3:4 (7).

104. Significantly, R. Tzadok HaKohen explains in this light the accusation leveled against Yirmeyahu for prophesying doom for those refugees of Yehudah who were determined to flee to Mitzrayim. At first, these refugees approached Yirmeyahu on their own initiative to pray on their behalf to G-d for guidance (Yirmeyahu 42:1-6): "May G-d be a True and Faithful Witness against us if we do not do everything for which G-d your L-rd will send you to us. Whether good or bad, we shall heed the voice of G-d our L-rd, to Whom we are sending you: that it be good for us when we heed the voice of G-d our L-rd" (ibid. 42:5-6). Yet the same refugees respond to Yirmeyahu's prophecy by reviling him as a false prophet: "You speak falsely! G-d our L-rd did not send you to say, 'Do not go to Mitzrayim to sojourn there.' For Baruch the son of Neriyyah [your disciple] instigates you against us ..." (ibid. 43:2-3). Comments R. Tzadok HaKohen on the apparent contradiction:

> Certainly they held Yirmeyahu to [be] a true prophet, since after all they inquired of him. However, they knew that there is in prophecy [an element of] error and imagination when [the prophet] has a self-interested

relationship [with his prophecy]. And this is the relationship of Baruch the son of Neriyyah, who did not want them to go to Mitzrayim, since he wanted to attain prophecy [Yirmeyahu 45 and *Tar. Yonathan* and com., loc. cit; *Mechilta* on Shemoth 12:1], and this is impossible outside the Land [of Yisra'el — see the text below and nn. 142-43]. And if the prophet does not clear away the [self-interested] relationship entirely, then, because of the relationship, he may imagine that it is the voice of G-d [that he hears], and it is not. This [possibility of error] is because, in reality, it is actually his own voice [that the prophet hears], only [in true prophecy] he perceives and knows that it is the voice of G-d that is speaking from within himself.

(*Dover Tzedek*, באה"ד וביאור זה [p. 161])

This interpretive dimension of prophecy — "*his own* voice," which the prophet perceives "is the voice of G-d that is speaking from *within himself*" — makes the possibility of error (and the challenge to overcome it) inevitable.

Because of this interpretive component, Maharil Diskin comments similarly that "the more the [prophet's] spirit is pure, the more clear and shining is the interpretation he sees" (*Shuth Maharil Diskin*, vol. II [end]). See also n. 105.

105. Interestingly, in light of the above statement by Maharil Diskin, R. Eli'ezer Shach explains the magnitude of G-d's "test" of Avraham in commanding him to slaughter his son Yitzchak:

> How could it have been conceivable [for Avraham] to have defied the command of G-d, Who has the capacity to confer life and death? And if one hears the words explicitly in [G-d] commanding [to do] such and such, how can this be called a "test" [i.e., how could Avraham have failed to submit to so overwhelming a mandate]? Surely there was no room [for Avraham] to rule leniently on how to explain the command to "take your son, your only one," etc. (BeReshith 22:2).
>
> But according to the true words cited above [by Maharil Diskin, loc. cit.], the resolution is well-settled and understood, since the prophecy of Avraham, too, was through "unclear glass" and required the interpretation of the prophet himself — who is Avraham. Therefore, Avraham had to interpret the allegory that he had been shown in such a manner [as to derive] that G-d told him to offer Yitzchak, his only son whom he loved, as a burnt offering. And by his soul being so pure and clear, he interpreted [the prophecy] thus, and he had no personal relationship [to his interpretation] to rule leniently by citing numerous reasons to interpret in a different manner.

(*Avi Ezri*, vol. I, on Yad Hil. Yesodei HaTorah)

The unparalleled greatness of Avraham — and of all the other prophets as well — lies not only in the prophet's capacity to receive the prophetic vision that is "made known" to him but also, at least as much, in his capacity to "know" its meaning by force of faithful, active interpretation, mediated by his own mind. See also n. 104.

106. See also Sh.HaSh.R. 4:11, Ru.R. *Peth.*:2, and *Yal.Sh.* Melachim:224. In addition, see *Koh.R.* 1:11.

107. We do, however, find similar questions posed to the prophet in Mosheh's initial prophecy (Shemoth 4:2; see *Ha'amek Davar*, loc. cit.) and in the prophecies of Amos (Amos 7:8 and 8:2) and Zecharyah (Zecharyah 4:2 and 5:2, 5).

It appears that, as prophecy ebbed, this interpretive capacity of the prophets waned. We find repeatedly in Zecharyah (one of the last of the prophets — see the text below and nn. 144-45) that the prophet beholds an image but cannot interpret it (see Zecharyah 1:9, 2:2, 4, 4:4-5, 11-13, 5:6, and 6:4). Likewise, Daniyyel solicits an explanation of his vision of the "Four Beasts" (Daniyyel 7:15-16). See also *Da'ath Tevunoth*, ch. 180.

108. See also *Tan. Chukkath*:6, *Pes. DeR. Kahana* 4 (36b), and *Pes. Rabbathi* 14 (61b). Alternate versions of this *midrash* are phrased more euphemistically: "Great is the power of the prophets, in that they *liken the form to its Former*," etc. Presumably, the import of the *midrash* remains unchanged. See *BeR.R.* 27:1; *Koh.R.* 2:20 (2) and 8:1 (1); *Mid. Tehillim* 1:4; and *Yal.Sh.* Yechezkel:340, Tehillim:833, and Koheleth:968, 977, and see com., loc. cit. See also *Moreh HaNevochim* 1:46, and see *Takkanath HaShavin*, ch. 12 (p. 113), quoted in the text. In addition, see R. Bachyai on BeMidbar 12:6, ד"ה במראה אליו אתודע, and *Rimzei HaMishkan* (Malbim) on Shemoth 25. Compare, however, *Torath HaOlah* (Rema) 1:14 and *Derech HaChayyim* (Maharal) on *Avoth* 3:14 (p. 143). See also R. Tzadok HaKohen, in *Dover Tzedek*, ד"ה באי"ד ולכ"א בבראי"ר (pp. 191-92); *Machshevoth Charutz*, ch. 9 (p. 65); *Resisei Lailah*, ch. 40 (p. 72); and *Peri Tzaddik*, "Kedushath Shabbath," Ma'amar 7 (pp. 36-37).

109. See also *Dev.R.* 1:3, *Mid. Tehillim* 14:1, and *Yal.Sh.* Yeshayahu:436.

110. I have translated "וביד הנביאים אדמה" as *"and by the hand of the prophets I am imagined"* in light of the Midrashic exposition that follows the one quoted. (See *Yal.Sh.* Yeshayahu:385.) See also Rambam's preface to *Moreh HaNevochim*; Ramban on *Yevamoth* 49b, ד"ה כל הנביאים נסתכלו וכו'; *Ra'aya Meheimna* on *Bo*; R. Bachyai on BeMidbar 12:6, ד"ה במראה אליו אתודע; *Da'ath Tevunoth*, chs. 180 and 184; and R. Tzadok HaKohen, in *Tzidkath HaTzaddik*, ch. 204, and *Peri Tzaddik*, "Kedushath Shabbath," Ma'amar 7 (p. 37). In addition, see *Zohar*, III, 280b.

111. See also *Mechilta* and Rashi on Shemoth 20:2 and *Yal.Sh.* Shemoth:286. In addition, see *HaKozari* 4:3; *Yad Hil. Yesodei HaTorah* 1:9; and *Da'ath Tevunoth*, ch. 180.

112. Note that the imaginative faculty is also prominent in another field of endeavor closely related to prophecy: prayer. See especially *HaKozari* 3:5, 11, and see *Tzidkath HaTzaddik*, chs. 208-9. (On the association between prophecy and prayer, see BeReshith 20:7 — "He is a *prophet*, and he will *pray* for you" — and com., loc. cit.)

113. It should be obvious from the foregoing that everything stated here regarding prophecy applies *strictly to all prophets other than Mosheh Rabbeinu*, who was so utterly different from all other prophets that only the imprecision of our speech allows us to employ the same label, *"navi* (prophet)," in describing both him and them (see especially *Moreh HaNevochim* 2:35). See also, for example, *Sifrei* on BeMidbar 30:2; *Yevamoth* 49b; *VaY.R.* 1:14; *Tan. Tzav*:13; and *Yal.Sh.* Shemoth:360, VaYikra:432, BeMidbar:784, Melachim:247, and Hoshea:528; and see Rambam's *Introduction to Perek Chelek, Yesod 7,* and *Yad Hil. Yesodei HaTorah* 7:6. In addition, see above, especially nn. 82, 89, 91, and 132.

114. Regarding the Talmud's analogy between dreams and prophecy, see also *HaIkkarim* 3:9; *Derech HaShem* 3:5 and *Da'ath Tevunoth*, chs. 180 and 190; *Shuth Maharil Diskin*, vol. II (end); *Tzidkath HaTzaddik*, ch. 203; and *Michtav MeEliyyahu*, IV, 165.

115. See also *BeR.R.* 44:17 and *Yal.Sh.* BeReshith:23, 77, and Shemu'el:139.

116. Rambam discusses the fundamental role of the imaginative faculty in prophecy at length. See especially *Moreh* 2:36-38 (and also ibid. 2:41, 45, 47).

117. The author of *Derashoth HaRan* is identified by most authorities as R. Nissim b. Re'uven (ca. 5100 [mid-fourteenth century, C.E.]), a student of Rashba and the noted commentator on Rif's *Sefer HaHalachoth*. Some identify the author as R. Nissim (ca. 5000 [mid-thirteenth century, C.E.]), a student of Ramban.

118. Regarding the role of the imaginative faculty in prophecy, see especially *HaKozari* 4:3. See also R. Bachyai (on BeMidbar 12:6, ד"ה במראה אליו אתודע), Maharal (*Gevuroth HaShem*, introduction 1 [pp. 2-3], and *Chiddushei Aggadoth* on *Yevamoth* 49b, ד"ה משה רבנו נסתכל באספקלריא המאירה), R. Levi Yitzchak of Berdichev (*Kedushath Levi* on BeReshith 15:1), Malbim (*HaTorah VeHaMitzvah* on Shemoth 3:2, 6:2, and 19:11; on BeMidbar 12:6-8; and on Devarim 13:2), R. Tzadok HaKohen (*Tzidkath HaTzaddik*, chs. 203-5; *Dover Tzedek*, באי"ד ולכי"א בבראי"ר [pp. 191-92]; *Takkanath HaShavin*, ch. 12 [p. 113]; and *Peri Tzaddik*, "Kedushath Shabbath," Ma'amar 7 [p. 37]), and R. Me'ir Simchah HaKohen of Dvinsk (*Meshech Chochmah* on BeMidbar 11:17). In addition, see R. David Kohen, *Kol HaNevu'ah: HaHiggayon HaIvri HaShimi* (Yerushalayim: Mossad Harav Kook, 1979), pp. 47-49 and 64-66.

119. See also Yeshayahu 40:25 and 46:5.

120. See also *Yal.Sh.* VaYikra:432 and Hoshea:528. In addition, see Ramban on *Yevamoth* 49b, ד"ה כל הנביאים נסתכלו וכו', and *Yefei To'ar* on *VaY.R.* 1:14.

121. See also *Yal.Sh.* Shemoth:244 and Rashi on Shemoth, loc. cit.

122. I have translated "'ירד ה'" (lit. "G-d will descend") as *"G-d will reveal Himself"* in accordance with *Tar. Yonathan* and *Tar. Onkelos*, loc. cit. See also *Moreh HaNevochim* 1:10, 27, and *HaTorah VeHaMitzvah* (Malbim) on Shemoth, loc. cit. In addition, see Ramban on BeReshith 46:1 and *Tifereth Yisra'el* (Maharal), ch. 33.

123. Regarding the special emphasis, "*This* (זה) is my L-rd," the Midrash states

further: "[Even] the infants were revealing Him with their fingers and saying, '*This* is my L-rd' " (*Sh.HaSh.R.* 3:7). See also *Yal.Sh.* Shemoth:245 and Rashi on Shemoth, loc. cit. In addition, see R. Tzadok HaKohen, in *Tzidkath HaTzaddik*, ch. 205, and *Machshevoth Charutz*, ch. 4 (p. 13).

124. See R. Tzadok HaKohen, in *Resisei Lailah*, ch. 15 (p. 17), and *Likkutei Ma'amarim*, ch. 16 (p. 219).

125. Note that the Hebrew word for world, "עולם," is derived from the root "עלם" (~ hide — as in "נעלם" ["hidden"]). By implication, the nature of this world is concealment. See also *Pesachim* 50a, *Kiddushin* 71a, *Koh.R.* 3:11 (3), *Yal.Sh.* Shemoth:171, and Rashi on Shemoth 3:15. In addition, see *Likkutei Ma'amarim* (R. Tzadok HaKohen), ch. 9 (p. 114), and *Pachad Yitzchak* (R. Yitzchak Hutner), "*Pesach*," *Reshimah* 4:6 (p. 304). See also n. 82.

126. See, for example, *Moreh* 3:32, where Rambam describes idolatry as an obsession with "*imaginary* things that lack substance."

127. See also *Moreh* 2:37-38.

128. This symbolism is implied in *Moreh HaNevochim* 2:30; see com., loc. cit. Malbim discusses it more explicitly (see *HaTorah VeHaMitzvah* on BeReshith 3:19).

129. Clearly, Rambam's position — that the *yetzer hara* is an internal force equated with the imagination (see *Moreh* 2:12, quoted in the text, and ibid. 3:22) — is reinforced by the perspective emergent from this essay. This position is also strongly supported by many later rabbinical sources that indicate or imply that the *yetzer hara* is an internal force. See the sources cited in n. 25, and see Radak on Tehillim 103:14, *Magen Avoth* (Rashbatz) and *Nachalath Avoth* (R. Yitzchak Abberavanel) on *Avoth* 2:11, and other sources cited in n. 28.

It should, nevertheless, be noted that this subject has been a point of contention since at least the period of the *rishonim* (early rabbinical commentaries). Thus, while Rambam evidently regards the *yetzer hara* as an internal force, Ramban (in the introduction to his commentary on Iyyov) states unequivocally that the *yetzer hara* is a supernatural entity and not an aspect of nature or an internal faculty. R. Aharon Walden raises the possibility that the roots of this dispute are to be found much earlier, in Chazal (see *Beith Aharon* on Tehillim 103, n. 35, and his analysis of the many sources cited, loc. cit.).

130. Obviously, this is the thrust of *Moreh* 2:12, quoted in the text. R. E.E. Dessler discusses this derivative of the imagination at length. (See *Michtav MeEliyyahu*, I, 112. See also R. Tzadok HaKohen, in *Dover Tzedek*, ד"ה כי תבוא וגו' [p. 73]; *Machshevoth Charutz*, chs. 3-4 [pp. 10-13]; and *Sichath Malachei HaShareth*, ch. 4 [p. 64].) Conversely, man's spiritual mission in this world hinges on channeling and refining the imaginative faculty. (See also R. Tzadok HaKohen, in *Tzidkath HaTzaddik*, chs. 207-9 and 219; *Dover Tzedek*, בא"יד ועל אותו יום [p. 172]; *Resisei Lailah*, chs. 30-31, 35, and 58 [pp. 42-43, 55-57, 174-75]; and *Likkutei Ma'amarim*, "*LeSiyyum HaShas*" [p. 236]. The imagination — and our need to

channel it — will be more extensively discussed, G-d willing, in the sequel to this essay.)

131. Regarding the singular greatness of prophecy, see, for example, *HaKozari* 1:109, 115, 2:12-14, 3:20, 4:3-5, 15-17, and 5:14; Rambam's *Introduction to Perek Chelek*, Yesod 6, and *Moreh* 2:36; and *Derech HaShem* 3:3-4.

132. In a sense, our conclusion — that prophecy as we know it (with the exception of Mosheh's) is predicated upon acquisition of the *yetzer hara* — is at least implied by the Midrash. In describing the overwhelming nature of the prophetic experience, Rambam states that "when all [the prophets other than Mosheh] prophesy, their limbs quake, and the strength of the body fails, and their thoughts are confounded.... [They become] frightened and terrified and faint" (*Yad Hil. Yesodei HaTorah* 7:2, 6; see also *Introduction to Perek Chelek*, Yesod 7). The Midrash describes the origin of such an overwhelming reaction: "Until Adam sinned, he would hear the sound of [G-d's] speech while standing on his feet and not be frightened. *Once he sinned*, when he would hear the sound of [G-d's] speech, he would be frightened and hide.... *Once he sinned*, he would hear the sound harshly [terrified (*Mattenoth Kehunnah* on BeM.R. 11:3)]" (*Sh.HaSh.R.* 3:6 [5], *BeM.R.* 11:3, *Mid. Shemu'el* 17:4, *Yal.Sh.* Tehillim:795). The fright associated with prophecy, experienced by Adam after sinning and by all later prophets other than Mosheh, is derivative of the imaginative faculty. Therefore, Adam did not experience it prior to his sin (and consequent acquisition of the *yetzer hara*), and Mosheh did not experience it (see *Introduction to Perek Chelek* and *Yad Hil. Yesodei HaTorah*, loc. cit.), since the imaginative faculty was irrelevant to his unique level of prophecy (see nn. 82, 89, 91, and 113). The level of prophecy experienced by all other prophets, then, entered this world with the *yetzer hara*.

133. Interestingly, we also find an additional creative dimension associated with the prophets' careers. Rambam states that "each and every one [of the prophets who were the leading scholars of their generations] would write for himself to the best of his ability ... *the matters that were innovated in each generation* in laws that had not been learned from the tradition but instead [had been expounded] through one of the Thirteen Principles of Exposition and upon which the Great Court had agreed" (introduction to *Mishneh Torah*). From this, R. Naftali Tz.Y. Berlin concludes more emphatically, "The prophets would write for themselves *scholarly innovations* in Torah" (*Harchev Davar* on Shemoth 34:27).

134. Significantly, in the version of this *aggadah* appearing in *Yalkut Shimoni*, this "lion of fire" is never identified. After it emerges, in response to the plea by the men of the Great Assembly for withdrawal of that which "destroyed the Beith HaMikdash and burnt the Sanctuary and killed the righteous," the prophet (Zecharyah) states merely, "*This is it!*" (*Yal.Sh.* Nechemyah:1071). While we may refer to it as the "*yetzer* of idolatry" when it is expressed destructively, such a designation is clearly inadequate given the true char-

acter of this faculty as the basis of all spiritual creativity.

135. See also *Shemu'el II* 6:2, *Melachim II* 19:15, *Yeshayahu* 37:16, *Tehillim* 80:2 and 99:1, and *Divrei HaYamim I* 13:6. In addition, see Ramban on *Shemoth* 25:1, 21, and on *VaYikra* 1:1.

136. See also *HaKozari* 4:3, in com. on *Yehoshua* 3:11.

137. See, for example, *BeR.R.* 66:2; *Sh.R.* 1:5, 33:1, 34:3, and 51:4; *VaY.R.* 30:13; *BeM.R.* 1:3, 12:4, 13:2, and 15:8; *Sh.HaSh.R.* 1:4a (2), 3:7, 8 (1), 5:1, and 7:1 (1); *Tan. Tissa*:4, *Pekudei*:2, 11, *Emor*:17, *BeChukkothai*:3, *BeMidbar*:3, *Naso*:11, and *BeHa'alothecha*:6; *Mid. Tehillim* 3:6 and 33:1; and *Yal.Sh.* BeReshith:17, Shemoth:365, VaYikra:652, BeMidbar:683, 711, Malachi:587, Tehillim:625, and Shir HaShirim:986, 992. See also *HaKozari* 3:23; R. Avraham b. Ezra and Ramban on *Shemoth* 25:1; and R. Ovadyah Seforno, *Or HaChayyim*, and *Ha'amek Davar* on *Shemoth* 25:8.

138. See also *Kol Yehudah*, loc. cit., ד״ה ונגנז הארון.

139. It should be stressed that "individual quality" is insufficient by itself as the basis of prophecy. Chazal cite several individuals who would have been worthy of prophecy had external circumstances not interfered. In particular, consider Baruch the son of Neriyyah (*Yirmeyahu* 45 and *Tar. Yonathan* and com., loc. cit, and *Mechilta* on *Shemoth* 12:1), Ezra (*Sanhedrin* 21b and *Yer. Megillah* 1:9 [10a]), Hillel the Elder (*Sotah* 48b, *Sanhedrin* 11a, *Yer. Sotah* 9:16 [45b], *Yer. Horayoth* 3:5 [15a], *Sh.HaSh.R.* 8:9 [3], and *Yal.Sh.* Shemoth:261), the students of Hillel (*Babba Bathra* 134a [and Rashbam, loc. cit., ד״ה ראוים שתשרה] and *Avoth DeR. Nathan* 14:1 [and *Sukkah* 28a]), Shemu'el HaKatan (*Sotah*, *Sanhedrin*, *Yer. Sotah*, *Yer. Horayoth*, *Sh.HaSh.R.*, and *Yal.Sh.*, loc. cit.), R. Eli'ezer b. Hurkanos (*Yer. Sotah* and *Yer. Horayoth*, loc. cit.), and R. Huna (*Mo'ed Katan* 25a).

See also *HaKozari* 3:65; *Yad Hil. Yesodei HaTorah* 7:5 (and *Lechem Mishneh*, ibid. 7:1) and *Moreh HaNevochim* 2:32; *HaIkkarim* 3:11; and *Avodath HaKodesh* (R. Me'ir b. Gabbai), "Sithrei Torah," ch. 24. In addition, see R. Isaac Sender, *Sefer Machazeh Elyon* (New York: n.p., 1987), pp. 224-44.

140. Regarding the linkage between the Beith HaMikdash and prophecy, see also *HaKozari* 2:26-28, 3:21-22, and 4:3, 11.

141. See also *Derashoth HaRan*, *Derash* 8, and *Chiddushei R. Yonathan* (R. Yonathan Eybeschuetz) on *Berachoth* 4a, ד״ה לדוד שמרה נפשי. In addition, see *Sefer Machazeh Elyon*, pp. 234-36.

142. See also *Sifrei* on *Devarim* 18:15 and *Yal.Sh.* Devarim:919. In addition, see *Mo'ed Katan* 25a. See also Ramban and *Torah Temimah* on *Devarim*, loc. cit.

143. Regarding the linkage between Eretz Yisra'el and prophecy, see also *HaKozari* 1:95, 2:12-14, 23-24, 3:11, 21-22, 4:3, 11, 17, and 5:23. In addition, see Rashi on *Babba Bathra* 15a, ד״ה כתבו יחזקאל; *Beith HaBechirah* (R. Menachem b. Shelomoh HaMe'iri), preface to *Avoth* (pp. 18-19); *HaIkkarim* 3:11; and *Tzafenath Paneach* (R. Yosef b. Mosheh Trani) on *BeHa'alothecha*, ch. 3.

Furthermore, apropos of the role of the imaginative faculty in prophecy and its equivalence with the *yetzer hara*, R. Tzadok HaKohen discusses the unique clarity of the imagination in Eretz Yisra'el (see *Sichath Malachei HaShareth*, ch. 1 [p. 8], and see *Tzidkath HaTzaddik*, ch. 205, and *Dover Tzedek*, ד״ה כי תבוא וגו' [p. 73]).

144. See *Megillah* 17b and com., loc. cit.; Rashi on *Babba Bathra* 15a, ד״ה אנשי כנסת הגדולה; and the introduction to *Mishneh Torah*.

Chaggai and Zecharyah prophesied during the return to Tziyyon and the reconstruction of the Beith HaMikdash, as evident both in the recorded dates heading their prophecies and in Ezra 5:1 and 6:14. Chazal identify Malachi alternately as Mordechai or as Ezra (see *Megillah* 15a and *Tar. Yonathan* on Malachi 1:1). The Talmud describes Chaggai, Zecharyah, and Malachi, together with Daniyyel, as contemporaries (see *Megillah* 3a and 15a and *Sanhedrin* 93b; see also *Nazir* 53a, *Zevachim* 62a, *Chullin* 137b, and *Bechoroth* 58a). In the transmission of *Torah shebe'al-peh*, "Chaggai, Zecharyah, and Malachi received from the [earlier] prophets; the men of the Great Assembly received from Chaggai, Zecharyah, and Malachi" (*Avoth DeR. Nathan* 1:3).

145. See also *Yoma* 9b, *Sotah* 48b, *Yer. Sotah* 9:13 (44a), *Sanhedrin* 11a, and *Sh.HaSh.R.* 8:9 (3). More generally, Chazal list withdrawal of "the holy spirit [of prophecy]" among the principal deficiencies of the second Beith HaMikdash with respect to the first. (See *Yoma* 21b; *Yer. Ta'anith* 2:1 [8a] and *Korban HaEdah*, loc. cit., ד״ה אש; *Yer. Makkoth* 2:6 [5a]; *Yer. Horayoth* 3:2 [12b] and *Penei Mosheh*, loc. cit., ד״ה ושמן המשחה ורוח הקדש; *BeM.R.* 15:10; *Sh.HaSh.R.* 8:9 [3]; *Tan. BeHa'alothecha*:6; and *Yal.Sh.* Chaggai:567. See also *Babba Bathra* 12a-12b.)

Regarding the cessation of prophecy at the beginning of the period of the second Beith HaMikdash, see also *HaKozari* 1:87, 2:23-24, and 3:39, 65; *Sefer HaMitzvoth* (Rambam), conclusion of "*Sharashim*," and *Yad Hil. Beith HaBechirah* 4:1 (and *Hassagoth HaRa'avad* and *Kesef Mishneh*, loc. cit.) and *Hil. Kelei HaMikdash* 10:10; *HaIkkarim* 3:11; *Avodath HaKodesh*, "*Sithrei Torah*," ch. 24; *Haghoth HaGra* on *Seder Olam R.*, ch. 30; R. Tzadok HaKohen (*Tzidkath HaTzaddik*, ch. 256; *Dover Tzedek*, בא״יד והנה מצד הזה [p. 142]; *Machshevoth Charutz*, ch. 17 [pp. 139-40, 142-45]; *Resisei Lailah*, chs. 13 and 56 [pp. 14, 158, 160-62]; *Divrei Soferim*, ch. 38 [p. 41]; *Poked Akkarim*, ch. 2 [p. 10]; *Sichath Malachei HaShareth*, "*Yer. Rosh HaShanah 1*" [pp. 71-72] and "*Tan. Parashath Mishpatim*" [p. 76]; and *Peri Tzaddik*, "*Kedushath Shabbath*," *Ma'amar* 7 [p. 38]); *Meshech Chochmah* on BeMidbar 11:17; and *Michtav MeEliyyahu*, III, 277-78, and IV, 105 and 174.

146. See also *Meshech Chochmah* on BeMidbar 11:17, which quotes and explains the Vilna Ga'on's commentary.

147. See also *Sichath Malachei HaShareth*, "*Yer. Rosh HaShanah 1*" [pp. 71-72]; *Resisei Lailah*, ch. 13 [p. 14]; and *Divrei Soferim*, ch. 38 [p. 41]. In addition, compare *Michtav MeEliyyahu*, III, 277-78, and IV, 105 and 174, which quotes and explains this concept of R. Tzadok HaKohen's.

148. The concept of man as a microcosm of the world is expressed repeatedly in classic Jewish thought (as well as in many trends in general philosophy),

with varying implications. See, for example, *Mish. Sanhedrin* 4:5, *Berachoth* 10a, *Avoth DeR. Nathan* 31:3, and *Tan. Pekudei*:3, and com., loc. cit. See also R. Se'adyah Ga'on, in com. on *Sefer HaYetzirah*; *Torath Chovoth HaLevavoth* 2:4; *HaKozari* 2:26 and 4:3, 25; *Sefer HaOlam HaKatan* (R. Yosef b. Tzaddik); R. Avraham b. Ezra, in com. on BeReshith 1:26 and on Shemoth 25:40; *Moreh HaNevochim* 1:72; *Sefer HaMishkal* (R. Mosheh b. Shem Tov de Leon), *"Perek Sod HaNefesh"*; *Torath HaOlah* (Rema) 2:2 (3); and *Derech HaChayyim* (Maharal) on *Avoth* 5:21. In the context of our *aggadah* and its portrayal of the "lion of fire," see also *Etz Yosef* and *Anaf Yosef* (on *Yoma* 69b, loc. cit.) and *Chiddushei Aggadoth* (Maharsha, on *Sanhedrin* 64a, loc. cit.), which understand the Gemara as symbolically referring to the human microcosm.

149. See also Yoma 9b, Sotah 48b, Yer. Sotah 9:13 (44a), Sanhedrin 11a, and Sh.HaSh.R. 8:9 (3). In addition, see *Babba Bathra* 12a-12b.

Regarding the meaning and role of the "divine echo," see also *HaKozari* 3:11, 73, and *Moreh HaNevochim* 2:42.

150. See also *Dover Tzedek*, באי"ד והנה מצד הזה (p. 142).

151. See also the introduction to Sha'arei HaKedushah (R. Chayyim Vital), which states that "the work of prophecy continues also now, even though prophecy [itself] has ceased." In addition, see *Poked Akkarim* (R. Tzadok HaKohen), ch. 2 (p. 9).

152. See also BeR.R. 61:1, Mid. Tehillim 1:13 and 16:7, *Avoth DeR. Nathan* 33:1, and *Yal.Sh.* BeReshith:109 and Tehillim:614, 667. In addition, see my essay "Unmasking Avraham's Slave: A Midrashic Analysis of Eli'ezer," *Jewish Thought*, 1, No. 1 (5750), 68, regarding the novelty of Avraham's Torah learning.

153. Concerning the powerful and decisive role played by Avraham's *yetzer hara* in his spiritual greatness, see also *Tzidkath HaTzaddik*, chs. 248-49 (pp. 128-29).

154. See also *Michtav MeEliyyahu*, III, 56, and see *Takkanath HaShavin*, ch. 5 (p. 17).

155. See also ibid. 1:12 (p. 233). In addition, see Prof. Yehudah Levi, "Yetzer Tov VeYetzer HaRa," *HaMa'ayan*, 25, No. 4 (5745), 50.

156. See also Yer. Chagigah 1:1 (1a), Yer. Sotah 3:4 (14b), Tos. Sotah 7:6, and BeM.R. 14:4. In addition, see *Avoth DeR. Nathan* 18:2 (*Nuschath HaGra*, loc. cit., n. 1) and *Mechilta* on Shemoth 13:2.

157. See also the sources in R. Tzadok HaKohen cited in n. 14. In addition, see *Tzidkath HaTzaddik*, chs. 218 and 248; *Machshevoth Charutz*, ch. 19 (p. 158); *Takkanath HaShavin*, ch. 5 (p. 17); and *Peri Tzaddik* on *Zachor*, ch. 1 (p. 173).

158. In a related sense, the Midrash comments on the prelude to the binding of Yitzchak, in which — although Avraham and Yitzchak beheld the apparition of a pillar of fire stretching from earth to heaven as a sign of G-d's presence manifest upon the mountain — Avraham's youths, *like the donkey*, saw nothing: " 'Avraham said to his youths, "You remain here with the donkey" '

(BeReshith 22:5) — [The 'youths' are] *a people that resembles a donkey"* (*Pir.DeR.E.* 31; see also *BeR.R.* 56:2, *VaY.R.* 20:2, *Koh.R.* 9:7, *Tan. VaYera*:23, and *Yal.Sh.* BeReshith:99). In addition, see *Yevamoth* 62a, *Kethubboth* 111a, *Kiddushin* 68a, *Babba Kamma* 49a, *Niddah* 17a, and *Yal.Sh.* BeReshith:100. See also Maharal, in *Netzach Yisra'el*, ch. 2 (p. 11); *Derech HaChayyim* on *Avoth* 5:19; and *Chiddushei Aggadoth* on *Nedarim* 32a, 'שהוריקן בתורה וכו'; ד"יה; and see "Unmasking Avraham's Slave," pp. 56-57 and 70, and pp. 77 and 79-80, nn. 44 and 85.

159. See also R. Mordecai Gifter, "Kol HaShirim Kodesh VeShir HaShirim Kodesh Kodashim," foreword to Shir HaShirim, eds. R. Nosson Scherman and R. Meir Zlotowitz (New York: Mesorah Publications, 1977), pp. xviii-xx — especially his discussion of this statement by R. Yitzchak b. Shemu'el of Akko, on p. xix.

160. Regarding the role of the yetzer hara as the mediator of enthusiasm, see also Torath HaMaggid, II, on Kiddushin 30a (p. 139), and see *Michtav MeEliyyahu*, IV, 289. (See n. 59.)

161. Regarding the designation "very good," see *BeR.R.* 9:7, *Koh.R.* 3:11 (3), *Mid. Tehillim* 9:1, and *Yal.Sh.* BeReshith:16 and Tehillim:643, quoted above.

162. See also *Shabbath* 89a, *VaY.R.* 24:8, and *Yal.Sh.* BeMidbar:752 and Tehillim:641.

163. See also *Berachoth* 61a, *BeR.R.* 14:4, and *Yal.Sh.* BeReshith:20. (In addition, regarding the absence of a *yetzer hara* in beasts, see my discussion of *Berachoth* 61a and *BeR.R.* 14:4, in n. 40.)

164. See also *Yal.Sh.* BeReshith:61 and Iyyov:914.

165. Regarding the role of the *yetzer hara* in precipitating man's sense of autonomy, see especially *Derech HaChayyim* (Maharal) on *Avoth* 3:15 (p. 148). See also R. S.R. Hirsch on BeReshith 3:5. (This issue of autonomy will be more extensively discussed, G-d willing, in the sequel to this essay.)

166. See BeReshith 3:16 and com., loc. cit. See also *Eruvin* 100b, *Avoth DeR. Nathan* 1:7-8, *BeR.R.* 20:6, *Pir.DeR.E.* 14, and *Yal.Sh.* BeReshith:31.

167. See BeReshith 3:17-19 and com., loc. cit. See also *BeR.R.* 5:9, 20:8, and 25:2; *Tan. BeReshith*:11; *Pir.DeR.E.* 14; and *Yal.Sh.* BeReshith:32, 42, and Divrei HaYamim:1072. In addition, see BeReshith 5:29 and com., loc. cit.

168. See also *Semachoth* 2:6 and *Yal.Sh.* Melachim:230.

169. See also *BeR.R.* 27:4 and *Yal.Sh.* BeReshith:47.

"LET EVERY LIVING BREATH PRAISE G-D":
The Finale of Sefer Tehillim

Shmuel Grunfeld

The essay that follows is based upon the source provided below:

Haleluyah! Praise the L-rd in His Sanctuary; praise Him in the firmament of His power.	הללויה! הללו-א-ל בקדשו; הללוהו ברקיע עזו:
Praise Him for His mighty acts; praise Him according to His abundant greatness.	הללוהו בגבורתיו; הללוהו כרב גדלו:
Praise Him with the sound of the *shofar*; praise Him with harp and lyre.	הללוהו בתקע שופר; הללוהו בנבל וכנור:
Praise Him with timbrel and dance; praise Him with flutes and pipe.	הללוהו בתף ומחול; הללוהו במנים ועגב:
Praise Him with resounding cymbals; praise Him with crashing cymbals.	הללוהו בצלצלי-שמע; הללוהו בצלצלי תרועה:
Let every living breath praise G-d. *Haleluyah!* (Tehillim 150)	כל הנשמה תהלל י-ה הללויה:

RABBI GRUNFELD, an alumnus of Yeshivah Rabbi Chaim Berlin of Brooklyn, New York, resides in Yerushalayim, where he teaches Talmud and other Judaic studies. He is the author of a new, highly acclaimed commentary on *haftaroth*, entitled *Beith HaSho'evah* (Yerushalayim: n.p., 1991).

"Let Every Living Breath Praise G-d" was adapted (by Daniel Haberman) from the author's introduction to *Beith HaSho'evah*, pp. 5-7.

1. INTRODUCTION

It is interesting to ponder why King David chose to close Sefer Tehillim with this list of musical instruments. Why were these instruments mentioned and not others that also appear in Tehillim? What is their significance as the grand finale of humanity's supreme book of praises to G-d?

A clue is provided by the last *mishnah* in *Seder Kodashim*:

> Said R. Yehoshua: This is as [the sages] said [of the ram]. When it is alive, its sound is one, but when it is dead, its sound is sevenfold. How is its sound sevenfold? Its two horns are [made into] two trumpets, its two thighs [into] two flutes, its hide into a timbrel, its large intestines into harp [strings], and its entrails into lyre [strings]....
> (*Kinnim* 3:6)

In striking parallel, the musical instruments mentioned in the *mishnah* all appear in Mizmor 150: *"Its two horns are [made into] two trumpets"*[1] corresponds to *"praise Him with the sound of the shofar"* (ibid. 150:3); *"its two thighs [into] two flutes"* corresponds to *"praise Him with flutes"* (ibid. 150:4); *"its hide into a timbrel"* corresponds to *"praise Him with [the] timbrel"* (ibid.); and *"its large intestines into harp [strings], and its entrails into lyre [strings]"* corresponds to *"praise Him with harp and lyre"* (ibid. 150:3). The *mishnah* seems to be based on — and perhaps even a commentary on — our *mizmor*. By understanding the symbolism of the *mishnah*, we may begin to fathom the depth of these closing words of Sefer Tehillim.

2. SINGING TO THE VERY END — AND EVEN BEYOND

What is the *mishnah*'s point in its parable of the ram's sound becoming sevenfold in death? Just when the ram would seem to be lost to the world and least valuable — in death — it actually becomes the basis of great creativity. In the same vein, in fact, the *mishnah* continues:

> ... R. Shimon b. Akashya says: The elderly among the ignorant, as they age, become increasingly confused of mind, as it is said, *"He removes the speech of orators, and the sense of elders He takes away"* (Iyyov 12:20). But with elderly Torah scholars, this is not the case.

> On the contrary, as they age, they become increasingly composed of mind, as it is said, *"With the aged is wisdom, and length of days [brings] understanding"* (ibid. 12:12).
>
> (Kinnim, loc. cit.)

As a scholar grows old and feeble, one would expect his intellect to follow suit. Yet, like the sound of the ram, it grows only stronger and more valuable.

Reading Mizmor 150 in light of this *mishnah*, we can appreciate King David's concluding message to us. While the ram may appear to be dead and gone, it still, in a way, sings G-d's praises. People, too, can sing praises to G-d, no matter how desperate or lost their situation. Indeed, the true fruition of the ram's song comes only after its death.

Our *mizmor* concludes, *"... praise Him with crashing cymbals. Let every living breath praise G-d.* Haleluyah!" (ibid. 150:5-6). The call to "praise Him with *crashing cymbals*" is rendered by the Targum, "praise Him with *cymbals of alarm*": We must praise G-d even in times of alarm and anguish. Ultimately, there is not a moment that is unfit for glorifying G-d. Thus, R. Me'ir expounds the closing verse, "Let *every living breath* (כל הנשמה) praise G-d": "For *each and every breath* (כל נשימה ונשימה) that a person takes, he is obligated to extol his Creator" (*Dev.R.* 2:37).[2]

3. THE ALL-EMBRACING SONG OF PRAISE

In the midst of all the musical instruments listed in our *mizmor*, King David includes "dance": *"Praise Him with timbrel and dance"* (ibid. 150:4). This suggests that we should utilize all our energies in praising G-d. First, the *mizmor* specifies praising G-d with "the sound of the *shofar*" (ibid. 150:3), an act of great skill and know-how,[3] which employs the mouth and lungs. It then speaks of praising G-d with *"harp and lyre ... [and] with timbrel"* (ibid. 150:3-4), instruments played by hand. Finally, it introduces "dance" as a means to praise G-d with the legs and body, as it is said, "And David *was leaping about with all his might* before G-d" (Shemu'el II 6:14).

Ultimately, it is not even man alone who is thus engrossed in praising G-d. The Targum identifies the "pipe (עגב)" (Tehillim 150:4) as the *"abuv,"* which is made not from animal bone but from a mere plant — and not from cedar or any other fine wood at that, but from a simple reed.[4] Likewise, "resounding cymbals" (ibid. 150:5) are cymbals made of copper,[5] an inanimate material. The musical instruments in Mizmor 150 derive, then, from diverse sources: the realms of the animal, the plant, and the inanimate. Every aspect of Creation is swept up in the singing of G-d's praises.

Furthermore, perfection is no prerequisite of this singing. Apropos of the "pipe" and the "resounding cymbals" of our *mizmor*, Chazal comment:

> The pipe in the Temple was smooth and thin and made of a reed, and it was from the days of Mosheh, and its sound was pleasant. [By] the king's command, it was overlaid with gold, and its sound was no longer pleasant. They removed the [gold] overlay, and its sound was as pleasant as it had been.
>
> The cymbal in the Temple was of copper, and it was from the days of Mosheh, and its sound was pleasant, and it became impaired. The sages sent for craftsmen who came from Alexandria of Mitzrayim, and they repaired it, but its sound was no longer pleasant. They undid the repair, and its sound was as pleasant as it had been.
> (*Arachin* 10b)[6]

The simplicity of the pipe and the flaw of the cymbal were integral parts of the unique songs they sang to G-d. By extension, even the flawed personality has the capacity to praise G-d — a praise that may be warmly received and treasured by the Holy One Blessed be He.

4. CONCLUSION

Each of the instruments mentioned in our *mizmor* features some negative connotation: The source of "the *shofar* ... harp and lyre ... timbrel ... [and] flutes" is the ram's carcass; the source of the "pipe" is an unadorned reed; and the "impaired" copper cymbal is a cymbal of "alarm." Indeed, *"for each and every breath"* — at every turn and with all of one's vitality and being — it is fitting to praise G-d, in times of joy as well as in times of sorrow. Every person, animal, plant, and inanimate object can and must sing G-d's praises. Perhaps for this reason King David, the "sweet singer of Yisra'el" (Shemu'el II 23:1), chose to end Sefer Tehillim with this *mizmor*. As humanity's supreme book of praises to G-d draws to a close, this is the message with which it leaves us. Never should we feel that the time is unripe or that we are unworthy to sing the praises of G-d. On the contrary, *"Let every living breath praise G-d. Haleluyah!"*

NOTES

1. The *mishnah*'s reference to "trumpets" from the ram's horns is clearly to the *shofar*. (See com. on the *mishnah*, loc. cit.)
2. See also *BeR.R.* 14:9.
3. See *Rosh HaShanah* 29b.
4. See *Arachin* 10b, quoted in the text, below.
5. *Yal. HaMachiri*, loc. cit., seems to identify the "resounding cymbals" of our *mizmor* with "the cymbal in the Temple," which "was of copper" (see *Tos. Arachin* 2:2 and *Arachin* 10b, quoted in the text, below).
6. See also *Tos. Arachin* 2:2.

HUMAN ACTION IN RAMBAM'S THOUGHT:
Individual Autonomy and Love of G-d

Yehudah Gellman

1. INTRODUCTION

Rambam was a profound philosopher, as well as a brilliant jurist, a metaphysician of historic proportions, and author of *Mishneh Torah*, the most comprehensive of guides to Jewish law and practice. He is one of the greatest religious figures of our tradition, as well as a major philosopher of the Western philosophical tradition.

Rambam's place as a religious giant is secured by his commentary on the Mishnah, by *Mishneh Torah*, by his epistles to various Jewish communities that had written to him seeking his guidance, and by his legendary devotion to the needs of the Jewish people. His place in the history of Western philosophy was earned by his monumental *Moreh HaNevochim* (*Guide of the Perplexed*), which addressed the issue of faith and philosophy within the Aristotelian tradition largely as taught by the Arabic

---

PROF. GELLMAN is a professor of philosophy and the holder of the Norbert Blechner Chair in Jewish Values in the department of philosophy at Ben Gurion University of the Negev and a professor of Jewish thought at Touro College in Yerushalayim. He is the author of numerous scholarly and popular essays on Jewish thought and philosophy.

philosophers. Rambam's treatment of that subject was the most extensive and novel yet offered, and the work has had a profound influence on generations of philosophers. The work continues to be studied in the universities of the world as a classic of medieval philosophy and as a precursor to major intellectual developments.

Inevitably, the question arises as to the relationship between Rambam's religious sensibilities and his philosophical teachings. More specifically, where did Rambam's inner life begin: Was it founded upon a philosophical thesis, which then shaped the contours of his religious sensibilities, so that Rambam's Judaism was determined by his philosophical opinions? Or did Rambam's specifically religious understanding determine the nature of the philosophical enterprise that he was to undertake, constituting a guiding context for the direction and thrust of Maimonidean philosophy?

A certain perception of Rambam, popular amongst philosophers and students of his religious works alike, is that the philosophical and religious parts of his teachings do not cohere satisfactorily. According to this perception, it seems quite difficult to synthesize into one world outlook Rambam's Aristotelian orientation and his total immersion in Halachic Judaism. This has contributed to the popularity of the distinction between the "exoteric" works of Rambam — the commentary on the Mishnah, *Sefer HaMitzvoth, Mishneh Torah,* and his various epistles and responsa — and the "esoteric" *Moreh HaNevochim.* The result has been a general ignoring of Rambam's Halachic works by professional philosophers and, if I may understate myself, the ignoring of *Moreh HaNevochim* by religious devotees of Rambam's other works.

I wish to present the case that Rambam was possessed of a profoundly *religious* conviction concerning the relationship of a person to G-d, and that this religious understanding served as the basis for the philosophical endeavors of his life. If I may so put it, Rambam was the father of "Maimonides" and not the other way around. Furthermore, I wish to argue that Rambam shaped his theoretical, philosophical thinking to have it yield a certain self-perception and attitude to G-d, on the part of the reader, which in turn were a *necessary condition* for the *religious* ideal he portrayed in his "popular" works. In this way, I hope to show that Rambam's philosophical understanding is ideally suited to the religious understanding he wishes to advance in his "nonphilosophical," Halachic works. I hope to illustrate how his philosophical stance was religiously motivated through the consequences of the self-perception that flows naturally out of his philosophy. In this way it will be shown that there was no inner alienation between Rambam and "Maimonides."

2. RAMBAM'S PHILOSOPHICAL SYSTEM

Moreh HaNevochim is the main locus of Rambam's philosophy, but it does not constitute a formal system. Nonetheless, a structure of foundational views and their corollaries can be discerned. In particular, one manner of systematizing the book is to note two foundational assertions.

The first foundational view is that the world and Torah have intelligible, rational structures. In other words, they accord with the Divine Wisdom (*Chochmath HaShem*), rather than with the Divine Will (*Retzon HaShem*) alone — since the Divine Will is subservient to the Divine Wisdom. With regard to the world, Rambam writes:

> Such is the belief of the multitude of the men of knowledge in our Law, and this was explicitly stated by our prophets: namely, that the particulars of natural acts are all well arranged and ordered and bound up with one another, all of them being causes and effects; and that none of them is futile or frivolous or vain, being acts of perfect wisdom.
> (*Moreh* 3:25, p. 505)[1]

Likewise, Rambam writes with regard to the Torah:

> Just as there is disagreement among the men of speculation among the adherents of Law whether His works, may He be exalted, are consequent upon wisdom or upon will alone ... there is also the same disagreement among them regarding our Laws, which He has given us. Thus there are people who do not seek for them any cause at all, saying that all Laws are consequent upon the will alone.... It is, however, the doctrine of all of us — both of the multitude and of the elite — that all the Laws have a cause, though we ignore the causes for some of them and we do not know the manner in which they conform to wisdom.
> (*Moreh* 3:26, pp. 506-507)

This view applies as well to *chukkim*, and not only to *mishpatim*. However, the wisdom implicit in the latter is known to the multitude, while the wisdom of the former is known only to those who have studied deeply.[2]

The second foundational view is that the human cognitive endowment, though limited in scope, is capable of knowing the rational structures of the world and of Torah. This view is found throughout *Moreh HaNevochim*. The following are early examples:

> It was because of this something, I mean because of the divine intellect conjoined with man, that it is said of the latter that he is *in the image of G-d and in His likeness*.
>
> (*Moreh* 1:1)

> For the intellect that G-d made overflow unto man and that is the latter's ultimate perfection was that which Adam had been provided with [sic] before he disobeyed.
>
> (*Moreh* 1:2)

While the sin of Adam precipitated a fundamental transformation in human nature on various levels — including the extent to which the human intellect can express itself — the intellect per se was not essentially impaired by this sin.[3]

These two assertions provide the foundation for many of the views found in *Moreh HaNevochim* and elsewhere. Thus, since reality is viewed as a stable, rational order, a "naturalizing" of various phenomena (that would otherwise be understood in terms of divine intervention in the natural order) is dictated. There is, for example, a reluctance to interpret miracles as being in violation of a fixed natural order:

> [The Sages] say that when G-d created that which exists and stamped upon it the existing natures, He put it into these natures that all the miracles that occurred would be produced in them at the time when they occurred.... If this statement is as you will see it, it indicates the superiority of the man who made it and the fact that he found it extremely difficult to admit that a nature may change after the Work of the Beginning or that another nature may supervene after that nature has been established in a definite way.
>
> (*Moreh* 2:29)

Other naturalizing examples are that prophecy is something to be achieved by training, rather than conferred on the prophet in an interventionist way from on high;[4] and that divine providence is viewed as essentially a human achievement, not entailing divine intervention. The perfection of a person's intellect activates the "divine overflow" to connect up with the individual intellect, thereby "of necessity" affording a greater degree of divine providence.[5] Further, this foundational doctrine makes possible a tendency to naturalize reward and punishment, including the world to come.[6] It also entails that no divine pronouncement can be inconsistent with the rational order of reality.[7]

In addition, that the Divine Wisdom is the basis of Torah makes possible the preference of a teleology immanent in the commandments themselves over a deontological approach to the laws. That is to say, it allows an interpretation of the commandments in terms of their good consequences in a practical sense rather than solely in terms of the ultimate obligation to obey G-d.[8] Thus, Rambam writes:

> The Law as a whole aims at two things: the welfare of the soul and the welfare of the body. As for the welfare of the soul, it consists in the multitude's acquiring correct opinions corresponding to their respective capacity.... As for the welfare of the body, it comes about by the improvement of their ways of living one with another. This is achieved through two things. One of them is the abolition of their wronging each other.... The second thing consists in the acquisition by every human individual of moral qualities that are useful for life in society so that the affairs of the city may be ordered.
>
> (*Moreh* 3:27)

This perspective determines Rambam's approach to the reasons for the Torah laws, with a surprising number of the latter explained as intended to produce a well-ordered society.

The validity of human cognition is the basis for the obligation to demonstrate "by the methods of speculation ... the rational matter that we receive from the Law through tradition" (*Moreh* 3:54). "The opinions in question," says Rambam, "should first be known as being received through tradition; then they should be demonstrated ..." (ibid.). Therefore, when a person comes to his final judgment, whereas he is first asked whether he set times to acquire Torah knowledge (the tradition), he is also asked whether he engaged in *chochmah* (speculation).[9]

This trust in human reason is also the basis of Rambam's view of Biblical interpretation: What can be proved to the human intellect is evidence of a correct understanding of the Biblical text.[10] Hence, Rambam intimates that, if the Platonic theory that Creation proceeded from pre-existent, undifferentiated matter could be demonstrated, it would be incumbent upon us to interpret the Torah's Creation account accordingly.[10] Finally, this second foundational view helps shape Rambam's doctrine of the oral teachings in Judaism. For according to that doctrine, only a narrow base of oral law was revealed to Mosheh at Sinai. The rest of the oral teaching is an accretion onto that base, of human origin, and issuing out of autonomous human judgments.[11]

3. THE SELF-PERCEPTION THAT FOLLOWS FROM RAMBAM'S PHILOSOPHICAL VIEWPOINT

There exists a profound difference in human self-perception between Rambam's naturalistic-tending metaphysic and optimistic epistemology, on the one hand, and a philosophy that posits a divine order that may pre-empt the natural order as a matter of course and an immanent G-d-man relationship that transcends a severely limited human reason, on the other hand.[12] As will be demonstrated in this section, Rambam's philosophy calls for a deep sense of human responsibility in the presence of G-d. A person must constantly recognize the infinite sustaining power of G-d as the basis of his very existence and of the stable environment in which he lives and acts. At the same time, in a world essentially enclosed within its natural boundaries, the manner in which the person is to succeed within that stable order is up to him. No divinely initiated, interventionist salvation is to be expected. On the contrary, we are to assume that our actions always have their natural consequences and that our hopes and wishes will only become true if consistent with the world as we know it. G-d will not change the natural order so as to conform to our needs, although He has granted us in His infinite wisdom the cognitive ability to initiate courses of action competently and out of our own choice. Even then, there is no guarantee of success, but the congruence of our rational faculties to the created order makes sense of our choices and plans. This self-perception contrasts strongly with the sense of passively waiting for G-d characteristic of a metaphysic of supernatural intervention by G-d and supersedure of human reason by nonrational experience.

It is precisely this perception of self-initiated responsibility that Rambam teaches in his Halachic works. Hence the philosophical assumptions of *Moreh HaNevochim* issue into the conception of man in his other works as well.[13]

The focus of Rambam's exposition of human responsibility can be found in the latter half of *"Hilchoth Teshuvah"* ("Laws of Repentance"), in *Mishneh Torah*. There, Rambam presents a thoroughgoing, libertarian approach to human freedom, together with an explicit rejection of divine interference with human choice.

Chapter 5 opens with the endorsement of full human freedom:

> Every person has free will: If he wishes to turn himself in a good direction and be saintly, he is free to do so. And if he wishes to turn himself to an evil path and be wicked, he is free to do so.
> (Hil. Teshuvah 5:1)

That chapter continues by informing us that every person can choose to be as good as Mosheh or as wicked as Yarovam (ibid. 5:2) and that there is no inclining influence whatever on the direction a person chooses (ibid.). The chapter closes by defending absolute freedom in the face of G-d's decrees and prescience (ibid. 5:4-5).

Chapter 6 goes on to interpret *prima facie* divine intervention in Paroh's freedom in the Biblical story of the Exodus as his own self-defeat. Paroh himself chose to be so wicked that he could not repent and change his ways. Chapter 7 stresses that human freedom makes possible *teshuvah*, the turning of oneself in the direction of G-d. Chapters 8 and 9 contain a naturalizing tendency in the concepts of the world to come and reward and punishment. The naturalizing of these concepts, making them extensions of the natural order, deflects an interventionist understanding of divine action and places the responsibility for action entirely on the person.

The paradigmatic self-perception for this entire section of *"Hilchoth Teshuvah"* is that of King David.[14] David's request that

G-d show him the way (Tehillim 86:11) is presented by Rambam as actually expressing the hope that David's sins will not prevent him from *teshuvah*, as did Paroh's sins:

> This is what is meant by the requests of the righteous and the prophets in their prayers to G-d to help them with regard to truth. As David said, "Show me Your way" (Tehillim 86:11), meaning: Do not let my sins prevent me from the way of truth, from which I will know Your way and the unity of Your Name." Likewise, his plea, "And uphold me with a willing spirit" (ibid. 51:14), means: Leave my spirit to do Your will, and let not my sins prevent me from repenting. Instead, may the choice be in my hands so that I may return, understand, and know the way of truth. And in this way all similar verses [are to be understood].
>
> *(Hil. Teshuvah 6:4)*

What might have appeared to be a plea by David for G-d to interfere within his soul — to make for him the decisions that he feels too weak to make himself — becomes in Rambam's hands a plea essentially to be left alone so that he, David, will be able to find the strength and the way to repent of his sinful acts. He pleads only that his past sins not be allowed to prevent his own initiation of turning in the direction of G-d. There is no request for an active divine influence on the decisions themselves. They are to be entirely up to King David himself. Finally, Rambam concludes that "in this way all similar verses [are to be understood]" — securing paradigmatic status for his interpretation of David's prayers.

David wishes to be entirely free of G-d's intervention or inclining influence, to be self-reliant and self-initiating. In what sense, then, does G-d help one who wishes to turn to Him? Rambam continues:

> What, then, is [meant by] David saying, "G-d is Good and Upright; therefore He instructs sinners on the way. He guides the humble," etc. (Tehillim 25:8-9)? This [means] that He sent prophets to them declaring the ways of G-d and bringing them to repentance. And furthermore, He granted them the capacity to learn and to understand.... This is [meant by] what the Rabbis said, "One who comes to be purified is aided" (*Yoma* 38b), meaning: He will find himself aided in the matter.
>
> *(Hil. Teshuvah 6:5)*

Divine aid, then, is not interventionalist, but consists of providing and sustaining the stable background of which a person can choose to take advantage through the intellect G-d has given him. The "aid" King David receives pertains to the rational structure that was available to him all along. King David wishes to be allowed to operate freely within this background structure.

In fine, a clear view of the self-understanding of a person according to Rambam emerges from chapters 5-9 of "*Hilchoth Teshuvah*": an understanding of oneself as free and responsible for one's fate, in a world where G-d's intervention is minimized.

4. MEDICINE AND MAGIC IN LIGHT OF RAMBAM'S VIEW OF HUMAN FREEDOM AND RESPONSIBILITY

In his works in general, Rambam is concerned with promoting such a deep sense of human responsibility in his readers. I want to illustrate how this concern insinuates itself into his writings via an examination of his treatment of two practices, standing in opposing relationships to human responsibility: medicine and magic.

Medicine (*refu'ah*), broadly construed as both curative and preventative health care, plays an important religious role for Rambam. Unless a person is healthy, he will not be free to pursue knowledge of G-d, for "it is impossible to understand or contemplate wisdom when one is hungry and ill or ... in pain" (*Hil. De'oth* 3:3).[15] The pursuit of health, therefore, belongs to the "ways of G-d" (ibid.) and is a condition of true happiness.

In *Moreh HaNevochim*, Rambam posits two aims of the Torah: "perfection of the soul and ... perfection of the body" (*Moreh* 3:27). The latter is not "ultimate perfection" but subservient to the former: "For the first aim can only be achieved after achieving the second one" (ibid.).[16] For this reason, the Torah provides laws pertaining to bodily health. There is, however, an important difference between the Torah's legislation and medicine proper: The Torah treats the *generality*, not providing for the unique circumstances of individuals. But medical treatment "is particularized for every individual in conformity with his present temperament" (*Moreh* 3:34, p. 534). The Torah is "absolute and universal" (ibid., p. 535). Medicine, though, pertains to individual judgments.[17] So it is clear from his writings — including *Moreh HaNevochim* — that Rambam regarded medicine as lying on a continuum with divine legislation aimed at bodily perfection and thus essential to spiritual life.[18]

There is a second, related aspect of Rambam's attitude to medicine, revealed in his commentary on the Mishnah. The Tosefta[19] enumerates certain controversial actions undertaken by King Chizkiyyahu to which the sages consented, including hiding the so-called *Sefer Refu'oth* (*Book of Remedies*). Rambam explains *Sefer Refu'oth* to have been a book of forbidden, talismanic healings, or a book detailing harmful drugs and their antidotes, which was falling into abuse (com. on *Mish. Pesachim* 4:9). He then adds a strong polemic against an opposing interpretation of the nature of *Sefer Refu'oth* and why it was banned:

> I have heard the explanation that Shelomoh wrote a book of remedies such that, should a person fall ill, he would refer to it, follow its instructions, and be cured. And when Chizkiyyahu saw that people were not trusting in G-d in their sickness [but trusting in the book of remedies], he withdrew it and hid it. Besides the emptiness of this idea and its fancifulness, they have ascribed to Chizkiyyahu and his comrades stupidity that is not even to be ascribed to the lowest of the masses.... According to their defective and foolish imagination, if a person is hungry and eats bread, thereby most certainly being cured of the great ailment of hunger, shall we say that he withdrew his trust in G-d? We say to them: O fools! Just as I thank G-d when eating for providing me with something to remove my hunger and revive me and give me life, so I shall thank Him for providing a cure that cures my illness when I use it. I would not have troubled to contest this inferior interpretation were it not for its popularity.[20]
>
> (com., loc. cit.)[21]

The rejected interpretation would welcome the banning of a cure-all book, because its existence would lessen man's sense of dependence on G-d. This interpretation distrusts the sense of independence and self-reliance that it fears would follow from the curing of all illnesses. Rambam, however, favors the sense of independence that would follow the possession of a cure-all book, which would give rise to a sense of gratitude to G-d for making possible the curing of illness. He rejects the sense of helplessness that he fears would be engendered by the other interpretation.

The example of the eating of bread is especially instructive here, for we — not G-d — make bread. G-d provides the opportunity for us to till, plant, harvest, mill, and bake bread. The gratitude to G-d for the bread is in reality gratitude for the order of nature in which we live, in which, when we choose to make bread, our choice often meets with success.

Interestingly, for Rambam a "book of remedies" of sorts actually exists. In *Mishneh Torah*, Rambam includes a lengthy chapter of *"Hilchoth De'oth"* ("Laws of Character Traits") on proper diet, care of the body, and sexual moderation, which concludes with the following words:

> I guarantee that anyone who accustoms himself in these ways that we have instructed will never fall ill until he grows very old and dies, and he won't need a doctor, and his body will be whole and healthy all his days — unless his body was of a defective constitution from the start, or he had bad habits from early in life, or there was a plague or famine.
>
> (*Hil. De'oth* 4:20)

Thus, Rambam considers himself to have disclosed in this chapter a physical regimen that could possibly free a person from illness for life. One would then never need to ask G-d to heal him, but indeed one would have many an opportunity to thank G-d for the intellectual ability conferred upon him to keep himself healthy. Given the stable order of nature, whether a person is healthy or not (barring plague or famine or the like) is up to him.

The ideal, then, for Rambam, is the person who keeps *himself* healthy by a proper way of living and, if that fails, by curing himself with medical knowledge. Rambam is concerned with teaching a self-perception based on human responsibility and to combat a self-perception of weakness before G-d. Medicine takes its place as an instrument of self-responsibility within a naturalistic metaphysics.

In polar opposition to medicine is magic, including practices as diverse as necromancy, divination, the readings of omens, and magical healings. In *Mishneh Torah*, Rambam takes a consistent stand against such practices, even branding as forbidden Eli'ezer's sign (BeReshith 24:12-14) for determining which maiden he should choose for Yitzchak (*Hil. Avodath Kochavim* 11:4).²² But even for Rambam there is an exception:

> If one says, "This house that I built was a good sign for me," or, "This woman whom I married" or, "This animal that I bought was blessed — from the time I bought it I became rich": ... All of these and similar statements are permitted, since he did not [use one of these as an omen to] decide on a course of action or [to] refrain from acting, but merely made this as a sign for himself for a matter that had passed. [Consequently] this is permissible.
>
> (*Hil. Avodath Kochavim* 11:5)

There is a distinction, then, between the prospective and retrospective use of omens.

The formal rationale against permitting magical practices is their historical association with idol worship.²³ And this is the formal reason for including the ban on them in the section of *Mishneh Torah* entitled "*Hilchoth Avodath Kochavim VeChukkotheihem*" ("Laws of Idol Worship and Rites of Idolaters"). However, in *Moreh HaNevochim* (3:37), Rambam quotes the Talmudic dictum that "all that pertains to medicine does not pertain to Emori ways [i.e., prohibitions associated with idol worship]" (*Shabbath* 67a). Rambam comments: "They mean by this that all that is required by speculation concerning nature is permitted" (*Moreh*, loc. cit.). In addition, "It is allowed to use all remedies similar to those that experience has shown to be valid even if reasoning does not require them. For they pertain to medicine, and their efficacy may be ranged together with ... medicines" (ibid.). Thus, at the end of his discussion of magic and similar forbidden practices in *Mishneh Torah*, Rambam emphasizes:

> All of these things are false and shams, and ancient idolaters misled peoples with them to follow their ways. And it is inappropriate for [the people of] Yisra'el, who are especially wise, to be drawn after this nothingness or to consider that they are effective.... Anyone who believes in these or similar matters and thinks to himself that they are true and wise matters, but that the Torah forbade them, is foolish and ignorant.
>
> (*Hil. Avodath Kochavim* 11:16)²⁴

A condition, therefore, of the prohibition upon practices rooted in magic is that — unlike medicine — they do not conform to reason or experience. They must be irrational to be prohibited. However, their being irrational is not yet sufficient. One must also *act* on their advice. Thus, as we have seen, retrospective reading of omens is not prohibited.

One who believes that the Torah would ban a practice rooted in rational inquiry or validated by actual experience has a mistaken perception of his relationship to G-d, contends Rambam, as does one who believes that a legitimate book of remedies would be banned. Such a person believes that the Torah would encourage a sense of dependence upon G-d by depriving man of a means to determine the future and prepare for it. On the contrary, Rambam insists that practices based on reason or experience are not prohibited. The Torah prefers reason to uncertainty and dependence, in the sense discussed here.

Why, then, are false magical practices prohibited? We have already noted a formal reason, together with the condition of irrationality. However, these would not account for Rambam's distinction between the prospective and retrospective use of omens. To account for that distinction we must conclude that — for Rambam — magic, signs, and omens represent an attempt to abrogate human responsibility for one's fate, by bypassing the system of rational inquiry as the basis for one's choice of actions. They are an attempt to cajole hidden powers to divulge their secrets to man, beyond what man himself is capable of knowing. One who uses them rejects the risk of choice in favor of the safety of a facade of sure "knowledge." Magic reaches for a certainty about the future by turning to powers that man seeks but never finds.

This, I propose, is the reason why citing signs in retrospect is not forbidden. A retrospective citing of signs does not influence our course of action for the future, and hence it does not constitute an abrogation of human responsibility. It may be foolish, after all, but it does not attempt to replace human efforts with paranormal certainty. On the other hand, if such omens *could* provide true information about the future, they would not be forbidden. The law does not wish to impose limitations upon us that would create uncertainty about the future if we could determine the future by our own efforts. The law would prefer certainty about the future — and concomitant self-reliance — over uncertainty imposed by limiting the exercise of our reason.

Yet, Rambam realizes, there are those who might believe that these practices *are* rooted in wisdom but nevertheless are forbidden. Such people mistakenly believe that the law would prefer insecurity over even a knowable future to the self-reliance made possible by striving to know that future and thereby preparing for it responsibly and in confidence. Rambam feels compelled to expose such an opinion and reject it in favor of human responsibility. Just as medicine is lauded as the means through which we take responsibility over the preservation of our health and the sustainment of our lives, magic is deplored as an irrational attempt to seek an external certainty about life at the expense of personal responsibility. Medicine and magic are therefore polar opposites in Rambam's perception of human responsibility.

5. THE RELIGIOUS CONVICTION THAT MOTIVATES RAMBAM'S PHILOSOPHY

We have seen how Rambam's theoretical philosophy fosters a sense of radical human responsibility. In turn, as Rambam explains, this sense of radical responsibility liberates the individual to pursue the love of G-d. In *Mishneh Torah*, Rambam defines the "love of G-d," contrasting it with the "fear of G-d" as follows:

> One should not say, "I shall do the commandments of the Torah and engage in its wisdom so that I shall receive all the blessings written in it...." It is inappropriate to serve G-d in this manner, for one who serves [G-d] in this manner serves out of fear.... One who serves [G-d] out of love engages in Torah [study] and the commandments and goes in the paths of wisdom not for any worldly gain and not for fear of evil consequences and not in order to inherit the good — but does the truth because it is the truth.
>
> (*Hil. Teshuvah* 10:1-2)

While serving out of fear of G-d is drawn by hope of benefits or fear of punishment, serving out of love of G-d is disinterested worship, for no personal gain whatsoever.

Nevertheless, according to Rambam, fear of G-d and love of G-d are linked as stages in an educational progression. We all begin in the mode of fear, and must be reoriented into the mode of love:

> [Initially, people must be taught] to serve out of fear and in order to receive reward, until their intellect matures and they gain more wisdom. Then this secret [i.e., love of G-d] is revealed to them bit by bit, and they are gradually made accustomed to this matter, until they conceive and know it and then serve out of love.
>
> (Hil. Teshuvah 10:5)

Hence, Rambam recognizes that there must be an educational program that relates to people in their natural fear mode, and trains them to relate to G-d from the perspective of love. This training is gradual, shifting one's orientation bit by bit from fear toward love. Rambam's own writings constitute such an educational enterprise, in which the reader is redirected from serving out of *"fear"* — understood here by Rambam as self-interested worship — toward serving out of *"love"* — understood by Rambam as disinterested service of G-d purely out of recognition of His perfection.[25]

In general, the education of the reader in the direction of love of G-d assumes two simultaneous tracks. The first introduces the reader to philosophy, including the study of nature, physics, and metaphysics. These studies reveal the Divine Wisdom and engender a theoretical concept of G-d. Optimally, seeing G-d's wisdom precipitates the formation of a concept of G-d rooted in perfection — a concept carried to completion by the metaphysical concept of an incorporeal Being. The G-d of perfection makes possible disinterested worship, grounded in an appreciation of His perfection: the mode of love. This replaces a coarse concept of G-d, grounded in self-interest: the mode of fear.

In Rambam's *Mishneh Torah*, this first educational track — the confrontation with philosophy, broadly construed — has its explicit focus in *"Hilchoth Yesodei HaTorah"* ("Laws of the Foundations of Torah"). Chapter 1 presents a philosophical concept of G-d, and chapters 2-4 present an outline of physics and metaphysics. The following several chapters appear as an elaboration of the knowledge that leads to love of G-d. In chapter 2, Rambam states:

> What is the way to the love and fear [of G-d]? When a person

contemplates His wondrous and vast deeds and creations and sees therein His infinite wisdom, he immediately loves and glorifies and adores [Him], and has a great desire to know the Great Name.... And when he considers these matters themselves, immediately he recoils in fear and knows that he is a small, lowly, dim creature standing with trivial, minimal knowledge before Him Whose knowledge is perfect.... In accordance with these matters, I am explaining major principles in the deeds of the Master of the universe that they may be a preface, for one who understands, to love G-d.

(*Hil. Yesodei HaTorah* 2:2)

Indeed, following this introduction, Rambam proceeds to present his outline of physics and metaphysics: his "preface ... to love G-d." *Mishneh Torah* is a legal work, intended for a general audience not necessarily familiar with philosophy. It is for this audience that Rambam writes, attempting to turn it — via the exposure to philosophy — in the direction of love of G-d, motivated by a concept of divine perfection.

This first track re-educates concerning *G-d*, the *object*-term in the person-G-d relationship. But it alone, while necessary, is not sufficient to produce love of G-d as a possible path. More is needed. There must also be a change in the perception of the *subject*-term in the person-G-d relationship: a change in the perception of *self*. The insufficiency of philosophy is due to the fact that it cannot overcome the sense of standing in need of G-d, which causes one to serve Him out of self-interest. One must redefine one's sense of selfhood so that one sees oneself as a self-initiating responsible being who worships G-d only "because it is the truth" (*Hil. Teshuvah* 10:2). In order for a person's philosophical knowledge to have a practical impact on his life, he must be imbued with a sense of his innate cognitive ability and his competence as an agent. He will then depend upon G-d for every moment of his existence and for the stable world in which he finds himself living and acting, but he will not wait for G-d to determine his fate. His fate will depend on how he acts. Either way he chooses, G-d will maintain the natural order in which the choice plays out its course. To the degree that a person feels helpless or defective, he will feel himself incapable of extricating himself from his predicament. He will be in danger of turning to G-d to save him, feeling that without G-d's saving intervention on his behalf, all will be lost.

Thus, the self-perception of weakness or of relative helplessness naturally inclines to the fear mode of service of G-d. That is why Rambam in his writings wants to foster in the reader a deep sense of human responsibility. The reader is made to feel that what becomes of him is basically in his own hands, given G-d's sustaining basis of being. The reader is made to feel that he is a self-initiating self-chooser, not dependent on G-d in a way that implies his own inadequacy as an agent or as a cognitive being. Armed with a sense of self-responsibility, the reader is freed from the motive of seeking self-aid, in order to pursue the goal of love of G-d: a relationship based on disinterested worship. This explains the importance of the sections in *"Hilchoth Teshuvah"* in which Rambam portrays human freedom and responsibility, and explains why those sections are followed by the chapter on love of G-d.

6. CONCLUSION:
LOVE OF G-D AND HUMAN RESPONSIBILITY

This new self-understanding, engendered by the earlier chapters of *"Hilchoth Teshuvah,"* makes possible a turn toward the true service of G-d out of love. Thus, *"Hilchoth Teshuvah"* ends by returning us to the themes of *"Hilchoth Yesodei HaTorah"* and the study of philosophy, meeting up with the first track of Rambam's educational program:

> In accordance with knowledge is love, whether it be a little or a lot. Therefore, a person must commit himself to understand and comprehend science and philosophy,[26] which make known to him his Creator, to the extent that a person is capable of understanding and comprehending, as we have explained in *"Hilchoth Yesodei HaTorah."*
>
> (*Hil. Teshuvah* 10:6)

The two tracks work cooperatively. A deep sense of freedom and of competence in cognition and action makes possible a relationship with G-d not grounded in one's own needs for oneself. The study of science and philosophy opens the reader to a new understanding of G-d, based on wisdom and perfection. In self-responsibility, a person can develop love of G-d with no motivation other than "because it is the truth," allowing the new G-d concept to transform his very life.

We have seen how the philosophical teachings in *Moreh HaNevochim* form the basis for a philosophy of human responsibility. And now we appreciate how the motif of Aristotelian thought serves as the philosophical rationale for Rambam's previously established religious insight into the human condition. The individual's self-transition to a thoroughgoing sense of human responsibility sets him free from the fetters of action-dependence to pursue true love of G-d. Thus, the goal of teaching the love of G-d may be seen as the foundation of all foundations in Rambam's thought, the bedrock upon which his choice of philosophical orientation is grounded.

NOTES

1. All quotations from *Moreh HaNevochim* and page references are based on the translation of Shlomo Pines (Chicago: Univ. of Chicago Press, 1963).
2. See *Moreh* 3:26.
3. See *Moreh* 1:1-2.
   Ed. note: For an additional discussion of the sin of eating the fruit of the "tree of knowing good and evil" and the consequent transformation in human nature, see also " 'You Will Be Like G-d': Chazal's Conception of the *Yetzer HaRa*," also appearing in this issue of *Jewish Thought*.
4. See *Moreh* 2:36-48.
5. See *Moreh* 3:17-18.
6. See *Yad Hil. Teshuvah* 8.
7. See *Moreh* 2:25 and elsewhere. In addition, we should note that Rambam's view that the Divine Wisdom is the ontological grounds of reality is the basis for the Maimonidean view of the stability of reality and of the possible and impossible (see *Moreh* 3:15). These are fixed in accordance with the Divine Wisdom.
8. See *Moreh* 3:27 and on.
9. See *Moreh* 3:54, commenting on the Talmud's description of man's final judgment (see *Shabbath* 31a).
10. See *Moreh* 2:25.
11. See Rambam's *Introduction to the Mishnah*, chs. 1-4. See also *Yad Hil. Mamrim* 1-2.

12. Other classic approaches to Jewish thought, particularly those influenced by the Kabbalah, are predicated on just such assumptions as a divine order that ideally (when man is worthy) pre-empts the natural order and an immanent G-d-man relationship that transcends the bounds of human reason. Indeed, these assumptions may well be regarded as foundational views in many of the great classics of Jewish thought, which are at variance with Rambam's approach, most notably *Sefer HaKozari* (which predated Rambam). See, for example, *HaKozari* 1:63-67, 79, 87, 99, 109, and elsewhere throughout the book. In later works, in which the influence of Kabbalistic ideas is more keenly sensed, these ideas are often even more emphatically developed. See, for example, *Derech HaShem* 1:2, 5, 2:1-3, 5, 8, 3:1-4, and elsewhere throughout the book.

13. There are those who view the naturalizing approach of Rambam as expressive of his preference of universalism over particularism. (In particular, see David Hartman, *Maimonides, Torah, and Philosophic Quest* [Philadelphia: Jewish Publication Society, 1976].) A naturalized conception of miracles, for example, would then allow an understanding based on universal reason; interventionism fosters Jewish particularism. It is, however, my contention that this explanation is insufficient.

    I am suggesting that careful scrutiny of Rambam's writings indicates that the issue of concern is radical responsibility versus dependence. The denial of magic in favor of reason, discussed below, cannot be explained by the universalist/particularist dichotomy. Neither can Rambam's distinction between permissible retrospective and forbidden prospective magical practices be so explained. But both of these can be explained by the responsibility/dependence dichotomy that I propose. The latter is thus more comprehensive. See Hartman, ch. 4, and my discussion of magic, below.

14. *Ed. note:* Significantly, Chazal note King David's paradigmatic role in *teshuvah* as he "who established the yoke of *teshuvah*" (*Mo'ed Katan* 16b, *Avodah Zarah* 5a).

15. See also *Yad Hil. De'oth* 4:1 and *Shemonah Perakim*, ch. 5. In addition, see my essays "Maimonides' 'Ravings'," *Review of Metaphysics*, 45 (Winter 1991), pp. 309-28; and "Maimonides and the Cure-All Book," in *Maimonides on Science and Medicine*, ed. Samuel Kotteck (forthcoming).

    All the more striking in light of this is Rambam's ruling on Torah study: "Every Jewish man must study Torah whether he be poor or rich or whole of body or suffering from pain..." (*Yad Hil. Talmud Torah* 1:8). However, R. Joseph B. Soleveitchik (in his public *yahrtzeit* lectures in memory of his wife, Tonya Soloveitchik [delivered in 5728], and his father, R. Moshe Soloveitchik [delivered in 5730]) explained this law as pertaining not to the acquisition of Torah knowledge but to the obligation to set fixed times for Torah study, such obligation directed toward the existential experience of studying the word of G-d, whether wisdom is acquired or not. It may further be added that the study to which Rambam refers in *"Hilchoth Talmud Torah"* pertains to the study of the *tradition*, whereas in *"Hilchoth De'oth"* the reference is to *speculative knowledge* gained individually. See this distinction in *Moreh HaNevochim* 3:54, discussed in the text and in n. 9, above.

Ed. note: See also R. Yosef Dov HaLevi [Soloveitchik], *Shi'urim LeZecher Abba Mari z.l.*, II (Yerushalayim: Akiva Yosef, 1985), 12-16.

16. *Ed. note:* See also *Shemonah Perakim*, ch. 5, and *Yad Hil. De'oth* 3:3.

17. See *Yad Hil. De'oth* 4:21, where Rambam refers to the variegated treatments of medicine, dependent on whether the treatment is preventative or curative.

18. It is interesting to note an apparent inconsistency in Rambam's views on health as presented here (and in *Shemonah Perakim*, ch. 5) and as presented elsewhere in *Moreh HaNevochim*. Specifically, in considering the four types of perfection that Rambam lists in the final chapter of *Moreh HaNevochim* (3:54), one notes that his second level of perfection pertains to "bodily constitution and shape ... that individual's temperament being most harmonious, his limbs well proportioned and strong as they ought to be" (ibid.). Rambam asserts that "utility for the soul is absent from this species of perfection" (ibid.). The argument has been advanced that this assertion contradicts Rambam's position on health as presented here and elsewhere in *Moreh HaNevochim* and his other works. (See Alexander Altmann, "Maimonides' 'Four Perfections,' " in *Essays in Jewish Intellectual History*, by Alexander Altmann [Hanover: Brandeis Univ. Press, 1987], p. 68.) It is important to see that this is *not* a correct interpretation.

This "second perfection" pertains not merely to health, as proponents of this assertion erroneously contend, but primarily to human strength at its maximum. So Rambam adds in his description of this perfection, "Even if the strength of a human individual reached its greatest maximum, it would not attain the strength of a strong mule, and still less the strength of a lion or an elephant" (ibid.). Notice that only the *strength* of a lion exceeds that of a human, while the *health* of a lion need not exceed that of a person. Also, Rambam says that the pinnacle of this second perfection lies in "transporting a heavy burden or breaking a thick bone," both of which rest on a continuum of strength, not necessarily of health. And so, Rambam can perfectly well assert that from this perfection of great strength, as opposed to mere health, no great utility for the body can be derived. How much more so may it be said that no great utility can be derived from it for the soul! As we have seen, however, Rambam's view of the importance of physical *health* is — consistently — very different. So we see that Rambam's views in the final chapter of *Moreh HaNevochim* are perfectly consistent with the view we have attributed to him here.

19. *Ed. note:* In his commentary, Rambam states, "This *halachah* is a *tosefta* [and not a *mishnah*]" (com. on *Mish. Pesachim* 4:9). (See also *Tosefoth Yom Tov* and *Shinnuyei Nuscha'oth*, loc. cit.) Indeed, while this *tosefta* appears in the standard Vilna Mishnah as *Mish. Pesachim* 4:9, it does not appear in the

Mishnah as quoted in either the Talmud Bavli or the Talmud Yerushalmi. In the Talmud Bavli (*Berachoth* 10b, *Pesachim* 56a), it is introduced with the words *"tanu rabbanan"* ("the Rabbis taught"), indicating an extra-Mishnaic statement of the Tanna'im (Mishnaic sages), quoted from the Tosefta or Baraitha. (See also *Yer. Pesachim* 9:1 [55a].) A similar statement (that includes the reference to hiding *Sefer Refu'oth*) appears in the Tannaic work *Avoth DeR. Nathan* (2:4).

20. *Ed. note:* The interpretation that Rambam rejects so vehemently is presented by Rashi (com. on *Berachoth* 10b, ד"ה שגנז ספר רפואות, and on *Pesachim* 56a, ד"ה וגנז ספר רפואות). See also commentaries on *Mish. Pesachim* 4:9. Ramban presents the philosophical and Talmudic bases for this interpretation in detail (com. on VaYikra 26:11). For alternative explanations of the views of Rashi, Rambam, and Ramban regarding these issues, see *Michtav MeEliyyahu*, III, 170-74, and see R. Yehudah Copperman, "*Iyyun BeFerush HaRamban al HaTorah*," *HaMa'ayan*, 22, No. 2 (5742), 1-16.

21. English translations of Rambam's commentary on the Mishnah are based on the Hebrew translation (from Arabic) of R. Yosef Kappach, *Mishnah im Perush Rabbeinu Mosheh ben Maimon* (Yerushalayim: Mossad Harav Kook, 5719).

22. *Ed. note:* Rambam's ruling here (like virtually all his rulings in *Mishneh Torah*) is derived from Chazal: "Rav said: Any [proposed] divination that is not like [the divination of] Eli'ezer, slave of Avraham ... is not [true] divination" (*Chullin* 95b). However, the Halachic implications of this Talmudic statement are disputed, and Rambam clearly favors a broad interpretation, ruling that such divination is punishable by *malkuth* (flogging). See *Hassagoth HaRa'avad* on *Yad Hil. Avodath Kochavim*, loc. cit., where Ra'avad differs sharply with Rambam, and see com. on Rambam, loc. cit. See also *Tosefoth* on *Chullin* 95b, ד"ה כאליעזר עבד אברהם (and Maharsha, loc. cit.); *Chiddushei HaRan*, loc. cit., ד"ה והאמר רב כל נחש וכו'; and *Chiddushei HaRitva*, loc. cit., ד"ה ויהונתן בן שאול. In addition, see Radak on Shemu'el I 14:9; *Beith HaBechirah* (Me'iri) on *Sanhedrin* 68a, ד"ה יש מקצת דברים בחקות הגוים; *Tur Yoreh De'ah* 179 and *Beith Yosef, Bayith Chadash,* and *Perishah,* loc. cit.; and *Bei'ur HaGra, Yoreh De'ah* 179:11.

23. See *Moreh* 3:37.

24. *Ed. note:* Nonetheless, within the spectrum of legitimate approaches to Jewish thought, other authorities contend this very approach that Rambam negates. In particular, the Vilna Ga'on rejects Rambam's approach with equivalent force:

> All who followed after him disagreed with him, inasmuch as many incantations are mentioned in the Gemara. But [Rambam] was drawn after [Aristotelian] philosophy, and he therefore wrote that witchcraft, [use of] divine names, incantations, demons, and amulets are all lies. But [later scholars] already beat him on his head, inasmuch as we find

> many stories in the Gemara involving divine names and witchcraft.... And the Torah testified: "[The staffs of Paroh's magicians] became vipers" (Shemoth 7:12). See *Zohar*, loc. cit. Likewise we find numerous amulets [mentioned in the Talmud] and countless incantations. But [Aristotelian] philosophy inclined him with its reasoning to interpret the Gemara all figuratively and to wrench it from its simple meaning. And — G-d forbid! — I don't believe any of it; all these statements are [to be understood] according to their simple meaning. They do nevertheless have a deeper, internal meaning: not the internal meaning of the philosophers, which is superficial, but that of the masters of [Kabbalistic] truth.
>
> (*Bei'ur HaGra, Yoreh De'ah* 179:13)

While the vehemence of the onslaught on Rambam has led some scholars to question attributing the actual wording to the Vilna Ga'on, this passage indeed conveys the sentiments of students of the Kabbalah. See also, for example, *Derech HaShem* 3:2.

Presumably, Rambam would contend that Talmudic allusions to witchcraft were made in deference to popular fears and not because Chazal actually subscribed to them.

25. *Ed. note:* Rambam's use of the term *"fear"* in this context is complex and obviously should not be taken to imply that he intends to minimize the ultimate teleological significance of the commandment to *fear* G-d (Devarim 6:13, 24, 8:6, 10:12, 20, 13:5). In Rambam's *Sefer HaMitzvoth*, the commandment to fear G-d is listed as fourth of the 613 commandments of the Torah (*Aseh* 4), following only the commandments to believe in G-d's existence, to believe in G-d's oneness, and to love G-d. Furthermore, the commandment to fear G-d is one of the ten commandments of the Torah discussed in "Hilchoth Yesodei HaTorah," the first section of Rambam's *Mishneh Torah*. In chapter 2, fear of G-d appears in a definitely positive sense, paralleling love of G-d:

> We are commanded to love *and fear* this honored and awesome L-rd, as it is said, "Love G-d your L-rd" (Devarim 6:5). And it is said, "G-d your L-rd *you shall fear*" (ibid. 6:13). And what is the way to the love and fear [of G-d]? When a person contemplates His wondrous and vast deeds and creations and sees therein His infinite wisdom, he immediately loves and glorifies and adores [Him], and has a great desire to know the Great Name.... *And when he considers these matters themselves, immediately he recoils in fear* and knows that he is a small, lowly, dim creature standing with trivial, minimal knowledge before Him Whose knowledge is perfect.
>
> (*Hil. Yesodei HaTorah* 2:1-2)

In this latter quotation, however, fear is not a sign of self-interested worship. What Rambam emphasizes in *Hilchoth Teshuvah* is the undesirability of a mode of serving G-d that is predicated upon ulterior motives, which he calls serving out of "fear." See also the author's discussion of this passage from *Hil. Yesodei HaTorah* in the text, below.

26. *Ed. note:* "חכמות ותבונות" (lit. "the [branches of] wisdoms and understandings") is translated here contextually as "science and philosophy."

Part II

KOHELETH REVISITED II:
On Mortality, Society, and G-d

Moshe M. Eisemann

1. INTRODUCTION

In a previous essay,[1] we drew primarily upon insights of Maharal to establish Koheleth as the paradigmatic *megillah* of *yirath Hashem* (awe of G-d), just as Shir HaShirim is the classic *megillah* of *ahavath Hashem* (love of G-d). By analyzing some key phrases that provide Koheleth with its body and nuance, we sought to prove that the *megillah* conjures up a far more optimistic vision of life than suggested by its popular image as a work of unrelieved negativism. In this essay, we explore the facets of life Koheleth viewed as central to the awe-inspired servant of G-d. In the process, aspects of life most commonly perceived as morbid are injected with surprising positivism through the unique perspectives offered by King Shelomoh, Koheleth's illustrious author.

RABBI EISEMANN is the *mashgiach* of Yeshiva Ner Israel of Baltimore. A prolific writer and a leading Torah scholar, he authored the translation and commentary of the ArtScroll-Mesorah Tanach series' *Yechezkel* (New York: Mesorah Publications, 1977) and *Divrei HaYamim I* (New York: Mesorah Publications, 1987).

2. MAN AND MORTALITY

"Death is Good"?

What aspect of life most concerns the *oved miyirah*?

Strangely, or perhaps not so strangely, it is death. As *Zohar* comments, " '... *the L-rd engaged in an act of creation [in order] that they should stand in awe of Him*' (Koheleth 3:14) — What did He create? He created the angel of death" (*Zohar* 3:98b).

Throughout life, death is a pervasive presence. Every moment brings death closer and is inextricably coupled therewith.[2] This is as it should be: " '*The L-rd saw all that He had wrought, and, behold, it was very good ...*' (BeReshith 1:31) — '*Good*': That is the angel of *life*. '*Very good*': That is the angel of *death*" (BeR.R. 9:1). The very essence of life becomes "good"[3] only because of its transience. Thus, the Midrash relates that when R. Meir was once writing the aforementioned verse in a *sefer Torah*, he inadvertently substituted "טוב מות" ("death is good") for "טוב מאד" ("very good") (ibid. 9:15). This error was no mere oversight. R. Meir's quill was guided by the turmoil of his thoughts. Why, he asked himself, was life so sweet? He concluded that only the inevitability of death made life worth living. Life was indeed "טוב מאד" only because of "טוב מות."

> It is better to go to a house of mourning
> than to go to a house of revelry,
> for that is the end of all men — and the living will take it to heart.
> (Koheleth 7:2)

This verse articulates a simple enough thought. Yet what are we to make of the idiom "יתן אל לבו" — literally, "[the living] will put it into his heart"? The heart is our most versatile organ. As the Midrash tells us, the heart sees, hears, speaks, wanders, falls, stands, rejoices, cries, finds comfort, suffers, feels encouraged, feels sorrow, breaks, swells with pride, is obdurate, deceives, thinks deeply, thinks creatively, plans, desires, strays, is satisfied, subjugates itself, endeavors, loses its way, trembles, is alert, loves, hates, envies, examines, is torn, and ponders; it is like fire, it is like stone.[4] Some order and discipline must be brought to this bewildering array of capabilities. The heart must be infused with intimations of mortality.

> The heart of the wise is in the house of the mourners;
> the heart of the fool is in the house of revelry.
>
> (ibid. 7:4)

The wise take the advice given two verses earlier. They go to the house of mourning and absorb the lesson that life — especially one circumscribed by the inevitability of death — can teach. Death becomes their constant companion, dominating their consciousness even when they are not confronted with it. Their hearts are in the mourner's house even when they themselves are far away.

Yet we feel uncomfortable with this approach to death. Something within us rebels against such morbidity. Preoccupation with death, we feel, drains life of its color and music. The intimation of mortality chills our hearts. It is, within the context of our positive perception of living, as incongruous and unwelcome as the haggard face of a mourner amid the twirl and gaiety of a wedding.

Does not Sefer Koheleth's obsession with death confirm its reputation as a chronicle of doom?

We submit that it does not. To understand why, however, we must fathom the dicta of Chazal quoted above. Why is death so "very good"?

A Realistic Hierarchy of Values

R. Chaim of Volozhin relates a meeting between an ordinary mortal and a man from Luz, a place where, according to tradition, people live forever.[5] The Luzite was keenly interested in how mortals coped with daily living. He assumed that, for people who expected to live only seventy or eighty years,[6] food, clothing, and shelter would be minor concerns. Concentrating on such peripherals made sense in Luz, where life — lived eternally — was a serious matter. But on earth? Did it make sense to eat well the better to feed the worms? To dress stylishly even as you awaited shrouds? To build houses that would stand for centuries when, after a few decades, your grave would be your home?

Needless to say, he was shocked by the answers he received.[7]

The story makes an important point: Life's hierarchy of values must reflect reality. The transient cannot make the same demands as the permanent resident. The mortal who answered the Luzite had obviously not internalized the lessons of Koheleth, and, to the extent that we identify with this respondent, neither have we.

How then does Koheleth suggest that we deal with the ubiquitous reality of death? Clearly, we are not to smother our joy and creativity in morbid, self-defeating anxiety and sorrow. Death must become a tool for life. But how is transience to generate eternity?

"Fill the Earth and Conquer It"

> I developed hatred for all the labor
> I invested under the sun,
> for I will have to leave it to whomever will follow me.
> Who knows whether he will be wise or foolish?
> [Yet] he will control all the labor I invested
> and upon which I lavished so much wisdom under the sun;
> this too is vanity.
>
> (ibid. 2:18-19)

How are we transients to view our temporary home? How much are we to identify with the houses and businesses in which we invest so much creativity? Is there a place in Judaism for the love we tend to develop for our surroundings, the physical realities that make up so much of our lives?

This question centers upon a correct understanding of G-d's blessing to the male and female He created: *"fill the earth and conquer it"* (BeReshith 1:28). Ramban explains that we conquer the earth by forcing it to yield its bounty. Everything the earth has to offer is ours. We are to mine its treasures, uncover its secrets, unleash its energies. It is G-d's gift to us, an opportunity to join Him in creation and construction.

What are we to make of this blessing? Are we to be intimately involved in developing our world? Does the world legitimately demand our attention and energies because it is ours and we should therefore care about it? Or do we remain strangers in this paradise, functioning herein because such is G-d's will but never really becoming part of it?

Significantly, G-d's blessing of conquest is recorded in BeReshith 1, the earlier of the Torah's two Creation narratives, in which the first humans are nameless, functioning only as male and female. The blessing does not appear in BeReshith 2, where Adam and Chavvah have already assumed their identity and individualism. For the objective duty to develop the earth devolves upon the masses, who are differentiated only by gender. Adam[8] and Chavvah, the strivers and educators,[9] have a different agenda.

The difference between Jew and gentile was later institutionalized by Yitzchak in blessing his two sons.[10] Ya'akov was granted the bounties of this world only insofar as they would contribute to his spiritual growth. Esav, by contrast, received these gifts unconditionally.[11] Ya'akov's element is the world to come; he relates to this world merely as an antechamber: Whatever does not insure his entry into the palace is meaningless for him.[12] For Esav, however, the antechamber *is* the palace. It is his only reality.

This, then, is Koheleth's dilemma: How should we relate to the circumscription of our lives and the possibility that the very causes, legitimate or not, to which we devote our best efforts will end up under the thumb of an incompetent fool who will quickly destroy all that we've built up with so much love and dedication?

To resolve this dilemma, let us note how Koheleth introduces it: Koheleth hates life, we are told, because he disdains everything he has observed *"under the sun."*[13] The implication is clear: By adopting an attitude uncramped by a life lived *"under the sun,"* one can cope with Koheleth's frustrations.

And indeed there is such an attitude: If the development of the world is not an end in itself but only a means of facilitating passage from antechamber to palace, then "success" and "failure" undergo subtle redefinition. The bridge I build may perform in an exemplary manner, yet it may be counted a dead loss. The outside world has been substantially improved, but my inner world may have been shattered in the process. Conversely, the bridge may never carry a single traveler, and yet, if G-d is pleased with my effort, I have lived constructively.

Rejoicing in Our Labors

> There is nothing better for man
> than that he should eat and drink
> and permit himself to rejoice in his labors;
> this too, it is clear to me, is a gift from G-d.
> (Koheleth 2:24)

Here we have the answer: We must rejoice not in the success of any venture but in the *labor* that attended it.

An entirely new, positive attitude toward life's tasks now ensues. Protected from the fears and frustrations that inevitably arise in pursuing our goals, a *joie de vivre* surfaces, which results in an enthusiastic shouldering of effort and involvement. Where the prospect of failure holds no terror, one does not procrastinate. Indeed, in this spirit, Koheleth admonishes the uncommitted laborer:

> Amid sloth, the ceiling will disintegrate;
> and where hands hang idle, the house will leak ...
> He who waits for a fair wind will never sow;
> and he who watches the clouds will never reap ...
> Sow your seeds in the morning,
> [but] do not rest in the evening;
> for you know not which will turn out well, these or those,
> or whether perhaps both will be good.
> How sweet the light!
> How good for the eyes to behold the sun!
> For [even] if man were to live for many years,
> let him rejoice in all of them,
> and let him remember the days of darkness,
> for they will be many indeed.
> (ibid. 10:18, 11:4, 6-8)

The message is clear: Life is worthwhile. Do not waste it.

Let us now consolidate what we have learned: The pervasive reality of death reorders our priorities. Ends are downgraded to means, the fires of ambition are banked, and despair cedes to hope. We are freed from the corrosive naggings of frustration, because all effort — so long as it is honest, responsible, and noble — will inevitably be crowned by success.

Surely we feel a little better about the morbid "mistake" in R. Meir's *sefer Torah*. Perhaps the substitution of "טוב מות" ("death is good") for "טוב מאד" ("very good") is appropriate after all.

3. MAN AND SOCIETY

The Antithesis of *Avodah MiYirah*

We are never lonelier than when we move among people with whom we feel no kinship, and we are never more despondent than when society fails us and we sense ourselves to be utterly alone, even in a crowd. It is man's terrifyingly predatory nature that brings Koheleth to his lowest point:

> Observing once more,
> I saw all the victims who had been created under the sun;
> here were the tears of the downtrodden
> who have none to comfort them;
> their oppressors have power, but for them there is no comfort.
> So I regarded the dead who had already died
> as luckier than the living who were still alive.
> And more fortunate than both is he who has not yet been,
> who has not witnessed all the evil work that is done under the sun.
> (ibid. 4:13)

The facts, sadly enough, are clear and undeniable. But Koheleth insists on delving beneath the surface:

> And I realized that all labor and all ingenuity
> are driven by no more than jealousy between men....
> (ibid. 4:4)

Since the dawn of man, nothing has changed. The centuries might just as well not have passed, the toils and sorrows of history might just as well have been spared. Humanity has not progressed one whit beyond that first dreadful moment when Kayin — crazed by the same lust for self-assertion that King Shelomoh now bemoans — sullied the pristine earth with Hevel's blood.[14]

Understandably, of all the human failings Koheleth pillories with such vehemence, man's propensity to self-aggrandizement disturbs him most. Of all our flaws, this one stands most blatantly in opposition to the subservience that is the hallmark of *avodah miyirah*.

Man versus Animal

Let us take a closer look at Koheleth's plaint that *"... man's advantage over the animal is nothing, for all is empty of meaning"* (ibid. 3:19). Man's superiority over the animal world purportedly lies in his ability to look outside himself, beyond his immediate needs and wants, to a greater, preemptive Power. The careless and wanton cruelty of nature, the unceasing struggle for ascendancy and propagation, the uncompromising will to live so ably documented by the brooding Schopenhauer[15] — all derive from an absolute egocentrism that leaves no room for any consideration other than one's own survival. The same ruthless self-interest drives the acorn, the ocean, and the vulture, together with the billions of species that populate the earth and paradoxically benefit it by seeking their own perpetuation.

What of man?

In despair, Koheleth looks around and sees to his horror that man is no different. He may be more ingenious, more restlessly and tirelessly ambitious, but he is guilty of the same dreary myopia, the same conversion of subject to object, and the same self-defeating predisposition to battle.

The Need for Community

In response to this revelation, *"The fool folds his hands, consuming his own flesh"* (ibid. 4:5). The sensitive soul withdraws turtle-like into itself, with pessimism breeding spiritual isolationism. What one cannot abide one must eschew.

But Koheleth's riposte comes hard and fast: We cannot cut ourselves off from our community any more than we can deny our own selves. Just as the starving body ultimately gnaws away at its own flesh, pathetically scrounging for the resources that so patently lie elsewhere, so must we destroy ourselves in isolation.

Like it or not, we are social beings, fated to travel through life together. Clearly, then, there must be ways of coping. G-d cannot possibly wish us to be swept away by the passions that evidently animate the corrupt society described by Koheleth earlier.

And here, what Koheleth does *not* say seems as significant as what he says. He does not, as we might have anticipated, call for a world in which love reigns supreme. Such a simple remedy! Surely the resulting ideal relationships would preclude destructive jealousy. If I love my fellow as I do myself, then his accomplishments, possessions, and happiness are as important to me as my own. I begrudge him nothing, because I find my own fulfillment in his.

Of all this, Koheleth says nothing. Why not? If love conquers all, why not preach it?

Once more, our earlier thesis is confirmed. Koheleth is not Shir HaShirim. It addresses not the *oved me'ahavah* but the *oved miyirah*. It speaks to us as we are, not as we ought to be; it sees us and our world, warts and all. Written in prose rather than poetry, it seeks to instruct rather than to inspire; it delivers rather than dreams.

Not surprisingly given all that we have learned, our salvation, according to Koheleth, lies in enlightened, benign self-interest. The *oved miyirah* does not lose himself in an ecstasy of self-effacement. He is here, he is real. To devote his life to G-d's service, he must first come to grips with his humanity. He must strike a balance between needs and duties, between self and other. For one who seeks solace in self-delusion makes a very poor servant.

Redefining Goodness

In reality, we crave goodness. But "good" is not an absolute term. Its contours are flexible. Preconceptions need neither bind nor frustrate us. Let us, Koheleth suggests, rethink and redefine what we mean by "good."

It is not the hurly-burly of insatiable quest. *"One handful of satisfaction is better* [literally, *"more good"*] *than two handfuls of emptiness and unfulfilled desire"* (ibid. 4:6). We must therefore impose logical, definite limits on our ambitions. But that is only possible if we vacate center stage. The *I* will always hunger for more; only the *we* has a chance of assuaging its thirst.

> Observing once more, I saw futility under the sun.
> There is a lone person, who has neither son nor brother,
> whose exertions are endless,

> whose ambitions are never fulfilled;
> for whom, then, do I labor, denying myself pleasure?
> This too is futility, and it is a terrible thing!
> (ibid. 4:7-8)

Man has something over the animals after all: He does not relish working for himself alone. His sense of accomplishment is incomplete if he cannot share the fruits of his labor with another.

This is a momentous discovery, setting even base, unrefined man above the animal world. The idea is so radical that Koheleth unveils it gingerly, approaching it with reserve. He savors it first as an objective truth, expressing it in the third person: *"There is a lone person ..."* (ibid. 4:8). Only subsequently does he permit himself to internalize it and apply it to his own life: *"For whom, then, do I labor ..."* (ibid.).

Next Koheleth contemplates this newfound truth. In a world purposefully created, our instinctive aversion to solitude cannot be purposeless. What, then, is its function?

The Oneness of Friendship

> Two are better than one....
> For if they fall,
> one will lift up his fellow....
> (ibid. 4:9-10)

Initially, Koheleth sees our instinct for companionship as purely utilitarian. We need someone to help us up after a fall, to protect us in our moments of vulnerability. We cannot manage on our own. But this rationale is very primitive. It perceives one's fellow as object rather than subject, as someone to be used rather than someone with whom to share life.

> Also, if two lie together, it is warm for them;
> [but] as for a single person, how will he find warmth?
> (ibid. 4:11)

Once Koheleth embarks upon this path of discovery, there is no turning back. Insight begets insight, and experience cradles wisdom in its embrace. Hence, the next stage: If my friend can help me up after a fall, I can render him the same service. He and

I are one — two limbs of one body, two ideas animating one mind. We can lie in each other's arms, warming and sustaining. Taking becomes giving, and giving becomes a feast of love, a feast of sharing. Koheleth has found a friend.

> Now if [a robber (Rashi)] attacks the one,
> the two can stand up against him....
> (ibid. 4:12)

And friendship ennobles. Friends sacrifice for friends. When one is attacked, both are victims. They take up cudgels for one another, because ultimately they are one; there is no other.

> ...the threefold thread is not quickly broken.
> (ibid.)

What of this cryptic conclusion? Is there a perception of society that surpasses even our current enlightened vision?

Fellowship as Its Own Reward

Fellowship is its own reward. It requires no justification. The third man, whose hand need not lift the fallen, whose warmth need not restore the frostbitten, whose weapons need not repulse the enemy because there are sufficient defense forces without him — it is he who teaches Koheleth the ultimate value of the "other." As long as we think in terms of pairs, measuring human worth purely in utilitarian terms, the thread that joins us is readily severed. Postulate self-sufficiency and the desert island will serve as well as the village square. It is a sorry world indeed in which, because I don't need your help, I don't need you.

Only with the appearance of a third, apparently superfluous presence does Koheleth grasp what really animates our friendships. We are — he discovers — very different from animals. We value people not for what they do but for who they are. We bond because we want to be bonded. We need not be shackled by myopic self-absorption. We can vacate the center of our petty personal fiefdoms. We can look beyond ourselves and behold a man who owes us no explanations, and we can treasure him simply because he is!

4. MAN AND G-D

The Theology of Koheleth

Sefer Koheleth offers the theologian slim pickings. Man, not G-d, dominates the narrator's ruminations. Throughout the book, G-d is no more than a shadowy presence, merely one consideration among many as we grope along the complex paths of our this-worldly lives. Where G-d is mentioned at all, it is with summons to duty, not ecstasy. We are made to feel puny without hearing any call to greatness. The impossible is more pervasive than the possible. We are called upon to act rather than to dream, to obey rather than to aspire.

Granted, the last few chapters are — as noted in our earlier essay — an optimistic and joyful affirmation of life. But this life seems animated by temporal rather than religious goals. If we followed Koheleth's advice, we would be exemplary husbandmen but indifferent saints. Our roofs would keep out the rain, but our souls would wilt in an arid stupor.

In short, we are hard put to recognize Sefer Koheleth as a religious book. It delights our minds but seems to leave our hearts untouched.

And yet, at its very end, the book appears to redeem itself:

> The end of the matter, when all has been heard [is this]:
> Fear the L-rd and fulfill His commands,
> for that is the entirety of man.
> (ibid. 12:13)

Strikingly, fear and service of G-d are presented not as the most important aspects of man's life, not as those things that imbue all his other activities with meaning, but as *"the entirety of man"* (ibid.) — a religious statement if ever there were one!

But how does Sefer Koheleth's argument yield this conclusion? If G-d's name were excised from the book, its message, we feel, would hardly be weakened. The reflections of this most optimistic of philosophers upon the futility of life lived *"under the sun"* could just as easily have spawned a secular humanism in which fear of G-d would have little if any relevance. What, then, drove Koheleth to deem this fear *"the entirety of man"* (ibid.)?

The Torah according to Hillel

Koheleth's conclusion — that the religious imperative grows out of an essentially secular contemplation of man and society — uncannily parallels the definition of Judaism immortalized centuries later by Hillel HaZaken in his confrontation with the non-Jew who sought the essence of the Torah while standing on one leg.[16] Hillel, it will be recalled, reduced the sum total of Judaism to a negative formulation of a single commandment: *"Love your neighbor as yourself"* (VaYikra 19:18).

Unfortunately, that story is so well-known that Hillel's audacious assertion makes no ripple upon the smooth surface of our theological certitudes. Having been taught to read this passage simply as vindication of Hillel's patience and understanding as opposed to Shammai's unforgiving, uncompromising vision of truth, we tend not to realize that Hillel's assertion is absolutely revolutionary. What right has he, after all, to single out one *mitzvah*, which appears in the Torah without fanfare or any other form of particularization, and declare it central to the extraordinary extent that *"all else is commentary"* (*Shabbath* 31a)?

Furthermore, why does Hillel drain this *mitzvah* of its color and excitement by casting it in the pallid negative — "That which is hateful to you, do not do to your friend" (ibid.) — instead of the pulsating positive? Why pretend that we need only refrain from hurting another when, in reality, G-d demands so much more, trusting our ability to love?

Where the Torah challenges us, Hillel appears content to appeal to self-interest. He suggests that our feelings be our guide in determining appropriate behavior, a position that brings to mind the famous contention that even among robbers, a certain decency is imperative. The Torah is more altruistic than that; it does not command us to love solely in order to be loved. Where the Torah summons us to greatness, Hillel seems to recommend mere prudence. He sounds more like a broker tendering investment advice — or a social worker ever-ready with a one-size-fits-all palliative — than an inspired teacher tantalizing his students with intimations of grandeur.

Is this truly the essence of Judaism? Is the Jew no more than a civilized human being? If that is all we have to offer the world, has all the blood and horror of our dreadful history really been worthwhile?

Above all, and here we return to Koheleth, is Hillel not postulating a secular rather than a religious core to Judaism? He propounds the moral obligation to treat others as we ourselves wish to be treated — is this not the credo of the secular humanist? How, then, can this principle encapsulate Judaism?

The answer lies in another question: Where does G-d figure in the essential secularism of Hillel's thought? Rashi has a remarkable suggestion. The Torah speaks of loving our "רע" ("friend") as we do ourselves (VaYikra 19:18). Rashi points out that G-d too is our "רע."[17] He too has a right to demand that we treat Him considerately. Would we not want our own commands to be obeyed? Therefore, we must not disobey His.

The implications of this analogy are shattering: We cannot care for G-d until we learn to care for man. A secular, humanistic imperative bids us, once the truth of G-d's existence is assumed, to live as men of religion.

The theory is simple enough. Man is either self-centered or other-centered. If he recognizes only his own needs, disregarding others', then even G-d can be no more than peripheral to his concerns.

"All Else is Commentary"

We asked how Hillel had the right to turn one *mitzvah* out of many into the irreducible core of Judaism, and why he would seemingly devalue the positive command to love by recasting it as a negative command to refrain from doing to others what you would not want done to yourself. The answer to both questions may well be that Hillel was not reformulating the *mitzvah* to *"love your neighbor as yourself"* (ibid.). He was simply enunciating a psychological truth, which requires no Scriptural mandate. Much as R. Chayyim Vital claims concerning the ethical moment,[18] this aspect of human nature must be assumed even before the Torah is given. To paraphrase Hillel, the Torah is no more — and no less — than "commentary" on this elemental quality, for the purpose of Torah is to refine and develop all that is good and worthy in the human potential.

We recognize a similar thought process in Koheleth. Only those who have learned to live well with the world can aspire to live well with G-d. Only those who have developed their full human potential will ultimately realize that the "entirety" of their humanity is fear of G-d and conscientious adherence to His commands.

NOTES

1. See "Koheleth Revisited," Jewish Thought, 2, No. 1 (5752).
2. See Ramban on BeReshith 2:17.
3. See Ramban on BeReshith 1:3.
4. See Koh.R. 1:16.
5. See *Sotah* 46b.
6. See Tehillim 90:10.
7. I heard this parable from R. Elya Svei, *rosh yeshivah* of Yeshivah of Philadelphia, who cited it in the name of R. Chayyim of Volozhin.
8. See the commentary of the Tosafoth on *Babba Kamma* 38a, ד״ה אלא האדם, where R. Tam maintains that the word "אדם" (literally, "man") refers exclusively to a Jew, while "האדם" ("the man") describes any human being. *Tifereth Yisra'el* (*Avoth* 3:1, *Bo'az*) explains that the Torah uses "אדם" as a proper noun, the given name of the first man. Only Yisra'el, Adam's spiritual heir, can lay claim to that appellation. "האדם," in contrast, simply means "man," for if it were a proper noun, it could not take a definite article.
9. See R. S.R. Hirsch on BeReshith 3:20, where he explains why the first woman was called not Chayyah, as in "life force," but Chavvah, as in "יחוה־דעת" ("offers knowledge") (Tehillim 19:3).
10. See BeReshith 27:28-29, 39-40.
11. See Rashi on BeReshith 27:28.
12. See *Avoth* 4:21.
13. See "Koheleth Revisited," 13-15.
14. See BeReshith 4:1-15.
15. German philosopher Arthur Schopenhauer (1788-1860) was a highly pessimistic thinker. The tragedy of life and the evil inherent in the world were two of his most common themes.
16. See *Shabbath* 31a
17. See Rashi on *Shabbath* 31a, ד״ה דעלך סני לחברך לא תעביד.
18. See R. Chayyim Vital, *Sha'arei Kedushah* (Yerushalayim: Eshkol, 1985), pt. 1, *sha'ar* 2.

Rabbeinu Hakadosh and Chanukkah
Why Chanukkah Was Excluded from the Mishnah

Moshe Tz. Neriyah

The essay that follows is based upon the source provided below:

טעם שנס חנוכה לא נזכר כלל במשנה, לפי שרבנו מסדר המשנה היה מזרע דוד המלך ע"ה, ונס חנוכה נעשה על ידי בית החשמונאים, שתפסו המלוכה ולא היו מזרע דוד, וזה הרע לרבינו הקדוש ובכתבו המשנה על פי רוח הקודש נשמט הנס מחיבורו.

The reason the miracle of Chanukkah is not mentioned at all in the Mishnah [is as follows]: For our master, the compiler of the Mishnah, was of the seed of King David, peace be upon him, and the miracle of Chanukkah was accomplished by the house of Chashmona'im, which seized the kingship although [its members] were

---

RABBI NERIYAH is *rosh yeshivah* of Yeshivath Kfar HaRo'eh and founder of Yeshivot Bnei Akiva in Israel. His *Mo'adei HaRe'iyah* was recently rendered into English under the title *Celebration of the Soul* (Yerushalayim: Genesis Jerusalem Press, 1992). This essay was adapted (by Daniel Haberman) from an article entitled *"Maddu'a Lo Nishnu Hilchoth Chanukkah BaMishnah?"* (Kfar HaRo'eh: Yabi'a Omer Press, 5746 [1986]).

not of the seed of David. Now this disturbed Rabbeinu HaKadosh, and [therefore] when he wrote the Mishnah under the inspiration of the holy spirit, the miracle was omitted from his work.

(R. Avraham Yitzchak Shperling, *Ta'amei HaMinhagim*, p. 365)

1. INTRODUCTION

According to *Ta'amei HaMinhagim*, R. Yehudah HaNasi, scion of the house of David, took offense at the "power grab" of the Chashmona'im, who were not of Davidic descent.[1]

This explanation was seized upon by those who sought to defame the early generations.[2] These detractors gleefully depicted a resentful Yehudah HaNasi, who, envying the glories of the Chashmona'im, omitted the laws of Chanukkah from the Mishnah "like a creditor who jumps at the chance to collect an old debt" (*BeR.R.* 85:3, 92:9).

In including this theory in his *Ta'amei HaMinhagim*, R. Shperling presumably acted in good faith, relying on R. Mosheh Sofer (Chatham Sofer), of sainted memory, to whom he attributes this *ta'am* (without, however, providing an actual source). Yet it is highly doubtful, for the many reasons we shall cite, that Chatham Sofer ever made any such assertion. Indeed, although he was a prolific writer, we do not find the above explanation in any of his many books, responsa, or *derashoth*, or even in his novellae on tractate *Shabbath*, where he devotes much attention to the Talmudic discussion of Chanukkah. The sole source of this idea appears to be an oral tradition, one that is surely "Like vinegar to the teeth and like smoke to the eyes..." (Mishlei 10:26).

Rabbeinu HaKadosh

Rambam writes:

> Rabbeinu HaKadosh ... was singular in his generation and unique in his time, a man in whom all desirable [conduct] and [all] good traits were found, until he merited to be called "our holy master" by his contemporaries ... and he was the epitome of wisdom and stature ... piety and humility.
>
> (*Introduction to the Mishnah*, ch. 3)

To ascribe to such a person resentment and jealousy of the Chashmona'im — whom we recall in *"Al HaNissim"* as fully righteous people whose heroism saved Yisra'el in one of its most difficult periods — seems patently ludicrous. In fact, had Rabbeinu HaKadosh allowed petty personal considerations to affect him, our faith in that great and monumental work, the Mishnah, would be utterly shaken.

This essay will discredit the *ta'am* in question both logically and historically. In the process, we shall present several more plausible solutions to the riddle of why Rabbeinu HaKadosh omitted the laws of Chanukkah from the Mishnah.

2. WAS THE CHASHMONA'IM'S ASSUMPTION OF THE KINGSHIP SINFUL?

Commenting on the verse "The scepter shall not depart from Yehudah ..." (BeReshith 49:10), Ramban claims that because the Chashmona'im usurped the throne without being of Davidic descent, they were punished for disobeying the will of Ya'akov Avinu.

While Ramban was the first major commentator to make this claim, he also magnifies the Chanukkah miracle by finding a Biblical allusion to it: In his commentary on BeMidbar 8:2, he cites a midrashic view linking the lighting of Chanukkah candles to a divine promise made to Aharon HaKohen, forebear of the Chashmona'im, during the very first *"chanukkah"* ("dedication"): the dedication of the Sanctuary and its altar. Hence, according to Ramban, the sin of the house of Chashmonai in no way reduces Chanukkah's standing. Therefore, even if there were grounds for disavowing the Chashmonai dynasty, such grounds would not warrant a dismissal of the Chanukkah miracle.

As is well-known, Chatham Sofer was very fond of Ramban's *Commentary on the Torah*. As such, he was surely well aware of Ramban's comments on *BeHa'alothcha*, making it highly unlikely that Chatham Sofer actually said what has been attributed to him. This improbability shall become even clearer as we proceed.

In contrast to Ramban, Rambam apparently saw nothing wrong with a king being appointed from among the *kohanim* —

not from the seed of David — during the Chashmonai period. In describing the miraculous salvation that occurred at that time, Rambam even stresses the importance of the renewal of the kingship:

> The sons of Chashmonai, the high priests, triumphed and slaughtered [the Greeks], saving Yisra'el from [enemy] hands. They appointed a king from among the *kohanim*, and [thus] the kingship returned to Yisra'el....
>
> (*Yad Hil. Megillah VeChanukkah* 3:1)

According to this view, there was no Davidic candidate for royalty, no one whose authority would have been willingly accepted by the people.[3, 4]

Rashi seems to concur with Rambam's position, consistently referring to the Chashmona'im with unreserved praise. For example, commenting on a verse in Zecharyah that speaks of Yisra'el's redemption, Rashi interprets the verse's shimmering imagery as an allusion to the Chashmona'im:

> "G-d their L-rd shall save them on that day ... for [they shall be like] crown jewels, glittering on His soil" (Zecharyah 9:16) — For the *kohanim*, the sons of the Chashmona'im, who are bedecked with the crown jewels, breastplate, and tunic, will glitter (מתנוססים) with miracles (ניסים) in His land.
>
> (Rashi, ibid.)

Similarly, in his commentary on Sefer Daniyyel, Rashi speaks of

> Mattithyahu son of Yochanan, who will throw off the Greek oppressor.... The glory of kingship in Yisra'el, he will be a great commander and hero, as will all his seed after him, the sons of Chashmonai.
>
> (com. on Daniyyel 11:20)[5]

Maharal offers his own rationale for a non-Davidic monarchy, introducing an unexpected twist:

> With the rebuilding and return of the second Temple, Davidic monarchy did not resume.... This was by virtue of the exaltedness of Davidic rule; only the future would be worthy of the dawning of Davidic rule.[6]
>
> (*Netzach Yisra'el*, ch. 18)

Thus, according to most commentaries, there was nothing sinful about the Chashmona'im's assumption of the throne. It would therefore seem illogical to assume that Rabbeinu HaKadosh could not justify it based on the relevant sources.

3. MISREADING HISTORY

The Chanukkah miracle took place in the third year of the Chashmonai rebellion, well before the onset of Chashmonai rule. In addition, years later, the Chashmona'im were careful to proclaim Shime'on merely the *nasi*, not the king. They even posted a bronze plaque on Mount Tziyyon, declaring his appointment valid only "until the coming of the true prophet." It was Yehudah Aristobulus, two generations later, who became king.[7]

Why, then, should the Chanukkah miracle be tainted by a sin committed generations later? To paraphrase Yirmeyahu, "The sons have eaten sour grapes, and the *fathers*' teeth are set on edge" (Yirmeyahu 31:29)?

Furthermore, if indeed said sin were grounds for taking issue with the Chashmonai court that "fixed these days [of Chanukkah] as a festival" (*Shabbath* 21b), Hillel HaZaken, grandfather of the grandfather of Rabbeinu HaKadosh, should have done so. Why would resentment towards Chanukkah surface only later, with Rabbeinu HaKadosh?

Certainly, as *nasi*, Hillel had the authority to intervene. Yet, not only did Beith Hillel not reject Chanukkah, it championed the way of *"mehadrin min hamehadrin"* (ibid.), enhancing the commemoration of the miracle by legislating the lighting of an additional candle every night of the festival, for "in matters of sanctity, one increases and does not decrease" (ibid.). Clearly, Beith Hillel favored a constant magnification of the miracle.

Likewise, the elders of Beith Hillel and Beith Shammai wrote *Megillath Beith Chashmonai*, an account of the Chanukkah miracle.[8] Thus, far from contesting the miracle's obligatory character, Beith Hillel sought to ingrain and glorify it through a unique *megillah* akin to Megillath Ester.[9]

How, then, seven generations later, could Rabbeinu HaKadosh, a descendant of Hillel, have questioned the teachings of his forefathers and revered teachers?

Moreover, after rigorous Halachic analysis, had Rabbeinu HaKadosh decided that the prohibited "power grab" on the part of the later Chashmona'im retroactively discredited the entire Chanukkah enterprise, his authority and influence would have led to the holiday's annulment. Just as *Megillath Ta'anith* and the celebratory dates recorded therein were abolished (due to the destruction of the second Beith HaMikdash and its afflictions),[10] such should have been the fate of Chanukkah. If Chazal canceled the days listed in *Megillath Ta'anith*, which were only peripherally related to the Beith HaMikdash, certainly they would have discontinued Chanukkah, which is intimately bound up with the miracle of the *menorah* in the Temple.

Although Chanukkah is unique among these days in that Chazal assigned it a *mitzvah* (candle lighting), this did not stop Abayyei from suggesting: "Let Chanukkah be abolished and its *mitzvah* along with it" (*Rosh HaShanah* 18b). Therefore, the rabbis did have the authority to annul the *mitzvoth* instituted by the Chashmonai court. In addition, when R. Yosef explains that Chanukkah was not annulled "because it publicly commemorates a miracle" (ibid.), Rashi adds, "... hence, it is not *proper* to annul it." Thus, *propriety* was the issue, but annulment was an option.

Furthermore, the Talmud reports that certain sages "decreed a fast on Chanukkah" (ibid.). Had Rabbeinu HaKadosh sought to abolish Chanukkah, he could have based himself on their opinion.

4. A STRANGE FORMULATION

In explaining the absence of Chanukkah from the Mishnah, R. Shperling writes:

> ... when [Rabbeinu HaKadosh] wrote the Mishnah under the inspiration of the holy spirit, the miracle was omitted [or literally: "forgotten"] from his work.
>
> (*Ta'amei HaMinhagim*, p. 365)

How strange to suggest that Chanukkah was "forgotten." Is the Mishnah the product of one individual, who, in his great haste, forgot about the miracle of Chanukkah? On the contrary, the redaction of the Mishnah was a protracted project involving many scholars:

> Rabbeinu HaKadosh gathered together all the traditions and enactments ... and redacted, from all this material, the Mishnah.... Throughout his life, he and his colleagues were engaged in giving public instruction in the Mishnah; these colleagues were the greatest of the scholars, who were members of his court ... and attended his college.
>
> (Rambam, *Introduction to Mishneh Torah*)

What kind of "holy spirit" could have led Rabbeinu HaKadosh and his colleagues to forget to include the laws of Chanukkah in the Mishnah?[11] If the view from on high was against Chanukkah, why didn't Rabbeinu HaKadosh annul the holiday entirely?

In conclusion, while we don't know precisely what, if anything, Chatham Sofer said concerning Chanukkah's omission, presumably he did not say what has been attributed to him.

5. ALTERNATE SOLUTIONS

Chanukkah's virtual absence from the Mishnah has long fascinated both Torah scholars and historians. Having rejected *Ta'amei HaMinhagim*'s explanation of this oddity, let us examine various alternative approaches.

Political and Security Concerns

It is crucial that we assess Jewish relations with the Roman authorities at the time of the Mishnah's redaction:

> Emperor Hadrian, after subduing the rebels at Betar, lashed out like fire in anger at all of Yisra'el, putting an end to [its] holiday[s], new moon, and Sabbath.
>
> The reign of the next emperor, Antoninus, who was Rebbi's [i.e., R. Yehudah HaNasi's] friend, could almost be termed comfortable; the previous ban on Chanukkah, however, apparently remained in effect. Even a benevolent ruler could not allow a holiday of such national feeling to a people who had only recently fought to the death and had, at great cost [to Rome], been contained. For this reason, Rabbeinu HaKadosh could not publicly mention Chanukkah.
>
> (R. Yehoshua Yosef Preil, *Egglei Tal* [Warsaw, 5659] 1:3)

Similarly, concerning the death of R. Akiva's students ca. 120

C.E., R. Sherira Ga'on states that they were massacred, whereas Chazal hush up the matter, reporting only that these disciples died.[12] Clearly, political considerations did not permit publicizing the whole truth.

R. Re'uven Margaliot expands on this theme: Aware that this work would be subject to Roman scrutiny, Rebbi omitted mention of both messianic redemption and Chanukkah (except in passing).[11] For the celebration of a national victory (Chanukkah) and the dream of future sovereignty (Mashiach) would have alarmed the Romans.[13]

Likewise, regarding the Talmudic license, *in times of danger*, to light Chanukkah candles in private,[14] the commentary of Tosafoth traces this dispensation to a Roman ban on the *mitzvah*.[15]

Given the prevailing Roman antipathy, then, *Megillath Beith Chashmonai* remained hidden rather than being preserved "for posterity" (*Megillah* 7a).

Actually, the institution of Purim prompted similar security concerns. To Ester's request, "Commemorate me for posterity" (ibid.), the rabbis initially replied: "You will incite the ill will of the nations against us [who will accuse us of rejoicing at their downfall (Rashi)] ..." (ibid.).

The Laws of Chanukkah Predated the Mishnah

The most convincing theory regarding Chanukkah's absence from the Mishnah may be that the laws of the festival had already been collected and organized in Rebbi's time:

> It is ostensibly a great wonder why not one law of Chanukkah is mentioned in the Mishnah. Concerning Purim, there is an entire tractate, while [regarding] Chanukkah there is not even one *mishnah*.... However, it is not really a wonder, since all the laws of Chanukkah are written in the ninth chapter of *Megillath Ta'anith*, with all the *baraithoth* cited in tractate *Shabbath* and dealing with the laws of Chanukkah having been cited there. It was therefore unnecessary for Rebbi to reiterate them in the Mishnah, since *Megillath Ta'anith* was considered almost as prestigious as Scripture, with its authority surpassing that of the Mishnah, [as indicated by the fact that] its recording was permitted prior to when it became permissible to

record *"Torah shebe'al-peh"* (as explained by Rashi [in his commentary] on *Shabbath* 13b, *Eruvin* 62b, and *Ta'anith* 15b). Now we never find in the Mishnah repetition of *anything* recorded in *Megillath Ta'anith* ... the same rule and reason [applying] to the laws of Chanukkah.... Only after *Megillath Ta'anith* was annulled and people no longer studied it did they copy therefrom the laws of the Chanukkah candles, since Chanukkah [unlike the other days recorded in *Megillath Ta'anith*] was not annulled.
(R. Dov Nachman Horovitz of Vitebsk, *HaPeles*, Vol. 1 [5661], p. 184)

Hence, the existence of *Megillath Ta'anith* absolved Rebbi of the need to record the miracle of Chanukkah and its attendant laws in the Mishnah.[16]

Admittedly, some scholars maintain that the commentary portions of *Megillath Ta'anith*, written in pure Hebrew, were not part of the original Aramaic text but were initially transmitted orally.[17, 18] Yet this fact does not detract from the theory presently under examination. Rather, this oral commentary took the place of the laws of Chanukkah in the Mishnaic order of *Mo'ed*.

This theory holds true not only according to the opinion that Rabbeinu HaKadosh *arranged* the Mishnah[19] but even according to the view that he *wrote* it.[20] Since this oral commentary accompanied a written work — *Megillath Ta'anith* — and was studied alongside it, there were grounds for leaving both out of the Mishnah, just as Rebbi omitted many other important *baraithoth*.[21] Likewise, R. Chiyya and R. Oshiya saw no need to include the laws of Chanukkah in the Tosefta.

Common Knowledge Was Not Included in the Mishnah

Interestingly, the laws of *tzitzith* and *mezuzah* are not featured in the Mishnah. Rambam points out that because they were common knowledge at the time of the Mishnah's redaction, Rabbeinu HaKadosh saw no reason to speak of them.[22]

This theory may apply to the laws of Chanukkah as well.[23, 24] That Rebbi produced no *"Masecheth Chanukkah"* is therefore no proof of any hidden agenda of suppressing or diminishing the holiday.[25]

6. CONCLUSION

Why are the laws of Chanukkah not taught in the Mishnah? Three solutions have been advanced: Recording them would have been politically dangerous; it was unnecessary to cite what was common knowledge; or, most likely, these laws were already taught in *Megillath Ta'anith*.

Any of these proposals is surely preferable to ascribing malice to Rabbeinu HaKadosh, who was "singular in his generation and unique in his time ... the epitome of ... piety and humility" (Rambam, *Introduction to the Mishnah*, ch. 3).

NOTES

1. This conjecture has two weaknesses:

    One, R. Yehudah HaNasi's Davidic lineage derived only from the female side: He descended from Hillel, whose mother's ancestry dated back to David and Avital (see *Yer. Kilayim* 9:3, *Kethubboth* 62b, and *Iggereth R. Sherira Ga'on*). Legally speaking, "the family of the mother is not regarded as the proper family" (*Babba Bathra* 109b).

    Two, "a king of Yisra'el must be of the house of David *and* of the seed of Shelomoh" (Rambam, *Introduction to Perek Chelek, yesod* 12); Rabbeinu HaKadosh was not.

    If, then, he had no claim to kingship, why depict him as aggrieved?

2. *Ed. note:* The literal translation is "those who [as it were] diminish the divine image"; see *Yevamoth* 63b.

3. Also see R. Yosef Karo, *Maggid Meisharim* (*parashath MiKeitz*): "they agreed that the holy priests should rule."

4. *Ed. note:* Careful evaluation of *Yad Hil. Melachim* 1:8-10 indicates that Rambam considers non-Davidic rule generally unobjectionable. As for "The scepter shall not depart from Yehudah ..." (BeReshith 49:10), Rambam apparently interprets the verse as G-d's assurance that even if David's descendants sin, the Davidic dynasty will continue — an assurance denied the non-Davidic monarchs, whose perpetuation depends entirely on their piety. See *Sefer HaMitzvoth, lav* 362, however, where Rambam seems to contradict his position in *Yad*. The resolution of this contradiction is beyond the scope of this note.

    It should further be noted that Chashmonai rule constitutes one of three apparent violations of "The scepter shall not depart from Yehudah ..." throughout history, the others being the reign of King Sha'ul, a Benjamite; and the rule of the "kings of Yisra'el," beginning with Yaravam ben Nevat (who was appointed by the prophet Achiyyah HaShiloni). Regarding the parameters of the verse in question, see Ramban on BeReshith 49:10 and

Derashoth HaRan, derash 7.

5. Also see Rashi on Daniyyel 11:22.
6. R. Ya'akov Kaminetzky echoes Maharal's idea:

> The sages of Yisra'el did not insist on Davidic rule in the days of the house of Chashmonai.... To do so would have contravened the divine will: Davidic rule is a key element in the process of redemption, and they wanted to underscore the idea that the redemption remained incomplete, its time had not yet come.
>
> (*Oraitha*, Vol. 14 [Nethanyah, 5744], pp. 143-44)

7. See Prof. Gedalyah Alon, "*HaHishkichah Ha'Umah VeChochmeha Eth HaChashmona'im?*" *Mechkarim BeToldoth Yisra'el* (Tel Aviv, 5717), pp. 15-25.
8. See *Halachoth Gedoloth*, "Hil. Soferim."
9. The very license to record *Megillath Beith Chashmonai* bespeaks great respect for Chanukkah.
10. See *Rosh HaShanah* 18b.
11. Although Chanukkah is mentioned in the Mishnah (see *Bikkurim* 1:6, *Rosh HaShanah* 1:3, *Megillah* 3:6, *Ta'anith* 2:10, *Mo'ed Katan* 3:9, and *Babba Kamma* 6:6), its essential laws appear only in *Megillath Ta'anith* and in the Gemara.
12. See *Iggereth R. Sherira Ga'on* (Haifa 1921 ed.), p. 13; and *Yevamoth* 62b.

Ed. note: It should be noted that R. Sherira Ga'on provides no evidence of any massacre. His assumption is apparently based on the massive loss of students cited in *Yevamoth*.

13. See Re'uven Margaliot, *Yesod HaMishnah Ve'Arichatah* (Lvov, 5693), p. 22.
14. See *Shabbath* 21b.
15. See Tosafoth on *Shabbath* 45a, ד״ה מקמי חברי בשבתא. Also see Margaliot, p. 22.
16. Strikingly, in his introduction to *Midrash Aggadath BeReshith*, R. Avraham b. HaGra writes that his father referred to *Megillath Ta'anith* as "*Masecheth Chanukkah*." Similarly, the commentary of the Tosafoth on *Megillah* 7a, ד״ה נאמרה לקרות ולא לכתוב, identifies *Megillath Ta'anith* with Chanukkah. See R. Avraham Eliyyahu, *HaEshel* (commentary on *Megillath Ta'anith*) (Yerushalayim, 5669).
17. See Maharatz Chayyuth, *Kol Sifrei Maharatz Chayyuth* (Yerushalayim: Divrei Chachamim Publishers, 1958), Vol. 1, p. 154.

Ed. note: The author's reference to the Hebrew commentary on the Aramaic text of *Megillath Ta'anith* is based on a lengthy footnote by Maharatz Chayyuth in his *Ma'amar Divrei Nevi'im Divrei Kabbalah* (ibid.), where he concludes that the *megillah* comprises two parts:

a) A list of the semi-holidays on which fasting and eulogizing were prohibited. This original section of the *megillah* was written in Aramaic, the vernacular of Eretz Yisra'el during the second Temple period. Because a written record of these special days was necessary in order to observe them, special dispensation was granted to record *Megillath Ta'anith*, even as the recording of *Torah shebe'al-peh* remained strictly forbidden. *Megillath Ta'anith* was recorded by Chananyah b. Chizkiyyah b. Garon, a student of Hillel and Shammai. See *Shabbath* 13b.

b) Detailed descriptions of the miracles that occurred on these days. These accounts are recorded in pure Hebrew, indicating a different author. Maharatz Chayyuth contends that this section was not part of the original *Megillath Ta'anith* but was, like the rest of *Torah shebe'al-peh*, transmitted orally until Chazal saw fit to record it.

18. Indeed, Chanukkah has been linked with the notion of *Torah shebe'al-peh*:

> Chanukkah was the first of miracles "not meant to be written down" (*Yoma* 29a), the beginning of [the concept of a] rabbinic *mitzvah*; its root is *Torah shebe'al-peh*, as stated in the Gemara: "And where did He command us? R. Aviyya said: It follows from [the verse] 'do not stray from the word that they shall declare to you' (Devarim 17:11)" (*Shabbath* 23a).
>
> (R. Tzadok HaKohen, *Peri Tzaddik*, BeReshith, p. 150 [also see p. 141])

> "... they made [the eight days of Chanukkah] festive days of praise and thanksgiving" (*Shabbath* 21b) — This is characteristic of the notion of *Torah shebe'al-peh*.... Hence, the miracle of Chanukkah was not recorded (like Megillath Ester), nor was it written in the Mishnah.... Rather, they put a sign [lit. "letter"!] in the mouths of Yisra'el.
>
> (*Sefath Emeth*, BeReshith, p. 219)

> It is fitting that Chanukkah defies the realm of the written.... Observe how the Mishnah, too, omits the laws of Chanukkah candles. This is because their light is the light that was revealed by the great self-sacrifice involved in preserving the oral nature of the oral law.
>
> (R. Y. Hutner, *Pachad Yitzchak*, "Chanukkah" [New York, 5724], p. 11)

Yet Beith Shammai and Beith Hillel recorded *Megillath Beith Chashmonai*. Furthermore, according to the commentary of the Tosafoth, "Chanukkah was permitted, by rabbinic dispensation, to be written in *Megillath Ta'anith*" (com. on *Megillah* 7a, ד"ה נאמרה לקרות ולא לכתוב).

The following differentiation resolves this difficulty: The *events* of Chanukkah were allowed to be written down, whether in *Megillath Beith Chashmonai* or in *Megillath Ta'anith*; the *laws*, rooted in *Torah shebe'al-peh*, were to remain oral even after the Mishnah was recorded.

19. See Rashi on *Babba Metzi'a* 33b, ד"ה בימי רבי נשנית משנה זו; and *Iggereth R. Sherira Ga'on*.

20. See *Iggereth R. Sherira Ga'on*; Rambam, *Introduction to Mishneh Torah*; and Prof. Ch. Albeck, *Mavo LaMishnah* (Yerushalayim, 5719), pp. 111-15.

21. See *Yevamoth* 43a.
22. See Rambam, com. on *Mish. Menachoth* 4:2.
23. See R. Avraham Eliyyahu, *HaEshel* (Yerushalayim, 5669).
24. "From R. Sa'adyah, we know that *Megillath Beith Chashmonai* was available and popular among the people ... and that there was apparently a widespread custom to read it in synagogue on Chanukkah" (S.A. Vertheimer, *Battei Midrashoth* [Yerushalayim: Mossad HaRav Kook, 5710], pp. 311-13). *Tosefoth Rid* (*Sukkah* 42) also mentions this custom.
25. See Alon, p. 21.

Sha'ul and Amalek:
Anatomy of a Sin

Moshe Ch. Sosevsky

The essay that follows is based upon the source provided below:

Shemu'el said to Sha'ul,	ויאמר שמואל אל־שאול,
"G-d sent me to anoint you as king	אתי שלח ה' למשחך למלך,
over His people, over Yisra'el.	על־עמו על־ישראל.
And now hearken	ועתה שמע,
to the voice of the words of G-d.	לקול דברי ה':
"Thus said the G-d of Hosts:	כה אמר ה' צבא־ות,
I have taken account	פקדתי
of what Amalek did to Yisra'el:	את אשר־עשה עמלק לישראל;
that he lay in wait for him on the way	אשר־שם לו בדרך,
during [Yisra'el's] ascent from Mitzrayim.	בעלתו ממצרים:
"Now, go and smite Amalek;	עתה, לך והכיתה את־עמלק,
utterly destroy all that is his,	והחרמתם את־כל־אשר־לו,
and do not pity him.	ולא תחמל עליו.
You shall slay both men and women,	והמתה מאיש עד־אשה,
both infants and sucklings,	מעלל ועד־יונק,
both oxen and sheep,	משור ועד־שה,
both camels and donkeys."	מגמל ועד־חמור:

RABBI SOSEVSKY, *rosh yeshivah* of Yeshivat Ohr Yerushalayim, is the author of the "Commentary Digest" in *The Book of Samuel 2* — part of the *Judaica Books of the Prophets* series (New York: Judaica Press, 1978) — and is the editor of *Jewish Thought*.

Sha'ul gathered the people together,
   and he counted them in Tela'im:
   two hundred thousand infantry—
   and ten thousand men of Yehudah.
	וישמע שאול את־העם,
	ויפקדם בטלאים,
	מאתים אלף רגלי;
	ועשרת אלפים את־איש יהודה:

Sha'ul came to the city of Amalek; he fought in the brook.	ויבא שאול עד־עיר עמלק, וירב בנחל:

Sha'ul said to the Keini,
   "Go, depart, descend
   from among the Amaleki,
   lest I destroy you with him;
   and you acted kindly
   with all the children of Yisra'el,
   during their ascent from Mitzrayim."
   The Keini departed from among Amalek.
	ויאמר שאול אל־הקיני,
	לכו, סרו רדו,
	מתוך עמלקי
	פן־אספך עמו;
	ואתה עשיתה חסד
	עם־כל־בני ישראל,
	בעלותם ממצרים.
	ויסר קיני מתוך עמלק:

Sha'ul smote Amalek
   from Chavilah until the approach to Shur,
   which is before Mitzrayim.
	ויך שאול את־עמלק;
	מחוילה בואך שור,
	אשר על־פני מצרים:

He caught Agag, king of Amalek, alive,
   and all the people
   he utterly destroyed by the sword.
	ויתפש את־אגג מלך־עמלק חי,
	ואת־כל־העם
	החרים לפי־חרב:

Sha'ul and the people pitied Agag
   and the best of the sheep,
   the cattle, and the fatlings
   and the choice lambs and all that was good
   and would not utterly destroy them.
   And everything of little value and feeble
   they utterly destroyed. ...
	ויחמל שאול והעם על־אגג,
	ועל־מיטב הצאן
	והבקר והמשנים,
	ועל־הכרים ועל־כל־הטוב,
	ולא אבו החרימם;
	וכל־המלאכה נמבזה ונמס,
	אתה החרימו: ...

(Shemu'el I 15:1-9)

Shemu'el came to Sha'ul.
   Sha'ul said to him,
   "You are blessed of G-d;
   I have fulfilled the word of G-d."
	ויבא שמואל אל־שאול.
	ויאמר לו שאול,
	ברוך אתה לה';
	הקימתי את־דבר ה':

Shemu'el said,
   "And what is this sound of sheep in my ears
   and the sound of cattle, which I hear?"
	ויאמר שמואל,
	ומה קול־הצאן הזה באזני;
	וקול הבקר, אשר אנכי שמע:

Sha'ul said,
   "They brought them from the Amaleki, ויאמר שאול,
   as the people pitied מעמלקי הביאום,
   the best of the sheep and the cattle, אשר חמל העם
   in order to sacrifice to G-d your L-rd. על־מיטב הצאן והבקר,
   And the rest we utterly destroyed." למען זבח לה' א-לקיך;
ואת־היותר החרמנו:

Shemu'el said to Sha'ul,
   "Stay, and I shall relate to you
   what G-d spoke to me this night."
   He said to him, "Speak."

ויאמר שמואל אל שאול,
הרף ואגידה לך,
את אשר דבר ה' אלי הלילה.
ויאמרו (ויאמר ק') לו, דבר:

Shemu'el said,
   "While you are small in your eyes,
   are you not the head of the tribes of Yisra'el?
   G-d anointed you as king over Yisra'el.

ויאמר שמואל,
הלוא, אם־קטן אתה בעיניך,
ראש שבטי ישראל אתה?
וימשחך ה' למלך על־ישראל:

"G-d sent you on a mission;
   He said: Go and utterly destroy
   the sinners, Amalek,
   and fight against them,
   until they are consumed.

וישלחך ה' בדרך;
ויאמר, לך והחרמתה
את־החטאים את־עמלק,
ונלחמת בו,
עד־כלותם אתם:

"Why then did you not heed the voice of G-d,
   and you flew upon the spoil,
   and you did what was evil in G-d's eyes?"

ולמה לא־שמעת בקול ה';
ותעט אל־השלל,
ותעש הרע בעיני ה':

Sha'ul said to Shemu'el,
   "Indeed, I heeded the voice of G-d:
   I went on the mission
   upon which G-d sent me;
   I brought Agag, king of Amalek,
   and I utterly destroyed Amalek.

ויאמר שאול אל־שמואל,
אשר שמעתי בקול ה',
ואלך בדרך
אשר־שלחני ה';
ואביא את אגג מלך עמלק,
ואת־עמלק החרמתי:

"The people took from the spoil sheep and cattle,
   prior to their being destroyed,
   to sacrifice to G-d your L-rd in Gilgal."

ויקח העם מהשלל צאן ובקר,
ראשית החרם;
לזבח לה' א-לקיך בגלגל:

Shemu'el said,
   "Has G-d as much desire
   for burnt offerings and sacrifices
   as for heeding the voice of G-d?
   Behold, heeding is better than sacrifice,
   listening than the fat of rams.

ויאמר שמואל,
החפץ לה'
בעלות וזבחים,
כשמע בקול ה'?
הנה שמע מזבח טוב,
להקשיב מחלב אילים:

"For rebellion is like the sin of sorcery,   כי חטאת־קסם מרי,
   and stubbornness is like idolatry and *terafim*;   ואון ותרפים הפצר;
   because you disdained the word of G-d,   יען, מאסת את־דבר ה',
   He has disdained you from being king."   וימאסך ממלך:

Sha'ul said to Shemu'el, "I have sinned,   ויאמר שאול אל־שמואל, חטאתי,
   for I transgressed the commandment of G-d   כי־עברתי את־פי־ה'
   and your words: ואת־דבריך;
   for I feared the people,   כי יראתי את־העם,
   and I heeded their voice."   ואשמע בקולם:

(ibid. 15:13-24)

---

1. INTRODUCTION

Sefer Shemu'el starkly records King Sha'ul's failure to fulfill G-d's commandment in his battle with Amalek — a failure that cost Sha'ul his kingdom: "because you disdained the word of G-d, *He has disdained you from being king*" (Shemu'el I 15:23). Throughout the Bible, we find inordinate emphasis placed on the wrongdoings of great people. Yet Chazal inform us that generally these offenses were actually minute. Indeed, the Talmud contends that "whoever says that David sinned is but in error" (*Shabbath* 56a). Similar statements are made (ibid.) with respect to the questionable actions of various Biblical figures.[1] In *Derashoth HaRan*,[2] R. Nissim explains this apparent inconsistency: Since G-d judges every person according to the standard expected of him,[3] the subtle misdeeds of spiritual giants are tantamount to the actual offenses of lesser individuals.[4] Thus, the Bible's harsh description of the conduct of great people is fully consonant with the extraordinary potential G-d bestowed upon them and His commensurate expectations of them. Furthermore, such descriptions are intended to be instructive for us, expressed as they are in terms of our lesser spiritual levels.

In the case of King Sha'ul, the overstatement of his sins teaches us many things, among them the destructive power of jealousy and the pitfalls of leadership.[5] These themes are undoubtedly partly why the Bible portrays his transgressions in a manner with which common folk can identify. Yet, to apprehend Sha'ul's true stature, we must delve into not only *peshuto shel mikra* — the plain meaning of Scripture — but also what Chazal convey to us exegetically as *"midrasho shel mikra."*[6] Unlike King David, whose Tehillim offer eternal testimony to his soaring religious spirit, King Sha'ul remains enigmatic and therefore particularly vulnerable to misappraisal.

Hopefully, our meticulous evaluation of textual nuances will reveal something of King Sha'ul's full greatness and nobility. Yet Chazal caution that he is easily underestimated. The Talmud records the terrifying lesson R. Nachman b. Yitzchak was taught upon mocking Sha'ul:

> *"One year was Sha'ul in his reign"* (Shemu'el I 13:1) — Said R. Huna: [He was] like a one-year-old, who has never tasted the taste of sin.
>
> R. Nachman b. Yitzchak challenged: [Perhaps] it says [he was] like a one-year-old soiled with mud and with excrement?
>
> He was shown a panic in his dream [frightening demons agitated him (Rashi)].
>
> He said: I acknowledge you, O bones of Sha'ul son of Kish.
>
> Again he saw panic in his dream.
>
> He [then] said: I acknowledge you, O bones of Sha'ul son of Kish, *king of Yisra'el*.
>
> (*Yoma* 22b)

Elsewhere in the Talmud, even King David is stingingly rebuked for ignoring King Sha'ul's greatness:

> *"David spoke to G-d the words of this song on the day G-d saved him from the hand of all his enemies and from the hand of Sha'ul"* (Shemu'el II 22:1) — Said the Holy One Blessed be He to David: You compose a song over Sha'ul's downfall? Had you been Sha'ul and he David, I would have eliminated many "Davids" from before him[7] [for he is more righteous than you (Rashi)].
>
> (*Mo'ed Katan* 16b)

We therefore proceed cautiously, fearing that even our defense of Sha'ul will understate his true stature.[8]

2. PRELUDE TO BATTLE

"To Anoint You as King"

Prior to instructing King Sha'ul to destroy Amalek, the prophet Shemu'el emphasizes the context of this mission: "Shemu'el said to Sha'ul, '*G-d sent me to anoint you as king over His people, over Yisra'el*. And now hearken to the voice of the words of G-d'" (Shemu'el I 15:1). Why does Shemu'el reiterate that G-d had previously sent him to anoint Sha'ul as king over Yisra'el? Was not Sha'ul fully aware of this? Had he not felt the anointing oil trickling down his head?[9]

One is tempted to read Shemu'el's words as a veiled threat:[10] Should you fail in the assignment about to be given you, you will lose your kingdom. Yet this reading presumes that the prophet anticipated Sha'ul's failure, whereas Shemu'el's subsequent reaction to his prophecy of the king's downfall conveys shock and utter disbelief: *"It greatly distressed Shemu'el,* and he screamed[11] to G-d all night" (ibid. 15:11). Perhaps instead it was the prophet's quiet confidence in Sha'ul's fulfillment of his mission that prompted Shemu'el to recall his own role as anointer.

Alternately, Shemu'el may be alluding to the three commandments incumbent on the nation of Yisra'el immediately upon settling Eretz Yisra'el: "[first] to establish a monarchy and [second] to exterminate the seed of Amalek and [third] to build the Temple" (*Sanhedrin* 20b). Shemu'el may have simply referred to the sequence of these commands:[12] Now that Sha'ul had been anointed king, it was time to exterminate Amalek.[13,14]

Surely no one was better suited to fight Amalek than King Sha'ul, whose exemplary humility[15] and modesty[16] starkly contrasted with Amalek's arrogance.[17] Moreover, Scripture introduces Sha'ul with the accolade "there was no one among the children of Yisra'el better than he"[18] (Shemu'el I 9:2), and the Talmud likens him to "a one-year-old, who has never tasted the taste of sin" (*Yoma* 22b, quoted above). Such qualifications rendered him the ideal person to defeat Amalek,[19] the very essence of wickedness and sin — a nation Shemu'el described as *"the sinners,* Amalek" (Shemu'el I 15:18).[20]

"He Fought in the Brook"

Once Shemu'el assigns King Sha'ul this historic task, he seems to proceed vigorously, calling his people to war, quickly conscripting "two hundred thousand infantry — and ten thousand men of Yehudah" (ibid. 15:4), and marching them "to the city of Amalek" (ibid. 15:5). Just as we begin to anticipate a resounding victory against this eternal enemy of G-d, however, Sha'ul's resolve appears to evaporate, and the ensuing, all-important battle borders on the surrealistic. Having reached "the city of Amalek," Sha'ul does not attack it directly. Instead, the Bible states enigmatically, "he fought *in the brook*" (ibid.).

Is a brook a logical battlefield for such a major confrontation? Can 210,000 soldiers of Yisra'el vanquish a formidable opponent (wherever those Amalekim are) in a narrow body of water? Additionally, the verse speaks of *"the* brook." Which brook? Finally, although the term "וירב" (here trans. "he fought") apparently describes the fight, elsewhere it refers to mere quarreling.[21] So if the "battle" depicted here is not physical but verbal, what is the bone of contention?

Without resolving these difficulties, the Bible describes yet another turn in King Sha'ul's military campaign against Amalek: "Sha'ul said to the Keini, 'Go, depart, descend from among the Amaleki, lest I destroy you with him; and you acted kindly with all the children of Yisra'el, during their ascent from Mitzrayim' " (ibid. 15:6). After fighting "in the brook," Sha'ul interrupts his fulfillment of G-d's mission to assure safe passage to the Keini, a nomadic people descended from Yithro and residing amongst the Amalekim. Assuming that Sha'ul knew in advance about the Keini presence in the midst of Amalek, should he not have warned this innocent nation *prior* to the onset of battle? We may also wonder whether King Sha'ul's concern for the welfare of the Keini was justified when he should have single-mindedly dedicated himself to the divine command to "go and smite Amalek" (ibid. 15:3). Indeed, by withdrawing the Keini once hostilities had already begun, was Sha'ul not endangering his campaign?

The Law of the *Eglah Arufah* — The Decapitated Calf

The Talmud seeks to resolve these difficulties:

> "*He fought in the brook*" (ibid. 15:5) — Said R. Mani: [He fought] concerning *matters* of a "brook." When the Holy One Blessed be He said to Sha'ul, "go and smite Amalek [...you shall slay both men and women, both infants and sucklings, both oxen and sheep, both camels and donkeys]" (ibid. 15:3), he said, "If concerning one [murdered] soul, the Torah said, 'Bring an *eglah arufah*' [a decapitated calf for atonement; see Devarim 21], [concerning] all these souls, how much more so! And [even] if adults sinned, [in] what [way] did the children sin?" A divine echo came forth and said to him, "Do not be overly righteous!" (Koheleth 7:16).
>
> (*Yoma* 22b)[22]

According to R. Mani, the fighting "in the brook" took place not at the front but in King Sha'ul's mind, reflecting an inner struggle.[23] As Sha'ul was about to battle Amalek, the law of the *eglah arufah* haunted him, for this commandment — perhaps more than any other — teaches us the incalculable value of human life. If a murder victim is found outside city limits, the elders of the nearest town must decapitate a calf in a brook — "*the* brook" of Sha'ul's fight — to atone for their moral responsibility for the crime.[24] If the death of one individual warrants such an elaborate ceremony, Sha'ul reasoned, how could he slaughter an entire nation — men, women, children, and animals?

R. Mani's exposition resolves most of the textual difficulties in our passage. However, it seems extremely farfetched — both in linking the "brook (נחל)" of our verse to the "swiftly flowing stream (נחל איתן)"[25] (Devarim 21:4) in which the rite of the *eglah arufah* is performed and in suggesting that this commandment came to Sha'ul's mind at this juncture. Nevertheless, as noted, Chazal provide the Bible with its most original and penetrating interpretation. The *eglah arufah* appears in the Torah amidst four passages pertaining to the laws of battle (Devarim 20:1-21:14), some of which are clearly intended to safeguard moral sensitivity even in the face of dehumanizing warfare (Devarim 20:10-11, 19-20, and 21:10-14). Since "a king is initially crowned only to execute justice *and wars*" (*Yad Hil. Melachim* 4:9), the Torah's laws of warfare were surely well-studied by every king of Yisra'el. R. Mani suggests, then, that the righteous King Sha'ul undoubtedly reviewed these passages prior to battle.[26] Inevitably, therefore, the rite of the *eglah arufah* would have crossed his mind. And since this commandment seems unconnected to its surrounding passages (which concern warfare), Sha'ul concluded that its emphasis on the value of life must explain its appearance in a military context in the Torah.[27]

According to R. Mani's interpretation, however, King Sha'ul's arguments are riddled with contradictions: If he questions the justice of killing innocent children, why does he spare only Agag, the king of Amalek? Moreover, does not the very slaughter of the *eglah arufah* invalidate Sha'ul's objection to slaying innocent animals? Indeed, if he is challenging the Torah's moral authority to condemn Amalek, then how can the *eglah arufah*, itself a Torah law, bolster his case?

Evidently, R. Mani does not contend that Sha'ul's arguments led him to consider abandoning his mission, for he proceeds to destroy Amalek — men, women, children, and animals. Rather, R. Mani suggests that Sha'ul's misgivings detracted from what should have been his relentless resolve to fulfill the prophet's command. As we shall see, these errant thoughts largely determined the events that followed.

"The Keini"

We have already noted King Sha'ul's questionable concern for the Keini in the midst of battling Amalek, G-d's eternal enemy. Given R. Mani's contention that the sanctity of life preoccupied Sha'ul at this fateful juncture, perhaps he evacuated the Keini in order to prove to himself that — his military campaign notwithstanding — he remained sensitive to this sanctity. Yet, in proposing that Sha'ul's conduct toward the Keini was essentially self-serving, we again risk underestimating his true stature. In fact, Sha'ul guaranteed the Keini safe passage, even at so inopportune a moment, because he was obligated to do so — as he evidently inferred from the strange juxtaposition of two sections of the Torah.

After deducing that Yithro — progenitor of the Keini —

reached the encampment of the children of Yisra'el *after* the giving of the Torah,[28] despite the Torah's recording of his arrival beforehand (Shemoth 18), Ramban adds:

> If this is so, we need a reason why this section is written in advance here. R. Avraham [b. Ezra] said that this was due to the matter of Amalek: Having [just] mentioned the evil Amalek inflicted upon us and having commanded us to requite him according to his evil, [Scripture, by contrast, then] mentioned the good that Yithro did on our behalf,[29] *to instruct us that we should reciprocate with kindness*. And when we undertake the extermination of Amalek, as is incumbent upon us, we should warn the Keini [Yithro's descendants], who dwelt with [Amalek], and not destroy them together with [Amalek]. *And this was indeed done by Sha'ul, who said this to them.*
> (com. on Shemoth 18:1)

Radak (com. on Shofetim 1:16) echoes R. Avraham b. Ezra and Ramban, demonstrating that throughout Biblical history (including Sha'ul's treatment of the Keini) the people of Yisra'el repaid Yithro's kindness by bestowing benevolence upon his descendants at every opportunity.

We may now begin to appreciate the enormous incongruity facing Sha'ul as he proceeds to perform G-d's command to punish Amalek. Charged with destroying an entire nation, modest and forgiving[30] Sha'ul must garner all his mental energies and intensify his hatred of this despicable people.[31] Yet just before venting G-d's anger by obliterating Amalek, Sha'ul recalls his historic obligation to the Keini, which involves emotions that are diametrically opposed to his mission. He must protect the Keini, repaying them for Yithro's kindness toward Yisra'el. Could there be any greater test of his resolve to wreak G-d's vengeance on Amalek?[32]

Steadfastly, righteous King Sha'ul negotiates this difficult but necessary turnabout: Immediately after "the Keini departed from among Amalek" (Shemu'el I 15:6), *"Sha'ul smote Amalek, from Chavilah until the approach to Shur, which is before Mitzrayim. ... and all the people he utterly destroyed by the sword"* (ibid. 15:7-8). Even after his benevolence toward the Keini, Sha'ul does not shirk his obligation to annihilate Amalek.

Yet Sha'ul's resolve then seems to weaken: "He caught Agag,

king of Amalek, alive, and all the people he utterly destroyed by the sword. *Sha'ul and the people pitied Agag and the best of the sheep, the cattle, and the fatlings and the choice lambs and all that was good and would not utterly destroy them.* And everything of little value and feeble they utterly destroyed" (ibid. 15:8-9). Sha'ul's righteous determination appears to falter. In addition, Sha'ul and the people's pity on "the *best* of the sheep, the cattle, and the fatlings and the *choice* lambs" seems misplaced. Isn't pity normally directed toward the "feeble" — which, by contrast, "they utterly destroyed"?[33]

3. ASSIGNING VALUES TO THE *MITZVOTH*
"The Best of the Sheep, the Cattle, and the Fatlings"

It should be stressed that nowhere in our chapter does Shemu'el take Sha'ul to task for sparing Agag, for surely the capture of an enemy king constitutes the ultimate humbling of one's foe. It is a fate worse than death — as demonstrated by none other than Sha'ul, who had himself put to death rather than be captured by the Pelishtim (ibid. 31:4). Certainly he intended to kill Agag after publicly displaying him. Amalek's livestock was likewise doomed. Indeed, Sha'ul is never accused of lying in explaining to Shemu'el that these "best of the sheep, the cattle and the fatlings" are earmarked for sacrifice. What greater and more appropriate show of gratitude for his victory over Amalek than to sacrifice the enemy's livestock to G-d?

Additionally, it appears unlikely that the Torah's command concerning the obliteration of Amalek includes the destruction of its property. According to the Talmud, Yisra'el must exterminate only *"the seed* of Amalek" (*Sanhedrin* 20b). Similarly, in his *Sefer HaMitzvoth*, Rambam specifies that the obligation "to exterminate the seed of Amalek" includes "males, females, children, and adults" (*aseh* 188). Conspicuously missing is any requirement to destroy the livestock of Amalek.

By contrast, in his commentary on the Torah's commandment to destroy Amalek, Rashi quotes Shemu'el's command to slay "*both oxen and sheep*" (Shemu'el I 15:3), emphasizing that this commandment is intended to insure "that the name of Amalek will not be remembered even with regard to a beast — to say 'this beast belonged to Amalek'" (com. on Devarim 25:19). However, in *Minchath Chinuch*, R. Yosef Babad finds no legitimate source for this position. Furthermore, he notes, "from the incident of Sha'ul there is no proof [to substantiate Rashi's interpretation], since the Holy One Blessed be He commanded [Sha'ul] then through Shemu'el" (*Minchath Chinuch, mitzvah* 604), and any such temporal, prophetic command cannot be equated with the Torah's eternal mandate (ibid.).[34] Significantly, in Rashi's commentary on our passage, he explains that the prophetic command to slay "both oxen and sheep" was issued "because [the people of Amalek] were masters of witchcraft and would transform themselves to appear like beasts" (com. on Shemu'el I 15:3). This reasoning implies that, according to Rashi as well, there is no obligation *per se* to destroy Amalek's livestock; rather, such slaughter was necessary only to fulfill the Torah's commandment "to exterminate *the seed* of Amalek."

In sparing the animals for eventual sacrifice, then, King Sha'ul surely felt that somewhat greater liberties could be taken with prophetic commands than with Torah law. Apparently he was mistaken. Yet, given his otherwise total obliteration of Amalek, the secondary status of the command concerning the livestock, and the enormous emotional challenge of acting so ruthlessly toward Amalek immediately after expressing compassion toward the Keini, does not Sha'ul's loss of his kingdom in our chapter appear to be excessively harsh punishment for a minor infraction?

The key to pinpointing Sha'ul's sin lies in a well-known *mishnah*:

> [If] one says ... "[As] Your mercies extend to a bird's nest [so should Your mercies extend to us (Rashi)]" ... [we] silence him.
> (*Mish. Berachoth* 5:3, *Mish. Megillah* 4:9)

The Mishnah rules that if one who is leading the communal prayer service appeals to divine mercy based upon the supposed expression of this compassion in G-d's forbidding the removal of eggs or chicks from a nest before sending away the mother bird (Devarim 22:6-7), we silence him and replace him with an alternate. The Talmud explains his error: "he makes the ordinances of G-d into [acts of] mercy, whereas they are simply decrees" (*Berachoth* 33b).[35] Although G-d's commands are certainly not arbitrary and derive from His infinite wisdom, we are to perform them not because of their purported philosophical rationale but solely because they constitute His will.[36]

Had King Sha'ul recognized both tasks before him — the protection of the Keini and the extermination of Amalek — simply as G-d's will, he could have executed both with equal resolve and equanimity.[37] As R. Mani maintains, however, as Sha'ul stood ready to obliterate Amalek, thoughts of the *eglah arufah* detained him. This interpretation suggests the root of Sha'ul's downfall: He failed to reconcile the extermination of Amalek with the law of the *eglah arufah*, because he perceived the latter as affirming the value of life — and seemingly precluding the genocide of even the wicked Amalek. His obligation to extend compassion to the Keini therefore rendered him incapable of the ruthlessness necessary to "utterly destroy" Amalek.

"The Voice of G-d"

Upon defeating Amalek, Sha'ul proclaims to Shemu'el, "I have fulfilled the *word* of G-d" (Shemu'el I 15:13). In Shemu'el's ensuing rebuke, he asks in response, "Why then did you not heed the *voice* of G-d ... ?" (ibid. 15:19). In the beginning of our chapter, we find the same dichotomy in Shemu'el's instructions to Sha'ul: "And now hearken to the *voice* of the *words* of G-d" (ibid. 15:2). What distinguishes the *"voice* of G-d" from the *"word* of G-d"?

Perhaps the answer to this critical question is implicit in Shemu'el's initial description of Sha'ul's task: "Now, go and smite Amalek; *utterly destroy* all that is his, and *do not pity* him. You shall slay both men and women, both infants and sucklings, both oxen and sheep, both camels and donkeys" (ibid. 15:3). We propose that the *"word* of G-d" refers to the command to "go and smite Amalek" — men, women, children, and livestock — while the *"voice* of G-d" alludes to the spirit of the law. Executing Amalek did not suffice. To heed G-d's "voice," it was necessary to "utterly destroy" and to "not pity." The venting of divine *anger* against Amalek constituted an integral part of the command.

After acting compassionately toward the Keini, Sha'ul found

himself incapable of the utter destruction demanded by G-d. Since no explicit time limitation accompanied the prophet's command, Sha'ul intended to comply with the *"word* of G-d" by eventually slaughtering Agag and the spared livestock. Yet, by failing to "utterly destroy" Amalek and to "not pity," he did not heed the *"voice* of G-d."[38] Utter destruction precludes the sparing of anything, however noble one's intentions. Hence the resolution of one of the textual difficulties raised earlier: What is the meaning of "pity" in the Bible's record that "Sha'ul and the people *pitied* Agag and the best of the sheep, the cattle, and the fatlings and the choice lambs and all that was good and would not utterly destroy them" (ibid. 15:9)?[39] Evidently, "pity" here means not compassion but a weakening: an inability to "utterly destroy" Amalek viciously and uncompromisingly.

Given this key distinction between the "word" and "voice" of G-d, it is not surprising that, when Sha'ul tells Shemu'el, "... I have fulfilled the *word* of G-d," the prophet counters, "G-d sent you on a mission; He said: Go and *utterly destroy* the sinners, Amalek, and fight against them, until *they are consumed*. Why then did you not heed the *voice* of G-d ... ?" (ibid. 15:18-19).

"The People Pitied"

We have sought to establish that King Sha'ul's sin lay not in any outright defiance of G-d's command, but in his inability to comply with its spirit. Lest we underestimate Sha'ul's true stature, however, let us analyze the king's response to the prophet's criticism: "Sha'ul said to Shemu'el, 'Indeed, I heeded the *voice* of G-d: I went on the mission upon which G-d sent me; I brought Agag, king of Amalek, and I *utterly destroyed* Amalek. The people took from the spoil sheep and cattle, prior to their being destroyed,[40] to sacrifice to G-d your L-rd in Gilgal' "[41] (ibid. 15:20-21).

Assuming that Sha'ul never responds to the prophet dishonestly (for who more than Sha'ul could appreciate his mentor's greatness and the futility of any attempt to deceive him?), it is noteworthy that even after Shemu'el's rebuke, the king admits no wrongdoing. Rather, he emphatically denies his failure to *"utterly destroy"* Amalek with all the anger demanded by the *"voice* of G-d." It was the people who "took from the spoil" the best of the livestock — and not in defiance of G-d but, on the contrary, "to sacrifice to G-d." Perhaps Sha'ul argues (as suggested by *Be'er Mosheh*) that the command to destroy Amalek's livestock devolved solely upon himself, since he alone heard it from the prophet (whereas the people learned of it only through their king). Alternately, perhaps Sha'ul subscribed to the view (expressed in *Sefer HaYere'im* [ch. 465]) that the destruction of Amalek is a royal obligation, not a communal one. Either way, Sha'ul reasoned, as long as he himself had remained committed to slaughtering Amalek's livestock, the people could be excused if they had weakened somewhat in their resolve by sparing the best of the sheep and cattle for sacrificial purposes. In this sense, Sha'ul restates his first defense against the prophet's criticism: *"the people* pitied the best of the sheep and the cattle, in order to sacrifice to G-d your L-rd" (ibid. 15:14).

Shemu'el's response is apropos of Sha'ul's argument: "While you are small in your eyes, *are you not the head of the tribes of Yisra'el?* G-d anointed you as king over Yisra'el" (ibid. 15:17). As resolute as you believe you were, Shemu'el tells Sha'ul, you were evidently not firm enough, for had you, as king, been adamant, your people would not have challenged you. (Indeed, during King Sha'ul's previous major campaign, against the Pelishtim,[42] not one soldier tasted of the stream of honey in the forest[43] until the battle was over[44] — even though everyone was famished[45] — because of Sha'ul's oath[46] forbidding any eating.) By implication, then, any weakening of the people's resolve represents a weakening of their king's.[47]

Had the obligation to destroy Amalek comprised only technical destruction (the *"word* of G-d"), the sparing of livestock for sacrificial purposes might have been permissible and even admirable. Since, however, the command also included the *"voice* of G-d" — wreaking divine vengeance on the nation that epitomizes evil — the people's "pity" was sinful and worthless. Thus, Shemu'el appropriately admonishes Sha'ul: "Has G-d as much desire for burnt offerings and sacrifices as for *heeding the voice* of G-d? Behold, *heeding* is better than sacrifice, *listening* than the fat of rams" (ibid. 15:22). And, finally, Sha'ul acknowledges the bitter truth: "I have sinned, for I transgressed the commandment of G-d and your words: for I feared the people, and *I heeded their voice*" (ibid. 15:24). Sha'ul concedes that he "heeded *their* voice," not "the voice *of G-d*." You, Shemu'el — he says in effect — correctly assessed my state of mind: Although I thought I was steeled for the task at hand, my failure to stand up to the people — indeed, their very ability to defy me concerning the livestock — has exposed my weakness; the *voice* of G-d remained unheeded.

4. CONCLUSION

In illuminating Chazal's perspective on the deeds that cost King Sha'ul his kingdom, we may have glimpsed his tragic shortcomings, but we certainly are no less awed by his unique greatness. Even after his resolve is put to its supreme test by his thoughts of the *eglah arufah*, with its emphasis on the value of life, and by the compassion he is to show the Keini just before exterminating Amalek, Sha'ul rises to the challenge. He weakens but slightly in allowing the people to reserve some of the finest sheep and cattle for sacrifice — and this based on what he considers ample Halachic justification.

Yet, pronounces G-d's prophet Shemu'el, this insensitivity to the "*voice* of G-d" amounts to having "disdained the *word* of G-d" (ibid. 15:23); as a result, "He has disdained you from being king" (ibid.). For this seemingly minor infraction, King Sha'ul forfeits his kingdom. While his punishment appears unduly severe, it reflects his singularly great potential. Both the constant tests to which he is subjected[48] and the perfect righteousness demanded of him demonstrate King Sha'ul's towering spiritual stature. The Talmud relates that "the Holy One Blessed be He is exacting as a hairbreadth with those who surround Him [the righteous, who follow Him (Rashi)]" (*Yevamoth* 121b). Apparently, King Sha'ul belongs in that select company.

NOTES

1. These righteous individuals "sinned" either by failing to attain a moral level commensurate with their exalted stature, or by exercising flawed Halachic judgment. Regarding Sha'ul, several Talmudic references imply the latter offense. See *Eruvin* 53a and *Sanhedrin* 93b. For examples of sins that were

moral rather than actual, however, see *Shabbath* 56a and *Kethubboth* 9b.

2. See *derash* 6. *Derashoth HaRan* is generally ascribed to R. Nissim b. Re'uven (ca. 1350 C.E.), a student of Rashba and commentator on Rif's *Sefer HaHalachoth*, although some attribute it to Rabbeinu Nissim (ca. 1250 C.E.), a student of Ramban.

3. See *Yevamoth* 121b: "The Holy One Blessed be He is exacting as a hairbreadth with those who surround Him [i.e., the righteous]."

4. For a more thorough treatment of Chazal's view of the Biblical personality, see my essay "In Defense of Sha'ul," *Jewish Thought*, 1, No. 1 (5750), 101-8.

5. See *Derashoth HaRan, derash* 6, which outlines the lessons to be derived from the magnification of King David's sins.

6. See *Derashoth HaRan, derash* 6: "Nevertheless, our rabbis caution us based upon the true tradition that David did not in fact commit the sin ascribed to him by the Bible should the verses be read literally." See also Maharal MiPrag, *Be'er HaGolah, be'er* 3: "And so it is with all the '*derashoth*' found in the Talmud and the other *midrashim*; there is not one, large or small, whose words fail to [penetrate] the depth of the written text based on their true [understanding]."

7. Meiri explains this enigmatic statement in his introduction to Sefer Tehillim: "Had you been from one of the tribes foreign to royalty, and he from the tribe of Yehudah, which has been selected for royalty, I would have destroyed many 'Sha'uls' from before him." Compare *Yad Hil. Melachim* 1:7-9.

8. See Rashi ad loc., ד"ה משונה במעשיו, where he refers to Sha'ul as perfectly righteous. Also see *Mid. Tehillim* 7, where G-d demonstrates to David numerous ways in which Sha'ul is superior to him, at which point David admits his error.

9. See Shemu'el I 10:1.

10. See Rashi ad loc., ד"ה ועתה שמע: "Previously you acted foolishly [in ch. 13, where Sha'ul ignores Shemu'el's command to wait for him]; *now* be careful."

11. Compare R. Yitzchak's statement in *Rosh HaShanah* 16a: "A man's cry is effective whether before a decree [has been issued] or after a decree [has been issued]."

12. Our interpretation follows R. Yehudah, whose opinion is codified in *Yad Hil. Melachim* 1:1. R. Nehorai, however, argues that establishing a monarchy is not obligatory; it is merely a concession to the will of the people. See *Sanhedrin* 20b.

13. See Radak on Shemu'el I 15:1, ד"ה ועתה שמע.

14. In a pamphlet entitled "*Hadrath Melech*" (Yerushalayim, 1990), R. Menasheh Yosef HaLevi Miller indicates that, according to *Sefer HaYere'im* (ch. 465), the command to destroy Amalek is incumbent upon the king, while Rambam considers it a communal obligation (*Sefer HaMitzvoth*, end of positive

commands). See *Mishnah Berurah* 785:2 for differing opinions regarding the correct starting point when reading our chapter as the *haftarah* of *parashath Zachor*. R. Miller suggests that these views hinge upon the debate between *Sefer HaYere'im* and Rambam. Those who understand the command as royal begin with v. 1, which mentions Sha'ul's appointment as king. Those who deem it communal commence with v. 2, omitting the anointing of Sha'ul.

15. See *Tos. Berachoth* 4:16: "Why did Sha'ul merit royalty? Because of [his] modesty." Also see *Yal.Sh.* Shemu'el:108, 111.

16. See *Megillah* 11b.

17. See *BeM.R.* 13:3, " 'A man's arrogance shall bring him low' (Mishlei 29:23) — This refers to Amalek."

18. According to *Seder Olam*, which attributes a two-year reign to Sha'ul, David was already twenty-eight years old when this statement was made. Compare nn. 10, 11.

19. See R. Mosheh Yechiel HaLevi Epstein's commentary, *Be'er Mosheh* (Yerushalayim: Aleph Beith Publications, 1972), Shemu'el I, pp. 322-32, for an extensive evaluation of Sha'ul's unique suitability to battle Amalek.

20. For a more elaborate treatment of Amalek's personification of sin, see R. Yehoshua Bachrach, *Mah Bein Sha'ul LeDavid* (Feldheim: Yerushalayim, 1970), pp. 177-79.

21. See BeReshith 13:7, Shemoth 17:7, and Devarim 25:1.

22. The Talmud concludes: "Now when he said to Do'eg: 'Turn, you, and strike the priests ...' (Shemu'el I 22:18), a voice came from heaven and said to him: 'Do not be overly wicked!' (Koheleth 7:17)." The *midrash* refers to Sha'ul's failure to pity the men, women, children, and cattle of the priestly city of Nov, brutally ordering their death as rebels against the kingdom. The implications of this *midrash* are beyond the parameters of this essay. See Bachrach, pp. 37-46, for a more extensive analysis.

23. See Abarbanel and Malbim for interpretations more in accordance with the simple meaning of the text.

24. See Devarim 21:8 and *Sotah* 48b.

25. נחל means "brook" according to R. Ovadyah Bartenurah's commentary on *Mish. Pe'ah* 2:1 and *Tosefoth R. Akiva Eiger* ad loc. Rashbam (*Babba Bathra* 55b) and Rashi (*Babba Kamma* 61a), however, translate it as "valley." See R. Baruch HaLevi Epstein, *Torah Temimah*, Devarim 21:4, which cites numerous Biblical and Talmudic proofs that a נחל is a brook, yet suggests as a compromise that it is a wadi, which rages with water only during the rainy season.

26. The two Biblical passages immediately preceding the law of the *eglah arufah* begin: a) "When you come near a city to fight against it ..." (Devarim 20:10); b) "When you besiege a city ..." (ibid. 20:19). Conceivably, the *derash* of R. Mani is suggesting that the verse "Sha'ul came to the city of Amalek; he fought in the brook" (Shemu'el I 15:5) alludes to his coming upon the above

passages as they pertained to his battle against Amalek. Based on their sequence, he first came upon the laws concerning the besieging of a city (in this case, the city of Amalek) and then battled with his thoughts concerning "the brook" (i.e., the *eglah arufah*).

Other than the difficulties cited in this essay, an additional indication of the incongruity between "Sha'ul came to the city of Amalek" and "he fought in the brook" may be derived from BeReshith 26:17, "Yitzchak went from there and encamped in the brook of Gerar ...." On the phrase "the brook of Gerar," Rashi comments, "Far from the city," apparently assuming that any brook or wadi (see n. 22) is bound to be far-removed from any city. Also see Abarbanel and the Keli Yakar, who discuss the connection between the *eglah arufah* and its legislative context.

Furthermore, given that elsewhere the Talmud understands the word "ריבות (quarrels)" (Devarim 17:8) as an allusion to the *eglah arufah* (see *Sanhedrin* 87a), perhaps R. Mani's interpretation of the aforementioned verse in Shemu'el is supported not only by the word "נחל (brook)" but by the word "וירב (he fought)."

27. See *Hadrath Melech* for a lengthy evaluation of the pertinence of the laws of warfare to the battle against Amalek.

28. See *Zevachim* 116a, where the timing of Yithro's arrival is debated.

29. Ramban refers to Yithro's role in helping Mosheh Rabbeinu organize an effective judicial system. See Shemoth 18:13-27.

30. See Shemu'el I 10:27.

31. See *Yad Hil. Melachim* 5:5, "It is a positive commandment to remember constantly [Amalek's] evil deeds and ambush [of Yisra'el] in order to arouse hatred toward him ...."

32. See Shemu'el II 21:1-2 and Rashi ad loc., where a three-year plague during David's reign is attributed to a) his failure to eulogize Sha'ul properly, and b) Sha'ul's sin in ravaging the priestly city of Nov and executing the Gibonites. Rashi, citing *Yevamoth* 78b, comments: "Now do not wonder that the Holy One Blessed be He demands [Sha'ul's] honor and [simultaneously] demands retribution for his sin, for so it is written: 'who have performed His judgment' (Tzefanyah 2:3): Wherever His judgment is found, His performance [of good deeds] can also be found." Perhaps G-d uses Sha'ul to teach this lesson because of his inability to pursue kindness and retribution simultaneously. See Bachrach, "The Anointment of King David," *Jewish Thought*, 1, No. 2 (5751), 53-59, where it is indicated that David had this ability.

33. See Bachrach, *Mah Bein Sha'ul LeDavid*, p. 182.

34. *Minchath Chinuch's* inability to locate a source for Rashi's opinion is puzzling since *Sifrei* on Devarim 25:19 (and *Mechilta* on Shemoth 17:16) clearly supports his view: "The Holy One Blessed be He took an oath on his Throne of Glory not to leave any descendant of Amalek or camel or donkey [of

Amalek] under the heavens so that none would come to say, 'This camel belongs to Amalek.' " See, however, *Hadrath Melech* (p. 12), according to which the very need for a divine oath indicates that the destruction of Amalek's livestock is not part of the Torah's command. *Minchath Chinuch* evidently contends that the fulfillment of this oath necessitated the prophetic command to Sha'ul. Also see *Pes. Rabbathi* 12, which suggests that Sha'ul alone was selected to accomplish the utter destruction of Amalek.

35. See *Berachoth* 33b and Rashi ad loc., ד״ה מדותיו.

36. Compare *Rosh HaShanah* 28a: "Commandments were given not for pleasure [but as a yoke around (the Jews') necks (Rashi)]."

37. For a broader treatment of this idea, see Bachrach, pp. 170-72.

38. Compare n. 32.

39. להחרים (to utterly destroy) in its various forms appears a full eight times in this chapter.

40. See *Targum Yonathan* ad loc.

41. Perhaps Shemu'el's retort, "And what is this sound [lit. "voice"] of sheep in my ears and the sound [lit. "voice"] of cattle, which I hear?" (Shemu'el I 15:14), hints that sparing the livestock constituted a breach of the voice of the L-rd.

42. See Shemu'el I 14:1-31.

43. See ibid. 14:25-26.

44. See ibid. 14:24.

45. See ibid. 14:28, 31.

46. See ibid. 14:24, 28.

47. Indeed, the text states: "Sha'ul and the nation pitied ..." (Shemu'el I 15:9), the nation's pity indicating that Sha'ul had also pitied.

48. See Shemu'el I 13, where, with a well-equipped Philistine army of perhaps hundreds of thousands ("like the sand on the seashore" [ibid. 13:5]) poised to strike Sha'ul's six hundred unarmed soldiers at any time, he was expected to hold his ground and fearlessly await the prophet's arrival for up to seven days. To test Sha'ul, the prophet arrives at the last moment.

THE LAST KING OF YEHUDAH
The Tragic Saga of King Tzidkiyyahu

Yitzchak Levi, z.l.

1. INTRODUCTION

Tzidkiyyahu ben Yoshiyyahu was the last of the glorious kings descended from the house of David, who ruled the land of Yehudah for the four centuries during which the first Beith HaMikdash stood atop the mountains of Tziyyon.

Who was this man, whose actions led to the destruction of our magnificent Temple, the Babylonian exile, and the end of the Davidic dynasty? Could he have avoided the retribution foreseen by the prophets? Did his rule hasten it? Was he in command of the situation and yet Providence prevailed, or was he a victim of circumstance, stripped of his free choice in order that the divine will would be fulfilled?

One thing is certain: "[G-d] leads counselors away spoiled; judges He makes fools. He looses the bond of kings.... He re-

---

RABBI LEVI, z.l., was a popular lecturer in Tanach and contributed frequently to Hebrew-language journals until his untimely passing in the summer of 1991. He is the author of *Parashiyyoth BeSifrei HaNevi'im* on Yehoshua and Shofetim (Yerushalayim: Feldheim, 1988). This essay was translated (by Daniel Haberman) from the author's *Parashiyyoth BaNevi'im BeIkvoth Chazal* (Yerushalayim, 1991).

moves the heart of the leaders of the people of the land; He makes them wander in a wilderness, where there is no way" (Iyyov 12:17-18, 24). G-d is the Master of the universe; we are mere tools in His hand. Although we act of our own free will,[1] we carry out the calling of Providence.

Who was this man, then, who was assigned such a wretched role? What follows is an attempt to understand Tzidkiyyahu and his actions in the context of his generation and upbringing, according to Scripture and the words of Chazal.

2. BACKGROUND: THE DAYS OF YOSHIYYAHU

> *"The sons of Yoshiyyahu: the firstborn, Yochanan; the second, Yehoyakim; the third, Tzidkiyyahu; the fourth, Shallum"* (Divrei HaYamim I 3:15) — Said Mar: Shallum and Tzidkiyyahu were the same person.... But are they not each listed individually, as it is written: *"the third ... the fourth"*? [Rather,] what is the meaning of *"the third"*? The third of the sons. And what is the meaning of *"the fourth"*? The fourth to reign, as Yeho'achaz reigned first, then Yehoyakim, then Yechonyah, and finally Tzidkiyyahu.
>
> Our rabbis taught: Shallum and Tzidkiyyahu were the same person. Why, then, was he called "Shallum"? Because he was perfect in his deeds ["שלום" is expounded as "משולם" ("perfect")]. Others say: Because in his days, Davidic rule ended ["שלום" is expounded as "שלמה" ("ended")]. And what was his [real] name? Mattanyah, as it is said: "The king of Bavel [Nevuchadnetzar] appointed Mattanyah, [Yechonyah's] uncle, king in his stead; he changed his name to Tzidkiyyahu ("G-d is my *judgment*")" (Melachim II 24:17). [Nevuchadnetzar] said to him: "May G-d execute *judgment* upon you should you rebel against me!" ... And it is written: "And [Tzidkiyyahu] also rebelled against King Nevuchadnetzar, who had made him swear by G-d ..." (Divrei HaYamim II 36:13).
>
> (*Horayoth* 11b)[2]

Mattanyah-Tzidkiyyahu is born to righteous[3] King Yoshiyyahu in the twenty-first year of his rule, he being twenty-nine years of age. (Yoshiyyahu began his reign at age eight!) Tzidkiyyahu is born just three years after his father has repaired the Beith HaMikdash and eradicated idolatry from the Holy Land.

At an early age, Yoshiyyahu "began to seek the L-rd of David his father" (Divrei HaYamim II 34:3). Throughout the reign of Menasheh and Ammon, Yoshiyyahu's forefathers, the service of G-d was neglected, for pagan priests had captured the nation's spirit.[4] Only with great effort does Yoshiyyahu restore the sanctity of the people, the land, and the Temple.

The shocking discovery of a Torah scroll in the Beith HaMikdash occurs in those days.[5] Shafan the scribe reads the king the words "Cursed is he who does not uphold the words of this Torah ..." (Devarim 27:26); "the king rent his garments and said: 'It is my duty to uphold it'" (*Yer. Sotah* 7:4). Shafan continues reading: "G-d will lead you and the king you establish over you to a nation that you and your fathers have not known ..." (Devarim 28:36).[6] The king fears for his people's future on account of his forefathers' sins: "... for great is the wrath of G-d that is kindled against us because our forefathers have not hearkened unto the words of this book, to do according to all that is written concerning us" (Melachim II 22:13). At Yoshiyyahu's request, Shafan and others then consult Chuldah the prophetess; her response[7] — though reassuring to the king personally — only heightens his anxiety about the nation's future.

Consequently, Yoshiyyahu enters his people into a new covenant: "to walk after G-d and to observe His commandments, testimonies, and statutes with full heart and soul, to uphold the words of this covenant, which are written in this book" (ibid. 23:3). A great spirit of purity and holiness seizes the king and his people, whereupon "Yoshiyyahu removed all the abominations from all the territories of the children of Yisra'el, and he made all who were found in Yisra'el serve G-d, their L-rd; all his days they departed not from following G-d, the L-rd of their fathers" (Divrei HaYamim II 34:33).

During those days, a son is born unto the repentant king: Mattanyah-Tzidkiyyahu. Young Tzidkiyyahu hears of the great spiritual upheaval; of the angry prophecies of Yirmeyahu, who exhorts the people to complete penitence; and of the hiding of the ark and other items in anticipation of retribution.[8] For although King Yoshiyyahu has repented, "... G-d had not turned away from the fierceness of His wrath, which blazed against Yehudah, because of all the provocations with which Menasheh had provoked Him. G-d said: I will also banish Yehudah from My presence, as I have banished Yisra'el; I will detest this city that I have chosen, Yerushalayim, and the house of which I said, My name shall abide there" (Melachim II 23:26-27).

In this atmosphere of purification and consecration on the one hand and dread of destruction and exile on the other, the young prince of the house of David grows up. As the Assyrian empire crumbles, he surely hears both the royal court and the people debate whether to side with the rising power, Bavel, or with Mitzrayim.

To this debate, Yirmeyahu reacts strongly: "Also the children of Nof and Tachpanchess have broken the crown of your head. Have you not done this to yourself, in your forsaking G-d your L-rd, while He led you on the way? Now, what is there for you on the way to Mitzrayim — to drink the waters of Shichor? And what is there for you on the way to Ashur — to drink the waters of a river?" (Yirmeyahu 2:16-18). There is only one way to avoid calamity: "Withhold your foot from going bare, and your throat from thirst ..." (ibid. 2:25). Says the prophet in effect: It is not too late to repent; drink neither of Shichor nor of the Nile, but trust in the L-rd of your fathers truthfully and completely.

> After all this, Yoshiyyahu having repaired the Temple,
> Necho, king of Mitzrayim, came up to fight at Karkemish by Perath;
> Yoshiyyahu went out against him.
> [Necho] sent messengers to him, saying:
> "What have I to do with you, O king of Yehudah?
> [I come] not against you yourself this day
> but against the house with which I am at war,
> and the L-rd has instructed me to hurry;
> restrain yourself from [interfering with] G-d, Who is with me,
> that He not destroy you."
> And Yoshiyyahu did not turn his face away from him,
> but he sought an opportunity to fight him,
> and he did not listen to the words of Necho
> from the mouth of the L-rd;
> he came to fight in the plain of Megiddo.
> The archers shot at King Yoshiyyahu;
> the king told his servants:
> "Take me away, for I am badly wounded."

His servants carried him off ... and brought him to Yerushalayim;
he died and was buried in the graves of his fathers,
all of Yehudah and Yerushalayim mourning over Yoshiyyahu.
Yirmeyahu lamented Yoshiyyahu;
... behold, [these laments] are written in the Laments.
(Divrei HaYamim II 35:20-25)

The relative calm of Yoshiyyahu's rule is short-lived. Tzidkiyyahu is ten years old when his father, the king, falls in battle in the plain of Megiddo. It is hard to accept this divine decree as righteous inasmuch as it is executed "After all this, Yoshiyyahu having repaired the Temple ..." (ibid. 35:20).

> R. Shemu'el b. Nachmani said in the name of R. Yonathan: Why was Yoshiyyahu punished? Because he should have consulted with Yirmeyahu, yet he did not. What verse did Yoshiyyahu expound? "... no sword shall cross your land" (VaYikra 26:6) — even a sword of peace. Yoshiyyahu, however, did not realize that his generation found little favor in the eyes of G-d.
>
> (Ta'anith 22b)

Yoshiyyahu expounded the verse correctly; nevertheless, he should have conferred with the prophet. For a king does not know the hidden face of his people and whether his generation merits a miracle. Here, the condition was: "If you walk in My statutes, observe My commandments, and do them" (VaYikra 26:3). Only the prophet could have told Yoshiyyahu whether this condition had been fulfilled. Yet the king employed his own reasoning:

> "... he did not listen to the words of Necho from the mouth of the L-rd ..." (Divrei HaYamim II 35:22) — This [verse refers to] Yirmeyahu, who said to Yoshiyyahu, "Thus have I received from Yeshayahu, my master: 'I will set Mitzrayim against Mitzrayim ...' (Yeshayahu 19:2)." And [Yoshiyyahu] didn't listen to [Yirmeyahu]. Rather, [Yoshiyyahu] said to [Yirmeyahu]: "Did not Mosheh, the master of your master, say: '... no sword shall cross your land' (VaYikra 26:6)? And the sword of that wicked one is crossing my land and my borders!" He did not realize that his entire generation worshipped idols. He would send a pair of young scholars to remove [idols] from [the] houses; they would enter and find nothing [for a forbidden image was engraved inside the door ... half on one side and half

on the other (*Mattenoth Kehunah*)]. When they would leave, [the people] would say to them, "Close the door." Once they closed the door, the image would become apparent.

(*Eich.R.* 1:53)

Mournfulness and anxiety descend on the royal city of Yerushalayim. The dying king is brought in on the chariot of his second, and Yirmeyahu is present as Yoshiyyahu's soul departs:

> When [Yoshiyyahu] was dying, Yirmeyahu observed that [the king's] lips were moving, and he feared that, Heaven forbid, [Yoshiyyahu] was saying something improper because of his great pain; [then] he overheard him accepting the righteousness of [G-d's] decree against him, saying: "G-d is righteous, for I have rebelled against his word ..." (Eichah 1:18). Then [Yirmeyahu] pronounced him "The breath of our nostrils, the anointed of G-d ..." (ibid. 4:20).
>
> (*Ta'anith* 22b)

Accepting the righteousness of the divine decree, Tzidkiyyahu's father has departed for the world that is entirely good. With Yisra'el bereft of a leader at a critical juncture, Yirmeyahu laments Yoshiyyahu:

> How the gold has grown dim,
> the pure gold is changed....
> our end is near, our days are done, for our end is come. ...
> The breath of our nostrils, the anointed of G-d,
> has been captured in their snares —
> of whom we said,
> "In his shadow, we shall live among the nations."
>
> (Eichah 4:1, 18, 20)

3. LAYING THE GROUNDWORK FOR DISASTER

The people of the land enthrone Yochanan-Yeho'achaz, Tzidkiyyahu's older brother. Although Elyakim-Yehoyakim is two years older, Yeho'achaz is worthier of the throne.[9] He does not last, however. Returning from battle, Paroh Necho exploits Yehudah's weakness and exiles Yeho'achaz to Mitzrayim, for he has sinned: "She raised one of her cubs, he became a young lion; he learned to catch prey — he devoured men. The nations heard of him, he was caught in their snare; they dragged him off with hooks to the land of Mitzrayim" (Yechezkel 19:3-4).

Paroh Necho then installs Yehoyakim, thinking that he will faithfully shield Mitzrayim's northern border from the king of Bavel. But King Yehoyakim proves tyrannical:

> Woe unto him who builds his house with unfairness
> and his chambers with injustice;
> who makes his fellow man work without pay
> and does not give him his wages. ...
> For your eyes and heart are only on greed,
> on shedding innocent blood,
> and on committing violence and oppression.
> Therefore, thus says G-d
> concerning Yehoyakim ben Yoshiyyahu, king of Yehudah:
> They shall not eulogize him....
> He shall have the burial of an ass,
> dragged about and cast forth
> beyond the gates of Yerushalayim.
> (Yirmeyahu 22:13, 17-19)

Like Yirmeyahu, the prophet Uriyyahu ben Shemayahu of Kiryath Ye'arim also warns the king and his people of retribution and destruction. Fearing for his life, Uriyyahu flees to Mitzrayim, but the king's men bring him back. Yehoyakim then murders the prophet, hoping thereby to foil his prophecy.[10]

Initially, at least, the king's twisted scheme seems to succeed, for Yehudah enjoys three years of grace. In reality, however, Bavel is simply preoccupied with the conquest of Ashur. Having been installed by the king of Mitzrayim, Yehoyakim looks on and awaits the outcome of the power struggle between that country and Bavel.

Meanwhile, "The Holy One Blessed be He wanted to return the world to [a state of] null and void on account of Yehoyakim. [But] He looked at his generation, and His anger subsided" (*Arachin* 17a). Mindful of Yehudah's precarious position, Yirmeyahu continues to call for complete repentance:

> Perhaps they will listen and turn back,
> each from his evil way,
> that I may renounce the evil
> that I am planning to bring upon them....

> If you do not obey Me
> [by] walking in My Torah....
> I will make this house like Shiloh,
> and I will make this city a curse
> for all the nations of the earth ...
> And now mend your ways and your deeds,
> and heed the voice of G-d your L-rd,
> that G-d may renounce the evil
> that He has decreed upon you.
> (Yirmeyahu 26:3-4, 6, 13)

Alas, this grace period goes unutilized. In Bavel, Nevuchadnetzar ascends the throne, captures Nineveh, the royal city of Ashur,[11] and deals Paroh Necho such a blow[12] that he "never again ventured out of his land, for the king of Bavel had seized all that had belonged to the king of Mitzrayim, from the brook of Mitzrayim to the river Perath" (Melachim II 24:7). That year, the decree is sealed: Yisra'el will be exiled and Yerushalayim will taste the cup of wrath.[13] Yirmeyahu informs the people of Yehudah of this decree:

> From the thirteenth year
> of Yoshiyyahu ben Ammon, king of Yehudah,
> to this day — these twenty-three years —
> the word of G-d has come to me:
> I have spoken to you persistently
> but you have not listened.
> And G-d has constantly sent you
> all His servants the prophets,
> but you have not listened or inclined your ear to hear.
> [They came] to say:
> "Turn back now, each from his evil way
> and from the evil of your deeds,
> that you may remain on the soil
> that G-d has given you...."
> ... I will send and take all the families of the north —
> declares G-d —
> and My servant, Nevuchadnetzar, king of Bavel....
> This entire land shall be a ruin, an astonishment;
> those nations shall serve the king of Bavel seventy years.
> (Yirmeyahu 25:3-5, 9, 11)

As he matures, Tzidkiyyahu witnesses his older brother's corruption and tyranny. To silence G-d's word and decree, the king even imprisons Yirmeyahu.[14] Nevertheless, the prophet instructs his disciple, Baruch ben Neriyyah, to read the people the scroll of retribution. Says Yirmeyahu:

> Perhaps the house of Yehudah
> will hear all the evil I intend to do to them;
> that they may return, each from his wicked way,
> and I will pardon their iniquity and their sin. ...
> Perhaps their entreaty will be accepted before G-d,
> and they will return, each from his wicked way;
> for great is the anger and wrath
> that G-d has pronounced against this people.
> (ibid. 36:3, 7)

And indeed, great fear envelops the people and their leaders. They believe Yirmeyahu's prophecy but fear their oppressive king even more: "The officials said to Baruch: 'Go into hiding, you and Yirmeyahu; let no man know where you are!' " (ibid. 36:19). The generation remains capable of repentance and expiation, but its heart has been sealed by its stubborn king. Ignoring princely pleas not to burn the scroll, Yehoyakim orders the arrest of its bearers, the prophet and his disciple; "... but G-d hid them" (ibid. 36:26).

Having missed his last opportunity to save his generation and avert the evil decree, Yehoyakim is doomed:

> Of Yehoyakim, king of Yehudah, you shall say:
> Thus said G-d:
> You burned that scroll, saying:
> "Why have you written upon it to say:
> 'The king of Bavel will surely come and destroy this land
> and cause man and beast to cease from it'?"
> Therefore, thus said G-d concerning Yehoyakim, king of Yehudah:
> He shall have none sitting on the throne of David;
> and his corpse shall be cast out
> to the heat by day and to the frost by night.
> I will punish him and his offspring and his servants
> for their iniquity;
> I will bring upon them and upon the inhabitants of Yerushalayim

and unto the men of Yehudah
all the evil that I have pronounced amongst them —
but they would not listen.

                                                   (ibid. 36:29-31)

4. TZIDKIYYAHU'S REIGN

Nevuchadnetzar, G-d's weapon of war, takes control of Yehudah. The king of Mitzrayim dares not aid his vassal, Yehoyakim. For three years, the king of Yehudah is subservient, yet he still relies on that "reed staff" (Yechezkel 29:6), Mitzrayim. Unable to accept that Mitzrayim's time has passed, he defies the king of Bavel. For when a man trusts in the might of horses and the strength of his forearm, refusing to believe that the Holy One Blessed be He runs the world, he sees only what he wants to see, ignoring portents of calamity. We are shocked by Yehoyakim's obstinacy as he leads his people to the brink of the abyss. Mitzrayim has already suffered a crippling blow — even without Yirmeyahu's prophecies, the king should understand that times have changed.

How does his younger brother, Tzidkiyyahu, see the situation? Does he, too, lean towards Mitzrayim and advocate defiance of the king of Bavel? Or is he convinced by the prophecies, having already witnessed the beginning of their realization? Will he draw the right conclusion from Yehudah's sorry state? Since Tzidkiyyahu has now matured, the events of the day will surely help shape his opinions and policies once he takes power. We will soon see how he reacts to similar predicaments.

Meanwhile, Yehoyakim's reign is coming to an end: "G-d sent against him bands of Kasdim, bands of Aram, bands of Mo'av, bands of the children of Ammon; He sent them against Yehudah to destroy it; in accordance with the word of G-d, which He had spoken through his servants the prophets" (Melachim II 24:2). The diminishing kingdom of Yehudah is invaded from all sides.

In the third year of Yehoyakim's rebellion, "Nevuchadnetzar, king of Bavel, came to Yerushalayim and besieged it. G-d delivered into his hand Yehoyakim, king of Yehudah, and some of the vessels of the house of the L-rd ..." (Daniyyel 1:1-2). The king of Bavel orders Yehoyakim brought to Bavel in chains,[15] and he dies forthwith;[16] everything Yirmeyahu has prophesied about him has come to pass.[17]

The kingdom of Yehudah is now subjugated by the king of Bavel. At first, he installs Yehoyakim's son, Yehoyachin-Yechonyah, as king, but before he establishes himself on the throne, Nevuchadnetzar's subjects warn him concerning the new monarch: "So goes the proverb: The good-tempered whelp of an ill-tempered dog, do not raise; the ill-tempered whelp of an ill-tempered dog, how much less!" (VaY.R. 19:6). Nevuchadnetzar heeds their warning:

> "At that time, the troops of Nevuchadnetzar, king of Bavel, went up to Yerushalayim; the city came under siege. Nevuchadnetzar, king of Bavel, came upon the city; and his troops were besieging it" (Melachim II 24:10-11) — The Sanhedrin went out to meet him; they said to him: "Has the time come for this house to be destroyed?" He answered: "No — just hand over the one I enthroned, and I'll be on my way." They went and told Yechonyah: "Nevuchadnetzar wants you"....
>
> (VaY.R. 19:6)

Young King Yechonyah goes off to exile,

> ... he, his mother,
> his servants, his princes, and his officers....
> [Nevuchadnetzar] carried out of there
> all the treasures of the house of G-d,
> and the treasures of the king's house....
> He exiled all of Yerushalayim,
> and all the princes and all the *brave warriors* —
> ten thousand exiles —
> and all the *craftsmen* and the *smiths*;
> none remained, save the poorest people in the land. ...
> The king of Bavel appointed Mattanyah, [Yechonyah's] uncle, king in his stead,
> and changed his name to Tzidkiyyahu.
>
> (Melachim II 24:12-14, 17)

"*Brave*" (ibid. 24:14) — What bravery is there in men who go off to exile? How can men bound in chains and shackles do battle? Rather, they were bold-hearted in Torah....

"*Warriors*" (ibid.) — [They fought] in the give and take of combat in Torah.

"*Craftsmen* (חרש)" (ibid.) — One would speak and all would be silent ["חרש" is expounded as "מחריש" ("one who silences")].

"*Smiths* (מסגר)" (ibid.) — All would sit down before him to learn from him, and once he'd close [a topic], none would [re]open it ["מסגר" is expounded as "סוגר" ("close")].

(*Sifrei* on Devarim 32:25; *Seder Olam*, ch. 25)

"*Craftsmen* (חרש)" — When one of them began [to speak], all would become [overwhelmed] as though deaf.

"*Smiths* (מסגר)" — A matter closed by them could be opened by no one.

(*Gittin* 88a)

Over whom is Tzidkiyyahu appointed king? The sages (including the Sanhedrin), the princes of Yehudah, and the brave men have all gone into exile with Yechonyah. Of this spiritual elite, Yirmeyahu prophesies: "Thus said G-d, the L-rd of Yisra'el: Like these good figs, so will I favorably regard the exiles of Yehudah, whom I have driven out of this place to the land of the Kasdim. I will set My eye upon them for good, I will bring them back to this land.... I will give them a heart to know Me, for I am G-d; they will be My people, and I will be their L-rd...." (Yirmeyahu 24:5-7). This generation is worthy of saving the entire world.[18] Their exile will atone for sin; they will repent and rebuild the house of Yisra'el.

So who are Tzidkiyyahu's subjects? "...the poorest people in the land" (Melachim II 24:14). They are poor both in deeds and in Torah: "The Holy One Blessed be He wanted to return the world to [a state of] null and void on account of Tzidkiyyahu's generation" (*Arachin* 17a). They are "bad figs" (Yirmeyahu 24:2, 8); only the merit of Tzidkiyyahu's good deeds preserved them: "[But G-d] looked at Tzidkiyyahu, and His anger subsided" (*Arachin* 17a).

Yet even Tzidkiyyahu, "perfect in his deeds" (*Horayoth* 11b),[19] cannot save his generation, for G-d has promised: "I will make them a horror — an evil — to all the kingdoms of the earth; a disgrace and a proverb, a byword and a curse, in all the places to which I banish them. I will send the sword, famine, and pestilence against them; until they are exterminated from the land that I gave them and their fathers" (Yirmeyahu 24:9-10).

From the very outset, Tzidkiyyahu's rule is shaky both politically and spiritually:

> ... the king of Bavel came to Yerushalayim....
> He took of the royal seed,
> and made a covenant with him,
> and imposed an oath on him...
> To be a lowly kingdom, not to rise up;
> to observe his covenant and so endure.
> (Yechezkel 17:12-14)

Tzidkiyyahu rules over "a lowly kingdom" that has sworn in the name of the L-rd[20] "not to rise up." For Nevuchadnetzar knows that the kings of Yehudah will use any ploy to retain their territory's independence. Therefore, only by imposing on Tzidkiyyahu an oath in the name of Heaven, which cannot readily be absolved,[21] can Nevuchadnetzar restrain this powerful nationalism. Thus, the king of Bavel renames the king of Yehudah "Tzidkiyyahu" ("G-d is my *judgment*"): "[Nevuchadnetzar] said to him: 'May G-d execute *judgment* upon you should you rebel against me!' " (*Horayoth* 11b). The name "Tzidkiyyahu" will be a daily reminder of his subjugation to Bavel and his inability to rebel. His is indeed "a lowly kingdom."

Even as the Jews exiled to Bavel commence seventy long years of nurturing their hopes of redemption,[22] their brethren in Eretz Yisra'el have not learned their lesson:

> [False prophets] strengthen the hands of evildoers,
> so that none turns back from his wickedness....
> They say still to those who despise Me:
> "God has said: All shall be well with you";
> and to everyone who walks after the stubbornness of his heart
> they say:
> "No evil shall come upon you." ...
> they lead My people astray with their lies....
> (Yirmeyahu 23:14, 17, 32)

Yirmeyahu alone defies the pack of "prophets who delude ... who steal My words ... who use their own language and pronounce that [I] have said it ... who prophesy false dreams ..." (ibid. 23:16, 30-32). Only he warns of calamity:

> Behold, the storm of G-d goes forth in fury,
> a whirling tempest;
> it shall fall upon the head of the wicked.
> The anger of the L-rd shall not turn back
> till it has fulfilled and till it has completed His purposes;
> in the end of days, you shall clearly perceive it.
> (ibid. 23:19-20)

Yet no one heeds Yirmeyahu's words. The prophet roams the streets of Yerushalayim, searching for even one person who acts justly and seeks integrity:

> Then I said:
> These are just poor folk;
> they act foolishly,
> for they have not known the way of G-d,
> the judgment of their L-rd.
> I will get me to the great men
> and I will speak with them,
> for they have known the way of G-d,
> the judgment of their L-rd;
> but they all had broken the yoke,
> they had burst the bonds. ...
> And this people has
> a wayward and defiant heart;
> they have turned aside and gone.
> They have not said in their heart, "Let us revere G-d our L-rd...."
> Your iniquities have turned away these things;
> and your sins
> have withheld goodness from you. ...
> An appalling, horrible thing
> has happened in the land:
> The prophets prophesy falsely,
> the priests rule accordingly,
> and My people like it so;
> but what will you do at its end?"
> (ibid. 5:4-5, 23-25, 30-31)[23]

As it is written: "Your prophets have envisioned for you vanity and folly, and they have not exposed your iniquity to restore your captivity; they have envisioned for you burdens of vanity and deception" (Eichah 2:14). Such "burdens of vanity" are deceptive, but "[the] people like it so" (Yirmeyahu 5:31). For it is more pleasant to listen to false optimism — which makes no demands and encourages evildoers — than to listen to the words of the living G-d, which warn of impending retribution and call for radical change in thought and deed.

5. TZIDKIYYAHU'S GREAT TRIAL

Nevuchadnetzar places his confidence in loyal Tzidkiyyahu, granting him dominion over five of Yehudah's neighbors: Edom, Mo'av, Ammon, Tzor, and Tzidon. Tzidkiyyahu travels to Bavel to meet with Nevuchadnetzar;[24] their relationship of trust is strengthened.[25]

One officer accompanying Tzidkiyyahu, Serayah, carries a book of Yirmeyahu's prophecies concerning the downfall of Bavel.[26] The prophet instructs him to tie a stone to it, hurl it into the river Perath, and cry out: "Thus shall Bavel sink and not rise, because of the evil that I will bring upon it" (ibid. 51:64).

How should Tzidkiyyahu interpret these instructions? If Bavel's decline is inevitable, then it has played out its role, and the time for rebellion has come. Perhaps the very kings over whom Nevuchadnetzar has given him control will serve as messengers of Providence and be his allies.

Tzidkiyyahu receives the envoys of these kings in his capital, Yerushalayim, and conspires with them to liberate themselves from Bavel's yoke.[27] They see the political situation as ripe for revolt. Yehudah and its neighbors to the south, east, and north constitute a coalition of considerable strength within the young Babylonian empire; Paroh of Mitzrayim, who still dreams of revenge against Bavel, winks at them from afar.

Just then, Yirmeyahu appears before them, a yoke on his neck, and explains how G-d runs the world: Neither diplomatic opportunities nor ambitions create international upheavals, and false prophets — who merely express the desires of men — certainly cannot know the future. Only the Creator of the universe marshals the forces of the world and determines outcomes. He empowers whomever he pleases, disenfranchising him when the time comes. No man can frustrate G-d's plan or obstruct His will:

> ... thus said the G-d of Hosts, the L-rd of Yisra'el:
> Say thus to your masters:
> I made the earth,
> the man and the beast
> that are on the face of the earth,
> by My great might,
> and by My outstretched arm;
> and I have given it
> to whomever has seemed proper in My eyes.
> And now I have delivered all these lands
> to Nevuchadnetzar, king of Bavel, My servant....
> All the nations shall serve him,
> his son, and his grandson;
> until the time of his land comes too....
> Any nation or kingdom that does not serve him ...
> I will punish that nation, declares G-d,
> until I have destroyed it by his hand.
> And as for you, give no heed to your prophets ...
> who say to you, saying,
> "Do not serve the king of Bavel."
> For they prophesy falsehood to you;
> in order to distance you from your land;
> I will drive you out and you will perish.
> And the nation that brings its neck
> under the yoke of Bavel's king and serves him,
> I will leave it on its land, declares God;
> [that nation] will work it and dwell in it.
>
> (ibid. 27:4-11)

The words are clear and the point fundamental. G-d's prophet is neither for nor against rebellion — his opinion is irrelevant; in fact, he does not even express it. He conveys only the words of G-d, Who has decided that Bavel will continue to rule the world until "its measure is full" and "the time of [Nevuchadnetzar's] land comes too." Until then, Bavel will serve as "... My war club, [My] weapons of battle; with you will I shatter nations, with you will I destroy kingdoms" (ibid. 51:20). Once it fulfills its mission, however, "I will requite Bavel and all the inhabitants of Kasdim for all their evil that they have done in Tziyyon before your eyes, declares G-d" (ibid. 51:24).[28]

Yet the false prophets persist, headed by Chananyah ben Azzur. Even in these difficult times, they encourage the people, saying:

> ... the vessels of the house of G-d
> will shortly be brought back from Bavel. ...
> I have broken the yoke of the king of Bavel.
> In two years, I will restore to this place
> all the vessels of the house of G-d....
> And I will bring back to this place
> Yechonyah ben Yehoyakim, king of Yehudah,
> and all the exiles of Yehudah, who went to Bavel,
> declares G-d;
> for I will break
> the yoke of the king of Bavel.
>
> (ibid. 27:16, 28:2-4)

As stated, these false prophets express merely the people's desires and hopes of redemption and liberation. Even the prophet of truth, this time venting his own feelings, cries out enthusiastically: "Amen! May G-d do so! May G-d fulfill your words that you have prophesied, to bring back from Bavel to this place the vessels of the house of G-d and all the exiles!" (ibid. 28:6).[29]

But Yirmeyahu knows the truth, as the Almighty has told him:

> For thus said the G-d of Hosts, the L-rd of Yisra'el,
> concerning the vessels remaining in the house of G-d,
> in the house of the king of Yehudah and Yerushalayim:
> They shall be brought to Bavel, and there they shall remain,
> until the day I remember them, declares G-d,
> and I shall bring them up and restore them
> to this place.
>
> (ibid. 27:21-22)

Rebellion is premature; first, Yehudah must "serve [Nevuchadnetzar], his son, and his grandson" (ibid. 27:7).

Yirmeyahu seizes this opportunity to denounce the foolishness of the false prophets: "But listen now to this word, which I speak in your ears and in the ears of all the people: ... [As for] the prophet who prophesies peace, [only] when the word of the prophet comes true will it be known that G-d truly sent him" (ibid. 28:7, 9).[30]

Chananyah ben Azzur's breaking of the bars on Yirmeyahu's neck[31] proves to be mere theatrics: Two years pass, and "the vessels of the house of G-d and all the exiles" (ibid. 28:6) remain in Bavel. The wooden bars will be replaced by bars of iron.

Does Tzidkiyyahu learn from the past? Has the prophet won him over? Will he abandon his doomed thoughts of rebellion? Will he dare to lead his people in a spiritual revolution, as did his father, righteous King Yoshiyyahu? Only such a revolution can save the house of the L-rd from destruction and His people from exile.

Will this king of the house of David stand by G-d's prophet as he sounds the alarm? Will Tzidkiyyahu now coordinate his every action with the prophet, lest the king falter, as did his father in the plain of Megiddo?[32]

> Neither [Tzidkiyyahu] nor his servants
> nor the people of the land
> heeded the words of G-d,
> which He spoke through Yirmeyahu the prophet.
> (ibid. 37:2)

> [Tzidkiyyahu] did evil in the eyes of G-d his L-rd;
> he did not humble himself before Yirmeyahu the prophet,
> who spoke for G-d.
> He also rebelled against Nevuchadnetzar,
> who made him swear by the L-rd;
> he stiffened his neck and hardened his heart
> so as not to turn to G-d, the L-rd of Yisra'el.
> (Divrei HaYamim II 36:12-13)

Why does King Tzidkiyyahu, "perfect in his deeds" (*Horayoth* 11b), fail? Why is it that "in his days, Davidic rule ended" (ibid.)?

The king of Yisra'el is charged with spreading Torah and fear of G-d, elevating people spiritually and leading them to repentance. As Rambam writes:

> Whatever he does should be done by him for the sake of Heaven. His sole aim and thought should be to uplift the true religion, to fill the world with righteousness, to break the arm of the wicked, and

to fight the battles of the L-rd. The primary reason for appointing a king was that he execute judgment and wage war....

(Yad Hil. Melachim 4:10)

Furthermore, a Davidic king who emulates his forefathers

... meditates on the Torah, occupies himself with the commandments ... prescribed in the written and oral law, and prevails upon all of Yisra'el to walk in the way of [the Torah] and repair its breaches....

(ibid. 11:4)

Thus, not only must the king be righteous, he must "break the arm of the wicked" and repair the breaches of the Torah. Indeed, Tzidkiyyahu could have strengthened and supported the mission of the true prophet, whose piercing words called for complete repentance. That is Yirmeyahu's message to the king:

Render just verdicts morning by morning,
and rescue him who is robbed....
Thus said G-d: Do what is just and right;
deliver the robbed from the hand of the oppressor;
do no wrong, do no violence
to the stranger, the fatherless, and the widow;
and shed no innocent blood in this place.
For if you do this thing,
through the gates of this house
shall come kings of [the house of] David,
sitting upon his throne, riding in chariots and on horses,
he and his servants and his people.
But if you do not heed these words,
I swear by Myself, says G-d,
that this house shall become a ruin.

(Yirmeyahu 21:12, 22:3-5)

Doubtless, Tzidkiyyahu knows his kingdom is tottering; he also knows the only way to forestall its collapse. He is quite familiar with the uncompromising demands of the prophet, who, holding the moral high ground, neither favors those in high office nor caters to consensus. On several occasions, the king himself has turned to Yirmeyahu to guide him and pray for the people. Tzidkiyyahu lacks the courage to side with the prophet, however, and lend royal backing to his unceasing efforts to save whatever can be saved. Instead, "... [Tzidkiyyahu] did not humble himself before Yirmeyahu the prophet, who spoke for G-d" (Divrei HaYamim II 36:12).

> "[Tzidkiyyahu] did evil in the sight of G-d ..." (Melachim II 24:19) — For he could have protested [others' deeds], but he did not protest.
> (Sanhedrin 103a)[33, 34]

6. WEAKNESS AMID CRISIS

Three years pass since the first attempt to rebel against the king of Bavel. To rehabilitate Yisra'el, Tzidkiyyahu makes a covenant with the people: "That each should free his Hebrew manservant and each his Hebrew maidservant; that none should enslave his fellow Jew" (Yirmeyahu 34:9).[35]

Why does Tzidkiyyahu focus on the liberation of slaves? Surely, the prophet's words echo in the king's ears: "Do what is just and right; deliver the robbed from the hand of the oppressor" (ibid. 22:3). Knowing that, as king of Yisra'el, he must repair the breach of Torah, Tzidkiyyahu starts with the beginning of *parashath Mishpatim*: "When you acquire a Hebrew slave, he shall serve six years; and in the seventh, he shall go free, without payment" (Shemoth 21:2).

Perhaps Tzidkiyyahu also intends to foster national unity and fellowship in preparation for the decisive days ahead. For that very year, he again rebels against the king of Bavel, "relying on the kings of Mitzrayim" (*Seder Olam*, ch. 26).

Bavel's army wages war "on Yerushalayim and on all the remaining cities of Yehudah" (Yirmeyahu 34:7), crushing the revolt. Once more, the king of Mitzrayim saves his ally Tzidkiyyahu: "And Paroh's army set out from Mitzrayim; the Kasdim, who were besieging Yerushalayim, heard tidings of them; [the Kasdim] departed from Yerushalayim" (ibid. 37:5).

As soon as the siege is lifted, "normalcy" returns to Yehudah: "Afterwards, they turned about [and] brought back the manservants and maidservants whom they had freed; they forced them to [be] manservants and maidservants" (ibid. 34:11). Tzidkiyyahu's reform is short-lived; at the first sign of relief, the officers and the wealthy do as they please, ignoring their covenant with the king.

How does Tzidkiyyahu react? Does he exercise his authority

and enforce his covenant? Can he expect to fight a war if his command is flouted in his own capital? After all, not only are the people violating the covenant G-d had made with their forefathers upon taking them out of Mitzrayim, but they are defying the covenant their king has just established with them in the house of the L-rd!

Tzidkiyyahu, however, is afraid to open his mouth. He fears both his people and his officers, as did the first king of Yisra'el, Sha'ul ben Kish: "Said Sha'ul to Shemu'el: I have sinned, for I transgressed the commandment of G-d and your words: for I feared the people, and I heeded their voice" (Shemu'el I 15:24). This fear cost Sha'ul his kingship, yet he continued to consider himself worthy of Shemu'el's support.[36] Likewise, Tzidkiyyahu is afraid of his people but begs Yirmeyahu: "Please pray on our behalf to G-d our L-rd" (Yirmeyahu 37:3).

Similarly, just as Shemu'el castigated Sha'ul at the dawn of the kingship of Yisra'el,[37] Yirmeyahu puts Tzidkiyyahu in his place:

> ... thus shall you say to the king of Yehudah,
> who sent you to Me to inquire of Me:
> Behold, Paroh's army, which has set out to help you,
> will return to its own land, Mitzrayim.
> The Kasdim will return, and they will attack this city;
> they will capture it and burn it down by fire. ...
> You did not listen to Me, to proclaim a release,
> each to his brother and each to his neighbor;
> behold, I proclaim a release for you — declares G-d —
> to the sword, to pestilence, and to famine....
> ... the men who violated My covenant....
> The officers of Yehudah and the officers of Yerushalayim,
> the officials, the priests, and all the people of the land....
> I shall deliver them into the hand of their enemies
> and into the hand of those who seek their life....
> And Tzidkiyyahu, king of Yehudah, and his officers
> I will deliver into the hand of their enemies ...
> and into the hand of the king of Bavel's army,
> which has withdrawn from you.
> (ibid. 37:7-8, 34:17-21)

Paroh's forces get no farther than Azzah before the king of

Bavel and his army turn them back to Mitzrayim.[38] Once again, the Holy One Blessed be He shows Tzidkiyyahu that "A horse is a vain thing for deliverance; and for all its great power, it provides no escape" (Tehillim 33:17).

Does the king finally punish his officers and servants, who do as they please? Does he now heed the prophet's words?

A guard at the gate of Binyamin accuses Yirmeyahu of treason, of intending to defect to the Kasdim, and hands him over to the royal officers. They beat and imprison him without trial, without even consulting the king.[39]

Yet Tzidkiyyahu does not interfere — surely, his officials have only his and the country's good in mind. Simultaneously, however, he knows that the prophet speaks the words of the living G-d, devoid of self-interest; indeed, Tzidkiyyahu himself would like to hear them. Alas, this duplicity costs him his stature, forcing him to summon Yirmeyahu not regally but furtively, for fear of the royal officers' wrath:

> King Tzidkiyyahu sent and fetched [Yirmeyahu],
> and the king questioned him secretly in his house;
> he said: "Is there any word from G-d?"
> Yirmeyahu said: "There is";
> he said: "You will be delivered
> into the hand of the king of Bavel."
> (Yirmeyahu 37:17)

Yirmeyahu then pleads for his life:

> Yirmeyahu said to King Tzidkiyyahu:
> "How have I sinned against you,
> against your servants, or against this people,
> that you have put me in jail?
> And where are your prophets
> who prophesied to you, saying,
> 'The king of Bavel will never come upon you
> and upon this land'?
> Now, please listen, O my lord, the king;
> please grant my plea ...
> don't send me back to the house of Yehonathan the scribe,
> that I not die there."
> (ibid. 37:18-20)

The king can take the prophet out of prison in order to hear G-d's word, but Tzidkiyyahu cannot free him. For the king is captive to his officers and servants; they run the country. All he can do is ease the prophet's captivity: "King Tzidkiyyahu commanded that they place Yirmeyahu in the court of the guard, and that a loaf of bread be given to him daily from the bakers' street, until all the bread in the city was gone ..." (ibid. 37:21).

7. AN AGONIZING DECISION

We can only imagine the king's heartbreak. As he sees the savage enemy army encamped at the gates, he realizes that all his political maneuvering has backfired, and his officers and false prophets have misled him. In all its horror, Yirmeyahu's prophecy has come true. With no hope of outside support, Tzidkiyyahu must now rely on his Father in heaven.

What a bleak and tragic impasse: The holy city and the Sanctuary are besieged by an undefeated foe; the defenders do not stand a chance. The end is very near.

Should the king continue to fight and cling to the throne, or should he surrender and lead his people into exile?

Tzidkiyyahu knows well that his forefathers, the Davidic kings, sometimes yielded to overpowering enemies. Rechavam ben Shelomoh relinquished the ten tribes at the command of Shemayah the prophet.[40] Only a miracle saved Chizkiyyahu when Sancheriv besieged Yerushalayim.[41] Menasheh ben Chizkiyyahu was taken captive to Dammesek; only his repentance restored him to his throne in Yerushalayim.[42] And Tzidkiyyahu's father, Yoshiyyahu, fell in battle. But not one of them ever abdicated the throne. Perhaps Tzidkiyyahu should emulate King Sha'ul, who fought to the bitter end, though he knew the Pelishtim would prevail.

On the other hand, how can Tzidkiyyahu sacrifice so many lives to a lost cause, exposing men, women, and children to disease, famine, and the sword? How dare he endanger G-d's Sanctuary, which his fathers' fathers built and consecrated to the L-rd of Yisra'el?

How can a mere human being make such a fateful decision?

Once again, the king turns to the prophet:

> Please inquire of G-d on our behalf,
> for Nevuchadretzar [sic], king of Bavel, is warring against us;
> perhaps G-d will deal with us in accordance with all His wonders,
> and [Nevuchadnetzar] will go up from us.
>
> (ibid. 21:2)

Only an outright miracle can save Tzidkiyyahu, the house of Yisra'el, and the holy city. Surely, everyone is recalling the miracle that saved righteous King Chizkiyyahu from Sancheriv, king of Ashur, the awesome superpower: "perhaps G-d will deal with us in accordance *with all His wonders!*"

But unlike Chizkiyyahu's generation, Tzidkiyyahu's does not deserve a miracle. The prophet's response leaves no room for doubt:

> Thus said G-d, L-rd of Yisra'el:
> Behold, I am turning around
> the weapons that are in your hand,
> with which you are battling the king of Bavel and the Kasdim,
> who are besieging you outside the wall;
> I will gather them[43] into the midst of this city.
> I Myself will battle against you
> with an outstretched hand and with a mighty arm,
> with anger and rage and great wrath. ...
> And then — declares G-d —
> I will deliver King Tzidkiyyahu ... and the people ...
> into the hand of Nevuchadretzar [sic], king of Bavel...;
> he will put them to the sword — he will not pity them,
> and he will have no compassion, and he will have no mercy.
>
> (ibid. 21:4-7)

There will be no miracle, and it is too late for repentance. The centuries-old kingdom of Yehudah is finished.

The only hope — for individuals — is escape:

> And to this people you shall say:
> Thus said G-d:
> I set before you the way of life and the way of death.
> Whoever dwells in this city shall die
> by the sword, by famine, and by pestilence;

and whoever leaves and falls upon the Kasdim,
who are besieging you, shall live;
he shall have his life as booty.
(ibid. 21:8-9)

With their political independence gone, the people should at least try to save their lives and hope for better days. Yisra'el lives on forever, even in the darkness of exile.

Yirmeyahu also offers comfort but only in the distant future: He speaks of rebuilding, self-cleansing, and forgiveness; of "The voice of mirth and the voice of gladness ..." (ibid. 33:11); of a branch unto David's line and of priests serving in the house of the L-rd — but only after a grim period of exile and divine concealment.

> Thus said G-d:
> As surely as I have established
> My covenant with day and night,
> the laws of heaven and earth.
> So will I never reject
> the offspring of Ya'akov and David, My servant;
> I will never fail to take from his offspring
> rulers for the descendants of Avraham, Yitzchak, and Ya'akov;
> for I will return their captivity and have compassion on them.
> (ibid. 33:25-26)

These words of consolation, which the exiles take with them to the land of the Kasdim, strengthen both their faith in G-d and their hope of redemption.

8. TZIDKIYYAHU'S FINEST HOUR

In besieged Yerushalayim, all hope is lost. The few remaining soldiers, positioned on the walls, see a steady stream of refugees defect to the Kasdim, heeding Yirmeyahu's counsel that they at least save their lives. The people realize that the king cannot bring himself to surrender. Instead, he continues the war, goaded by his officers and false prophets, who regard Yirmeyahu as a defeatist.

To stem the tide of refugees, these officers seize on the prophet himself, imploring the king, "... please let this man be put to death, for thus does he weaken the hands of the men of war remaining in this city and the hands of all the people by speaking such things to them; for this man seeks not the welfare of this people, but their harm" (ibid. 38:4).

Tzidkiyyahu's officials have concluded that Yirmeyahu must be silenced at all costs; then, all will be well. Indeed, this is not the first time (or the last) that strong men have sought to bury the truth by killing the messenger, as if retribution will not come if one does not speak of it.

In a stricken voice, the pitiful king submits once again to their will: "He is in your hand; for the king cannot do anything against you" (ibid. 38:5).

What else can Tzidkiyyahu answer them? If he admits that the prophet speaks the truth, they will wonder why their king does not surrender. It is his ten-year reign that has "sunk his feet into the mire,"[44] and he cannot extricate himself.

Thus, Yirmeyahu is cast into a pit of mud to sink or starve. He is saved only by the devotion of Baruch ben Neriyyah (here known as "a servant of the king, a Kushite" [ibid. 38:7]),[45] who turns to the king in an impassioned plea to spare his master and teacher.

Here at last, King Tzidkiyyahu demonstrates his spiritual fortitude. Even after condoning the silencing of the prophet — as the good of the kingdom has seemingly demanded — Tzidkiyyahu defies his officers and instructs Baruch to take thirty men and rescue the exhausted prophet from the pit before he dies.[46] The king is distinguished in his deeds after all, "Just as a Kushite[47] is distinguishable by his skin ..." (*Mo'ed Katan* 16b).[48]

In ruling his kingdom, Tzidkiyyahu is clearly weak, ineffectual, and indecisive, fearing his officers and lacking initiative. Yet when called upon to save the prophet's life, the king resolutely and immediately decrees that Yirmeyahu be raised from the pit.

Apparently, when Tzidkiyyahu tells his officers, "[Yirmeyahu] is in your hand ..." (Yirmeyahu 38:5), the king never imagines that they might kill the prophet. True, they've demanded his death, but presumably only to silence him.

By saving Yirmeyahu, King Tzidkiyyahu redeems himself:

> ... thus said G-d concerning you:
> You will not die by the sword.
> You will die in peace,
> and with the burnings of your fathers,
> the former kings who were before you,
> so shall they make a burning for you....
> (ibid. 34:5)

> Tzidkiyyahu performed but one *mitzvah*: He pulled Yirmeyahu out of the muck [and thereby merited a peaceful death].
> (*Mo'ed Katan* 28b)

> Tzidkiyyahu, king of Yehudah, was perfectly righteous. Yet in Scripture,[49] all we find is that he ordered [Baruch ben Neriyyah] to pull Yirmeyahu out of the muck.
> (Tosafoth ad loc., ד״ה צדקיהו מלך יהודה)

Tzidkiyyahu is perfectly righteous, but only when he dares to defy his wicked officers does he acquire his reward: "You will die in peace" (Yirmeyahu 34:5) — they will honor you in death, just as they did the other noble kings of the house of David.

9. TZIDKIYYAHU'S LAST CHANCE

The prophet and the king meet one last time. Once again, hoping to avert tragedy, Tzidkiyyahu seeks G-d's word from the mouth of the prophet. Yirmeyahu offers an escape for the king, his household, and even the holy city and the Sanctuary. Will Tzidkiyyahu listen this time, or will he refuse to surrender? Will he find the courage to transcend his nature and extricate himself from the morass?

> ... the king said to Yirmeyahu,
> "... don't conceal anything from me."
> Yirmeyahu said to Tzidkiyyahu,
> "If I tell you, you'll surely kill me;
> and if I advise you, you won't listen to me."
> King Tzidkiyyahu swore secretly unto Yirmeyahu, saying:
> "As G-d lives ... I will not kill you,
> neither will I deliver you into the hand of these men
> who seek your life."
> Yirmeyahu said to Tzidkiyyahu: Thus said G-d ... :

> If you indeed go forth unto the officers of the king of Bavel,
> your soul will live,
> and this city will not be burned down by fire;
> you and your household will live.
> And if you do not go forth
> ... this city will be delivered into the hand of the Kasdim,
> who will burn it down by fire;
> and you will not escape from their hand.
>
> (ibid. 38:14-18)

The prophet has already learned how weak the king is. Twice he has turned Yirmeyahu over to the royal officers, who have persuaded the king to ignore the prophet's counsel. Why, then, should he speak now? Won't he only waste his words and risk his life?

Desperate to hear the word of G-d, Tzidkiyyahu undertakes a grave oath. But a powerless king stands before the prophet: Tzidkiyyahu swears to protect Yirmeyahu but not to obey him! The matter is no longer in the king's hands.

The prophet begs the king for the last time: It *is* in your hands! You can save the city, the Sanctuary, and your household! Rid yourself of both your fears and your evil counselors! Although the decree has been sealed, you can stay its execution.

> Said King Tzidkiyyahu to Yirmeyahu:
> "I worry about the men of Yehudah
> who have defected to the Kasdim,
> lest they deliver me into [the Yehudim's] hand and abuse me."
> Said Yirmeyahu: "They will not deliver [you];
> listen to the voice of G-d, to what I am telling you,
> that it may be well with you and your soul shall live.
> And if you refuse to go out [and surrender],
> this is the thing that G-d has shown me:
> And behold, the women ...
> shall be brought out to the officers of the king of Bavel,
> and [the women] shall say:
> 'The men who were your friends
> have incited you and vanquished you;
> now that your foot is sunk in mire,
> they have turned back [on you].'

> ... you will not escape from their hand;
> for you will be captured by the king of Bavel,
> and you will burn down this city by fire!"
> (ibid. 38:19-23)

Long paralyzed by doubts and anxieties, the king now has a new fear: The defectors may abuse him, having witnessed his hesitancy and capitulation to his officers, his tragic lack of stature in the besieged city.

Once again, the prophet pleads with the king to heed G-d's voice. Yirmeyahu brushes aside Tzidkiyyahu's fears and promises him a good end. Additionally, the prophet points to the ridicule that will result if the king does not surrender. Yirmeyahu warns Tzidkiyyahu: The city will be burned down on your account.

Drawing on all the oratory power of a prophet, Yirmeyahu employs all manner of persuasion and inducement. Yet his words are of no avail: In the end, the king has but one small request:

> Tzidkiyyahu said to Yirmeyahu:
> Let no man know of these words....
> (ibid. 38:24)

In case the royal officers learn of this secret meeting, Tzidkiyyahu invents an alibi for the prophet. What a poor, wretched king! After all Yirmeyahu's words — which Tzidkiyyahu believes in wholeheartedly — the king cannot overcome his fears and make the great personal sacrifice necessary to save Yisra'el. He remains in the grip of his officers; they must not find out that he has even thought of surrendering.

The prophet has done all he can; now, Yerushalayim is doomed.

10. DENOUEMENT

In the dead of summer, the sun's rays beat down on the heads of the remaining defenders. Harvest has passed, and the siege has dragged on for a year-and-a-half. Outside, the sword deals death, while inside there is hunger, pestilence, and dread.

On the ninth day of the fourth month, the city is breached.

Tzidkiyyahu can only flee, fulfilling Yechezkel's prophecy:

> And the prince who is among them
> shall carry [his gear] on his shoulder in the dark
> and shall go out;
> they shall break through the wall to carry out [his gear] thereby;
> he shall cover his face [in shame (Rashi)]
> that he not see the ground with his eyes.
> I shall spread My net over him,
> and he shall be caught in My snare....
>
> (Yechezkel 12:12-13)

> [The king] fled by way of an underground passageway that extended from his palace to the plains of Yericho. The Holy One Blessed be He arranged for a deer to run above ground along the length of the passageway; the Kasdim chased after it. When they reached the entrance to the passageway in the plains of Yericho, they spotted [the king] and caught him. As He said: "I shall spread My net over him, and he shall be caught in My snare" (ibid. 12:13).
>
> (Rashi, Melachim II 25:4)

> The army of the Kasdim pursued the king;
> they overtook Tzidkiyyahu in the plains of Yericho;
> and his entire army was scattered from him.
> They grabbed the king,
> and they brought him to the king of Bavel
> to Rivlah in the land of Chamath;
> and he passed judgment upon him.
>
> (Yirmeyahu 52:8-9)

The kingdom of Yehudah has come to an end. The last king has fled, only to fall into enemy hands. His royal city is set afire, the Sanctuary is destroyed, and the people are exiled to Bavel.

11. CONCLUSION

Ultimately, G-d's will prevails. However, He is "slow to anger and abounding in kindness" (Shemoth 34:6). Thus, for generations, the prophesied retribution is deferred:

> R. Chisda said in the name of R. Yirmeyah b. Abba:

> *"I went by the field of a lazy man ..."* (Mishlei 24:30) — This refers to Achaz.
> *"... and by the vineyard of a man void of understanding"* (ibid.) — This refers to Menasheh.
> *"And lo, it was all overgrown with thorns ..."* (ibid. 24:31) — This refers to Ammon.
> *"Nettles had covered its face"* (ibid.) — This refers to Yehoyakim.
> *"... and its stone wall was broken down"* (ibid.) — This refers to Tzidkiyyahu [who was righteous (Rashi)], in whose days the Sanctuary was destroyed.
>
> (Sanhedrin 103a)

Tzidkiyyahu is not responsible for "breaking down the wall," for the destruction of the Sanctuary. The field and vineyard have been neglected since the days of the wicked kings of Yehudah; the wall no longer guards anything of value.

> And now I will tell you what I will do to My vineyard:
> I will remove its hedge
> [I will remove from them My Shechinah (*Tar. Yonathan*)],
> that it may be ravaged;
> I will break down its wall
> [I will destroy My Sanctuary (ibid.)],
> that it may be trampled.
>
> (Yeshayahu 5:5)

The Shechinah has already departed from the Sanctuary six months earlier;[50] all that burns is wood and stone.

The last king of Yehudah can no longer forestall the retribution decreed back in the days of his forefathers on account of their deeds. His generation lacks the merit, and he lacks the strength.

> *"The sons of Yoshiyyahu: ... the third, Tzidkiyyahu; the fourth, Shallum"* (Divrei HaYamim I 3:15).
> *"Tzidkiyyahu"* (*"G-d is my justice"*) — He accepted the *justice* of [G-d's] decree against him.
> *"Shallum"* — For in his days, Davidic rule ended ["שלום" is expounded as "שלמה" (ended)].
>
> (Yer. Shekalim 6:1)

NOTES

1. *Ed. note:* See *Yad Hil. Teshuvah* 6:5.
2. *Ed. note:* Chazal assumed that clusters of names in Divrei HaYamim often refer to but one person. See *Megillah* 13a: "R. Shimon b. Pazi, when he began Divrei HaYamim, said thus: All your words are one, yet we know how to expound them. [You mention this one and that one, yet all refer to one person (Rashi).]"
3. "Before him there was never a king like him who turned to G-d with all his heart and with all his soul and with all his might, in accord with the entire Torah of Mosheh, nor did anyone like him arise after him" (Melachim II 23:25).
4. See Radak on Melachim II 22:8.
5. See Melachim II 22-23.
6. See *Yoma* 52b.
7. See ibid. 22:15-20.
8. See *Horayoth* 12a.
9. See ibid. 11b.
10. See Yirmeyahu 26:20-23.
11. See *Megillah* 11b.
12. See Yirmeyahu 46:2.
13. See *Seder Olam*, ch. 24.
14. See Yirmeyahu 36:5.
15. See Divrei HaYamim II 36:6.
16. See *Seder Olam*, ch. 25.
17. See Yirmeyahu 22:18-19, 36:30; and *VaY.R.* 19:6.
18. See *Arachin* 17a.
19. See *Mo'ed Katan* 28b and Tosafoth ad loc., ד"ה צדקיהו מלך יהודה; and *Shabbath* 149b.
20. See Divrei HaYamim II 36:13.
21. See *Nedarim* 65a and *Yad Hil. Shevu'oth* 6:7.
22. See Yirmeyahu 29:10.
23. See *Shabbath* 119b-120a.
24. See Yirmeyahu 51:59.
25. See *Seder Olam*, ch. 25 (end).
26. See Yirmeyahu 50-51.
27. See Radak on Yirmeyahu 27:1.

28. Bavel is punished despite its having served as G-d's tool. See Ramban on BeReshith 15:14 (end); and *Yad Hil. Teshuvah* 6:5 and Ra'avad ad loc.
29. See *Sotah* 41b for Chazal's opinion of Yirmeyahu's exclamation.
30. See *Yer. Sanhedrin* 11:5 and Rambam's *Introduction to the Mishnah*, ch. 2.
31. See Yirmeyahu 28:10-11.
32. See Melachim II 23:29.
33. *Ed. note:* Chazal's understanding of Tzidkiyyahu's "evil" typifies their approach to the misdeeds of the righteous. See *Shabbath* 55b-56a, where a sin of omission is equated with a sin of commission. For a broader treatment of this topic, see "In Defense of Sha'ul," *Jewish Thought*, 1, No. 1 (5750), 101-16.
34. Scripture also condemns Tzidkiyyahu for violating an oath taken in the name of G-d. R. Tam and Ra'avad dispute whether the Sanhedrin could have absolved this oath. See Ran on *Nedarim* 65a, ד״ה תניא המודר הנאה מחבירו; Tosafoth ad loc., ד״ה אמרו לו בפניו; Rosh ad loc., ד״ה המודר הנאה מחבירו; and *Chiddushei Aggadoth* (Maharsha) ad loc., ד״ה מאי מרדותיה אשכחיה כו׳.
35. See *Seder Olam*, ch. 26.
36. See Shemu'el I 15:26, 31.
    Ed. note: For an extensive analysis of Sha'ul's sin vis-e-vis Amalek, see "Sha'ul and Amalek," in this issue of *Jewish Thought*.
    The author's parallel between Sha'ul and Tzidkiyyahu is extremely apt. Both are deemed fully righteous by Chazal, yet both are severely criticized in the Bible (see Divrei HaYamim I 10:13-14 and Melachim II 24:19). Apparently, the *personal* piety of both was exemplary, but each fell short as a king and capitulated to the populace. Hence Sha'ul and Tzidkiyyahu's accountability for the wrongs perpetrated during their reigns. Yet both ultimately demonstrated their true mettle, Sha'ul by bravely battling alongside his beloved sons even though he knew he'd be killed (see Shemu'el I 31:2-3 and *Yal.Sh.* Shemu'el:28, ד״ה וימהר) and Tzidkiyyahu by defying his officers and saving Yirmeyahu's life.
37. See Shemu'el I 15:17-19, 22-24.
38. See Yirmeyahu 47 and *Seder Olam*, ch. 26.
39. See Yirmeyahu 37:12-16.
40. See Melachim I 12:22-24.
41. See Melachim II 19:35.
42. See Divrei HaYamim II 33:11-13.
43. *Ed. note:* "Them" refers either to the weapons (Rashi) or to the Kasdim (Radak).
44. See Yirmeyahu 38:22.
45. See *Sifrei* on BeMidbar 12:1, *Emek HaNetziv* ad loc., and *Pir.DeR.E.* 53. Also see *Mo'ed Katan* 16b. The Talmud and *Sifrei* differ on whether "a Kushite"

refers to the king or to his servant, Baruch ben Neriyyah.
46. See Yirmeyahu 38:10.
47. See n. 33.
48. Regarding the discrepancy between Chazal's glowing assessment of Tzidkiyyahu and the Bible's harsh appraisal of him as one who "did evil in the eyes of G-d" (Divrei HaYamim II 36:12), see n. 33.
49. *Ed. note:* According to these Talmudic citations, it seems that Scripture mentions only this one good deed of Tzidkiyyahu's — even though Chazal deem him fully righteous — because it was this heroic act that ultimately earned him his reward. Furthermore, the incident in question reveals his true character as Yirmeyahu's defender, despite his general inability to defy his officers and advisors whenever the prophet's life is not in danger.
50. See *Rosh HaShanah* 31a.

A MIZMOR FOR SHABBATH?
A Literary View of Mizmor 92

Dan Vogel

The essay that follows is based upon the source provided below:[1]

A *mizmor* for the Shabbath day: מזמור שיר ליום השבת:

It is good to praise G-d,   טוב להודות ה',
    to sing hymns to Your name, O Most High.   ולזמר לשמך עליון:

To proclaim Your kindness in the morning,   להגיד בבקר חסדך,
    Your faithfulness each night.   ואמונתך בלילות:

With a ten-stringed harp,   עלי עשור ועלי-נבל,
    with voice and lyre together.   עלי הגיון בכנור:

You have gladdened me by Your deeds, O G-d;   כי שמחתני, ה', בפעלך;
    I shout for joy at Your handiwork.   במעשי ידיך ארנן:

How great are Your works, O G-d,   מה-גדלו מעשיך, ה';
    how very subtle [or *profound*] Your designs.   מאד עמקו מחשבתיך:

DR. VOGEL is a professor of English at Michlalah — Jerusalem College for Women. He wrote this essay in memory of Rabbi David Mirsky, z.l., of Yeshiva University, New York. The author thanks Rabbis Nosson Geisler, Dr. Alter Halevi Hilewitz, Dr. Meshullam Margoliot, and Joseph Urivetsky, and Mr. Samuel Weiss, all of Yerushalayim, for their helpful criticisms and suggestions.

A brutish man cannot know,	איש־בער לא ידע;
a fool cannot understand this:	וכסיל לא־יבין את־זאת:
Though the wicked sprout like grass,	בפרח רשעים כמו עשב,
though all evildoers blossom,	ויציצו כל־פעלי און;
it is only that they may be destroyed forever.	להשמדם עדי־עד:
But You are exalted, O G-d, for all time.	ואתה מרום לעלם, ה'.
Surely, Your enemies, O G-d,	כי הנה איביך, ה',
surely, Your enemies perish;	כי־הנה איביך יאבדו;
all evildoers are scattered.	יתפרדו כל־פעלי און:
You raise my horn high like that of a wild ox;	ותרם כראים קרני;
I am soaked in freshening oil.	בלתי בשמן רענן:
I shall see the defeat of my watchful foes,	ותבט עיני בשורי,
and the fall of the wicked who beset me	בקמים עלי מרעים,
I shall hear.	תשמענה אזני:
The righteous one blooms like a date-palm;	צדיק כתמר יפרח;
he thrives like a cedar in Lebanon.	כארז בלבנון ישגה:
Planted in the house of G-d,	שתולים בבית ה'
they flourish in the courts of our L-rd.	בחצרות א־לקינו יפריחו:
In old age they still produce fruit;	עוד ינובון בשיבה;
they are full of sap and freshness.	דשנים ורעננים יהיו:
Attesting that G-d is upright,	להגיד כי־ישר ה'
He is my Rock, in Whom there is no wrong.	צורי ולא־עולתה בו:

(Tehillim 92)

---

1. INTRODUCTION

The only *mizmor* of Tehillim that is assigned to a day of the week is Mizmor 92, "מזמור שיר ליום השבת" ("A psalm for the Shabbath day"), and for nearly two thousand years, sages, scholars, and Shabbath observers alike have wondered why. As has been universally observed, not one word in Mizmor 92 refers to Shabbath, and its encomiums to the L-rd are unique neither to this *mizmor* nor to the day it purports to honor. Suggestions why the psalmist linked this *mizmor* to Shabbath range widely, taking us from the beginning of history to its end.²

2. AUTHORSHIP AND AUDIENCE

Many *midrashim* attribute our *mizmor* to Adam, stating that it was "composed by him on the first Sabbath of creation."³ The Midrash relates that Shabbath saved Adam from a decree of instant death after his sin, whereupon the day, as it were, said to him, "I and you will say this hymn to the Holy One Blessed be He" (*Yal.Sh.* Tehillim:843). As Adam's descendants, we continue this tradition. Alternatively, Adam composed Mizmor 92 after being assured that the L-rd had reprieved his son Kayin from execution.⁴

Yet this *mizmor* was forgotten by Adam's generation, and it remained unknown until Mosheh reintroduced it, concealing his name in the initial letters of its heading, "מזמור שיר ליום השבת," which form the word "למשה" ("for Mosheh").⁵ In his commentary on Tehillim, R. S.R. Hirsch maintains that Mizmor 92 was given to Mosheh that he might teach the Jewish people the sanctity of Shabbath, but how it was to serve this educational function without even mentioning the holiness of the day remains unclear.

In any case, we recite Mizmor 92 no fewer than three times during Shabbath: once at night, to usher in Shabbath, and twice the following morning — once within the preliminary service and once as the *mizmor* of the day. Following the Shabbath morning service, we also read *Mish. Tamid* 7:4, which lists the *mizmor* associated with each day of the week. The *mishnah* identifies six of these seven *mizmorim* by quoting the first significant verse of each. Regarding the *mizmor* for Shabbath, however, the *mishnah* cites only the introductory verse "A *mizmor* for the Shabbath day," emphasizing an eschatological vision: "It is the *mizmor* for the hereafter, for the day that will be wholly Shabbath and rest for eternity."

In this vein, the Talmud tells us that the world will last six thousand years, each day of the week alluding to a millennium. Shabbath corresponds to a seventh millennium, the "Shabbath" of the future, when all mankind will acknowledge God's sovereignty. This millennium will be the period between the end of the world and the resurrection of the dead, when God will be alone, for none will walk the earth.[6] If so, we might wonder, what is in Mizmor 92 for us?

That Mizmor 92 was thought to have a homiletical, personal dimension seems clear from its inclusion in the liturgy. Perhaps a literary approach to the *mizmor* will reveal its relevance both to Shabbath and, in turn, to those who recite it every week on that day.

This approach is one of *explication de texte*. In fact, it is but an extension of traditional hermeneutical exegesis, examining the structure and imagery of the Biblical poem. After devoting many years to close readings of non-Biblical poetry, I can think of no better application of this technique — sanctioned and sanctified by Rashi, Radak, and other traditional commentators — than in the service of isolating and explicating a sacred text like Mizmor 92. As Chazal tell us, " *'Like a hammer that shatters a rock'* (Yirmeyahu 23:29) — Just as this hammer [causes the rock (Rashi)] to be split into several fragments, so too one [verse from] Scripture may diverge into several explanations" (*Sanhedrin* 34a).

3. THE MACRO-STRUCTURE OF MIZMOR 92

Mizmor 92 contains sixteen verses. Discounting verse 1 as simply a signature verse attributing the *mizmor* to Shabbath, the remaining fifteen verses are symmetrically divided according to metrical balance:

Part I: verses 2-87 verses, each containing
an *ethnachta* (caesura)

Part II: verse 91 verse, no *ethnachta*

Part III: verses 10-167 verses, each containing
an *ethnachta*

A further breakdown, based on content, reveals an even more detailed, seven-stanza symmetry:

Stanza 1	Stanza 2	Stanza 3	Stanza 4	Stanza 5	Stanza 6	Stanza 7
verses 2-5	verse 6	verses 7-8	verse 9	verses 10-12	verses 13-15	verse 16
Man to G-d	Encomium	G-d vs. the Wicked	Fulcrum	G-d vs. the Wicked	G-d and the Righteous	G-d

Symmetry is not merely a pleasing artistic device. It betokens order, a careful edifice of technique and thought. As such, it reflects the close connection between Creation and Shabbath: out of chaos came order, a process culminating in Shabbath. Thus, the very formation of Mizmor 92 parallels the order and equilibrium of G-d's creation, satisfying our hunger for order in the universe. Likewise, we preface our recitation of each day's *mizmor* by noting its relationship to Shabbath in the weekly cycle (e.g., on Sunday we say, "Today is the first day in relation to Shabbath"; on Monday, "Today is the second day ..." etc.). This way, we too impose order on the chaos of the workweek, making Shabbath its pinnacle. "By counting the days of the week with reference to the forthcoming Sabbath," writes R. Nosson Scherman, "we tie our existence to the Sabbath."[7] On Shabbath, we sit back and contemplate the system of Creation.

4. THE MICRO-STRUCTURES OF MIZMOR 92: STANZA, VERSE, AND IMAGE

Stanza 1:
92:2. It is good to praise G-d,
    to sing hymns to Your name, O Most High.

Verse 2 announces that it is good to thank and praise G-d, a vague generalization expressed throughout Tehillim. Note, however, the sudden change from third person to second, from *"It is good to praise G-d ..."* to *"to sing hymns to* Your *name."* Having entered the presence of the King, as it were, we initially address Him formally, but immediately we turn to familiar language. Indeed, seven times throughout Mizmor 92, the Tetragrammaton is used in "direct" address, unbuffered by any preposition. These seven instances combine formality and familiarity, distance and closeness.

92:3. To proclaim Your kindness in the morning, Your faithfulness each night.

Verse 3 illuminates both the relationship between form and theme in Mizmor 92 and the connection between the *mizmor* and Shabbath.

The verse is beautifully balanced, the infinitive *"to proclaim"* introducing two parallel divine attributes and the time of day when each should be affirmed:

1.	2.
His kindness	His faithfulness
morning	night

"The purpose of parallelism," asserts Robert Alter, writing about Biblical poetry, "like the general purpose of imagery, is to transfer the usual perception of an object into the sphere of a new perception — that is, to make a unique semantic modification."[8] Here, then, *"morning"* parallels *"night,"* and each time of day parallels a divine attribute.

The sequence of "time followed by attribute" is reversed in the second hemistich, however, effectively completing a cycle: morning∩kindness∩faithfulness∩night. As we shall see, this cycle anticipates the overall circuit of the *mizmor*.

Furthermore, universal symbolism underlies the images of *"morning"* and *"night,"* demonstrating why the former is the time to relate G-d's *"kindness"* and the latter His *"faithfulness."* The light of morning symbolizes manifestation, and kindness must be manifest. The darkness of night represents fearsome hiddenness, when observation is impossible and faith alone must sustain us.

"In the morning," explains R. Scherman, "we express gratitude for already existing *kindness*, while in the evening we express our *faith* in something that has not yet taken place."[9] Thus, these symbols contain both personal and eschatological relevance. Alternatively, R. S.R. Hirsch interprets, "His rule and His will speak to us through each phenomenon of nature (להגיד בבקר) and through every event of history (בלילות)" (com. on Tehillim 92:2). Nature is a tangible manifestation of G-d's kindness; our history, a history of exile, demands intangible faith in our future redemption. Similarly, R. Scherman comments, "During the harsh night of exile, we refer to אמונתך, *Your faith*, because our faith, rather than our intellect, testifies to His goodness."[10]

Yet this comment is as ambiguous as the verse itself: Whose faith is implied here — G-d's, Yisra'el's, or both? Cast in the second person ("Your *faithfulness*"), the verse apparently pertains only to G-d. But can it also refer to Yisra'el's faith? All levels of indeterminate meaning are valid in *explication de texte*. Consequently, the psalmist here implies both sources of faith and both objects of faith, G-d's and Yisra'el's:

G-d's faithfulness	Yisra'el's faith
in Yisra'el	in G-d

We now see how Shabbath comes into all this: The historic exiles of the Jewish people are simply an extension of the exile of each workday from Shabbath. The L-rd showed His kindness in the six days of Creation; on the seventh, this manifestation ceased. The six days of the week therefore remain days of material manifestation, sensory activity, and work, days of viewing G-d's handiwork in nature and in life. On Shabbath, however, we are thrown back upon our faith. It is not a day of external tangibility; it is a day of inner certainty, of withdrawal, of striving for spirituality.

Mizmor 92 asserts that faith is no mere romantic dream, it is knowledge. The knowledge that each week eventually culminates in Shabbath reassures us that the "Shabbath" of the hereafter will eventuate as well, regardless of all indications apparently to the contrary. "נצחוני בני," as it were — "My children are victorious" (*Babba Metzi'a* 59b) over the evidence before their eyes.

Manifestation versus faith is the central conflict of Mizmor 92.

Let us now examine the variations on this theme in the ensuing images, syntax, and motifs of the *mizmor*.

Stanza 1:
92:4. With a ten-stringed harp,
    with voice and lyre together.

At first glance, verse 4 seems inconsonant with the emerging meaning of Mizmor 92. The verse refers to the long-lost era when the *mizmor* was sung in the Temple to the accompaniment of certain instruments. Yet these instruments themselves symbolize manifestation and faith. R. S.R. Hirsch, for example, doesn't even mention the first two instruments in his translation; instead, he interprets them as "full sound" and "plaintive tone," respectfully. In his notes, he contrasts "עשור," the ten-stringed instrument capable of producing a full sound, with "נבל," "whose strains correspond to the 'fading away' that comes at the end of life" (com. ad loc.). In our interpretation, then, the "full sound" is the "daytime" sound, while at night comes the "fading away," the "plaintive tone," the tone of faith.

92:5. You have gladdened me by Your deeds, O G-d;
I shout for joy at Your handiwork.

Verse 5 celebrates G-d's manifest labors, with the word *"deeds"* leading into the second stanza and its new perception.

Stanza 2:

92:6. How great are Your works, O G-d,
how very subtle [or *profound*] Your designs.

In this brief encomium, the psalmist reprises the theme of manifestation versus hiddenness by extolling G-d's visible *"works"* while expressing profound awe at the depths of His invisible *"designs."* These two opposites — observable deeds versus thoughts, which are a matter of faith — anticipate the thrust of the next stanza, which derides those who rely solely on what lies before their eyes.

Stanza 3:

92:7. A brutish man cannot know,
a fool cannot understand this:

92:8. Though the wicked sprout like grass,
though all evildoers blossom,
it is only that they may be destroyed forever.

What is it that the boors and fools of verse 7 and the wicked of verse 8 (all of whom may be associated with the mundane days of the week) cannot understand? The pronoun *"this"* points in two directions: It harks back to the previous verse, indicating that these simpletons cannot grasp anything that is not manifest before them. Yet it also introduces the next verse, where we learn that these individuals see only their proliferation, never suspecting their implicit doom.[11]

Again, the imagery — derived from nature — is universal. The simile *"like grass,"* referring to the world's most common vegetation, emphasizes the omnipresence of the wicked. Nonetheless, faith insists that they will yet be destroyed forever.[12] Furthermore, the psalmist will recall this very ubiquitousness of grass when he analogizes the righteous.

Stanza 4:

92:9. But You are exalted, O G-d, for all time.

Verse 9 comprises only four Hebrew words. This distinctive prosodic structure makes it visually, metrically, and thematically pivotal.

Unlike all the other verses of Mizmor 92, this verse has but a single clause: There is no *ethnachta*, no caesura. Nor is there any verb.[13] Thus, the verse itself acts as a caesura, a pause between the first and last three stanzas.

Introduced by the conjunction *"but,"* verse 9 connects verse 8's declaration that the wicked will dry up like grass and verse 10's promise that G-d's enemies will perish. Moreover, this transitional verse contrasts the doom of the evildoers with the eternity of G-d, preparing us for the form and theme of the second half of the *mizmor*.

Stanza 5:

92:10. Surely, Your enemies, O G-d,
    surely, Your enemies perish;
    all evildoers are scattered.

92:11. You raise my horn high like that of a wild ox;
    I am soaked in freshening oil.

**92:12. I shall see the defeat of my watchful foes,
and the fall of the wicked who beset me
I shall hear.**

The first seven verses of Mizmor 92 descended from the heights of praising the L-rd to the depths of unG-dly spiritual blindness. With verse 9 as its axis, the last seven verses begin with the fate of the evildoers and rise again to the climax of praising the L-rd. This cycle is analogous to our existence from one Shabbath to the next.

Pivoting on the phrase *"all evildoers,"* the *mizmor* finishes off the enemies of the L-rd and then turns to the rewards accruing to those who have sung of the manifestations of G-d's world and demonstrated their faith in the future. This vindication of the faithful is depicted in terms of the *"horn ... of a wild ox,"* a common Biblical symbol of pride and strength. Furthermore, the victors are *"soaked in freshening oil,"* a process of revivification, beautification, and consecration. The imagery climaxes in verse 12 in an exultant cry of complete and inevitable triumph.

Stanza 6:

**92:13. The righteous one blooms like a date-palm;
he thrives like a cedar in Lebanon.**

**92:14. Planted in the house of G-d,
they flourish in the courts of our L-rd.**

**92:15. In old age they still produce fruit;
they are full of sap and freshness.**

Having dispensed with the boors, the fools, and the wicked of verses 7-8, who fairly teem with the dross of the six weekdays, our *mizmor* focuses on their opposite, the *tzaddik*, who embodies the spirituality of Shabbath.

The psalmist is careful to maintain the symmetry of his poem. Just as the *"brutish man"* (Tehillim 92:7) was generalized into the *"wicked"* (ibid. 92:8), the singular *"righteous one"* (ibid. 92:13) is pluralized in verse 14. And just as the unG-dly were *"like grass"* (ibid. 92:8), the righteous are compared to date palms and cedars of Lebanon, classic Biblical symbols of fructivity, power, and longevity. In the Talmud, R. Chiyya b. Luliani wonders why both types of trees need be mentioned. He concludes that they complement each other with symmetry of their own: The cedar produces no fruit, but, even after being cut down, it renews itself; the date palm lacks this capacity for renewal, but it bears fruit. The righteous, then, encompass the best features of both trees.[14]

Furthermore, the psalmist introduces an upbeat irony by reprising a verb used before: The unrighteous, we remember, sprouted ("בפרח") like common grass (ibid. 92:8); now the righteous bloom ("יפרח") like a date palm (ibid. 92:13), and they grow not like lowly blades of grass, which wither within a season, but like the evergreen cedar of Lebanon, which will flourish ("יפרחו") in the house of G-d forever (ibid. 92:14), whereas the wicked will be "destroyed *forever*" (ibid. 92:7). In addition, to counterbalance this reference to old age (positive though it may be), *Mid. Tehillim* reads "שתולים" ("planted") (ibid. 92:14) as "שתילים" ("sprouts") — youngsters in the classroom, who will grow up to be righteous.[15] And even as they approach the end of their days, which presages their eternal "Shabbath," they remain vital and productive.

This is the promise embedded in Mizmor 92, recited each Shabbath "in the house of G-d" (ibid. 92:13). This is manifestation fulfilled.

Stanza 7:

92:16. Attesting that G-d is upright,
      He is my Rock, in Whom there is no wrong.

With the reprise of the infinitive "to proclaim" (ibid. 92:2), Mizmor 92 comes full circle. One last familiar image attests to what is manifest: Says the psalmist, "*[G-d] is my Rock*." Such is his granitelike belief in the L-rd's perfection and justice, regardless of the prevalence of evil. This faith is renewed each Shabbath, suggesting a complete, never-ending cycle from Shabbath to Shabbath, from one recitation of Mizmor 92 to the next. This geometric inevitability symbolizes the immeasurable faith that one day creation will turn back upon itself and regain its original paradisal state.

4. CONCLUSION

The literary approach of the psalmist is perhaps best placed in perspective by Robert Alter:

> G-d manifests Himself in part through language, and necessarily His deeds are made known by any one man to others ... chiefly through the mediation of language.... The psalmist's delight in the suppleness and serendipities of poetic form is not a distraction from [the] spiritual seriousness of the poems *but his chief means of realizing his spiritual vision* [italics mine], and it is one source of the power these poems continue to have not only to excite our imaginations but also to engage our lives.[16]

Through the mediation of word, image, prosody, and structure, we see how true this thesis is regarding Mizmor 92's relationship both to the day to which it is eternally ascribed and to the people who recite it faithfully every week.

NOTES

1. This translation is based on *Tanakh: A New Translation of the Holy Scriptures According to the Traditional Hebrew Text* (Philadelphia: Jewish Publication 1985), pp. 1218-19.

2. *Ed. note:* For but two of the many essays devoted to the connection between Mizmor 92 and Shabbath, see Yitzchak Ze'ev HaLevi Soloveitchik, *Chiddushei Maran Riz HaLevi Al HaTorah* (Yerushalayim, 1981), p. 6; and Chaggai Moshkovitz, "Mizmor Shir LeYom HaShabbath," *Shema'atin*, 60 (Teveth 1980), 13-16.

3. See *Pir.DeR.E.*, *BeR.R.* 22:13, and *Yal.Sh.* Tehillim:843.

4. See *BeR.R.* 22:13.
   Ed. note: Regarding the connection between Shabbath and repentance, see Mosheh Ostrer, *Tehillim Al Pi Derash Mosheh* (Brooklyn: Mechon Segulah, 1977), p. 215.

5. See *BeR.R.* 22:13 and Maharzu ad loc.

6. See *Rosh HaShanah* 31a and *Sanhedrin* 97a.

7. See *The Complete ArtScroll Siddur*, trans. and com. by Nosson Scherman (Brooklyn, 1984), p. 162n.

8. See Robert Alter, *The Art of Biblical Poetry* (New York, 1985), p. 10. Cf. Amos Chacham, ed., *Tehillim* (Yerushalayim, 1981), p. 180.

9. See *The Complete ArtScroll Siddur*, p. 96. This eschatological interpretation echoes Rashi's commentary on *Berachoth* 12a, ד"ה שנא׳ להגיד בבקר חסדך, and

Radak's on Tehillim 36:6, where the psalmist again refers to both kindness and faith in a single line. Kindness, says Radak, refers to the tangible, to animal fodder (an image that may anticipate the grass that symbolizes the earthbound fools and evildoers of Mizmor 92); faith signifies survival, the intangible promise of the future.

10. See *The Complete ArtScroll Siddur*, p. 320n. In contrast, according to *Mid. Tehillim*, morning represents the world to come, and night this world. This *midrash* implies that morning is the time of faith in a world to come, and darkness is the time of the manifestation of the existential world. Though interpretations of the images may differ, the theme of manifestation versus faith remains constant.
11. See Radak on Tehillim 92:7-8.
12. See *Pir.DeR.E.* 19.
13. *Ed. note:* One could argue that the verb here is implied, just as it is in verse 4, which may be viewed as a continuation of verse 3.
14. See *Ta'anith* 25a-b.
15. See *Mid. Tehillim* 92:12.
16. See Alter, p. 136.

JEWISH THOUGHT: A Journal of Torah Scholarship is a nonpartisan journal of traditional scholarship in *parshanuth HaMikra* (Biblical commentary and exegesis) and *machsheveth Yisra'el* (classic Jewish philosophy). It is a semiannual publication of the Union of Orthodox Jewish Congregations of America in conjunction with Yeshivat Ohr Yerushalayim in Israel.

Subscriptions are on an annual basis, two issues for $10, payable to *Jewish Thought*, c/o Orthodox Union, 333 Seventh Avenue, New York, NY 10001. The previous collection, *The 1993 Book of Jewish Thought*, is also available.

Appropriate scholarly essays in the areas of Biblical commentary and exegesis, Midrash, Aggadah, classic Jewish philosophy, and Jewish liturgy may be submitted for publication, contingent on the guidelines below.

GUIDE TO CONTRIBUTORS:

A) Content
1. Essays must be text-oriented, providing an analysis of either primary sources or specific topics illuminated by primary sources.
2. Essays must reflect original research, or adaptations or translations of research, hitherto unpublished in English.

B) Presentation
1. Essays must be written in a style suitable for an audience of both Torah scholars and learned laymen.
2. Essays must be prepared in conformity with *The MLA Style Sheet*. All sources must be properly referenced. Citations of quotations should be included parenthetically in the text, whereas more lengthy notes should be listed separately at the end of the essay.
3. Manuscripts should be approximately from ten to twenty-five pages long, double-spaced on one side of a page with adequate margins.

C) Editing
1. Essays accepted for publication may be edited. Authors will be notified about any significant changes.
2. All essays published will be synopsized in the table of contents and subdivided into subtitled sections. Authors may provide suggested abstracts and suggested subdivisions with their essays.

TO SUBSCRIBE TO

Jewish Thought

COMPLETE AND RETURN THIS COUPON

Name _____

_____

Address _____

_____

City/State/Zip _____

_____

Date _____

If this is a gift, complete your name and address below

Name _____

Address _____

City/State/Zip _____

- ❏ Annual Subscription (2 issues): $10 (U.S.)
- ❏ 3-year subscription (6 issues): $27 (U.S.)

  Single issues ($6 each):
- ❏ Volume 1, Number 1
- ❏ Volume 1, Number 2
- ❏ Volume 2, Number 1
- ❏ Volume 2, Number 2

My check, payable to *Jewish Thought,* is enclosed.

Mail to:
JEWISH THOUGHT
Orthodox Union
333 Seventh Avenue
New York, NY 10001